BLACK SATURDAY

BLACK SATURDAY
NOT THE END OF THE STORY
PEG FRASER

Black Saturday: Not the End of the Story

© Copyright 2018 Peg Fraser
All rights reserved. Apart from any uses permitted by Australia's Copyright Act 1968, no part of this book may be reproduced by any process without prior written permission from the copyright owners. Inquiries should be directed to the publisher.

Monash University Publishing
Matheson Library and Information Services Building
40 Exhibition Walk
Monash University
Clayton, Victoria 3800, Australia
www.publishing.monash.edu

Monash University Publishing brings to the world publications which advance the best traditions of humane and enlightened thought.

Monash University Publishing titles pass through a rigorous process of independent peer review.

www.publishing.monash.edu/books/bs-9781925523683.html

ISBN: 9781925523683 (paperback)
ISBN: 9781925835014 (pdf)
ISBN: 9781925835021 (epub)

Series: Australian History

Design: Les Thomas

Cover photograph: Strathewen 2009, by Katherine Seppings

 A catalogue record for this book is available from the National Library of Australia

Printed in Australia by SOS Print+Media: www.sos.com.au

CONTENTS

Preface vi

1 The Map: Black Saturday in Strathewen 1
2 The Jack: An Introduction to Strathewen 29
3 The Poetry Tree: Memorials 67
4 The Posters: Loss, Anger and Opportunity 95
5 The Mobile Phone: Narratives, Testimony and History 119
6 The Chook: Bushfire and Gender 157
7 The Hard Hat: Place, Home and Rebuilding 191
8 The Chimney: Conclusions 221
9 The Back Story 233

Acknowledgements 247
Oral History Interviews 249
Selected Reading List 251
Index 263

PREFACE

This is a story about stories. It is a cultural history of Strathewen, a tiny place on the northeast fringe of Melbourne. To its residents its history includes orchards, mudbrick houses, networks of old family farms, precious green space and room for kids to grow. But to many Victorians it is a name that is inextricably linked with a single day and the death and devastation it caused: Black Saturday. I originally went to Strathewen to document the bushfire of 2009 and its impact on the residents of the area, but the record of that day was just the beginning of a rich and complicated history about this place, and one that concerns all of us.

It is hard to believe that it is nearly ten years since the bushfires of 2009. From mid-January to late February, at the height of Victoria's hottest summer then on record, the state experienced its worst bushfire season. Black Saturday – 7 February 2009 – was the single worst day as catastrophic fires swept through vast tracts of bushland, obliterated small towns and threatened the outer suburbs of Melbourne. The scale of the disaster unfolded over the following days: 173 people killed; more than 2000 homes destroyed; 78 communities affected; 430,000 hectares of land burnt; more than 8000 livestock and domestic animals lost and untold numbers of native wildlife killed. Strathewen, a settlement of just 200 people, was particularly hard-hit: more than 10 per cent of its population died and 80 per cent of its buildings were destroyed.

As a historian and curator for the Victorian Bushfires Collection at Museum Victoria, I had hoped to document stories that would help

PREFACE

the rest of us understand what it was like to be in a major bushfire. Inevitably the research extended forwards and backwards, looking at the context and the consequences in one small community of Australia's greatest natural disaster. Even as I was researching and writing, people's circumstances, attitudes and decisions were altering and evolving. Many of the people interviewed for this book have, in the intervening years, changed their minds or their priorities or their homes. This is a natural part of coming to terms with what happened in the past and working out what will happen in the future.

So what's the point of documenting these stories if so many of their narrators have moved on? The pragmatic response is that when the next catastrophic bushfire comes along these stories will help us to understand survivors' experiences and observers' reactions. I hope they will illuminate both the successes and the failures and guide us to better decisions in prevention and response. But I think that they also serve a larger purpose, that of history's role in understanding the human condition. These stories remind us that people are individual, complex and ever-changing, and that – although these traits are heightened in the face of catastrophic change – they are common to us all. In order to truly understand and remember what happened on Black Saturday, we have to acknowledge and explore the human dimension of disaster.

Each of the chapters in this book starts with an object connected to Strathewen and to Black Saturday. All but one of these objects is in Museum Victoria's Bushfires Collection, a collection started in the aftermath of the fires. These things – from mobile phone to hard hat – become devices to look at some of the stories, questions, ideas and emotions that surround the bushfires.

For every object included in this book, thousands more exist only in memory. They are frequently mentioned in the oral histories, from small personal treasures to public buildings, from tea sets to tractors. The most powerful ones are connected to people who are deceased – photographs, heirlooms or utilitarian objects that people associated with family and friends. This is because the greatest loss was not material, but human. Twenty-seven people are named on the Strathewen memorial, twenty-three of them residents.[1]

I am grateful to all of the people who shared their experience of Strathewen and have agreed to add it to the public record: Mary Avola, Fred Bateman, Lyn (Lewis) Chambers, Leslye Chappelle, Robert Crisfield, Karen Gardam, Alan Horne, Joyce Horne, Jane Hayward, Barbara Joyce, Helen Legg, Angela McKenzie, Ian McKimmie, Vicki Mitchell, Laurie Nelson, Norma Nelson, Shane Pugh, Sylvia Shaw, Bronwyn Apted South, Darren Thompson, Fiona Truscott, Barrie Tully, Rae Tully, Jim Usher, June Warburton and Rosemary McKimmie Young.

I am also grateful to Ali Griffin and Bill Chisholm of Healesville who were the first people I interviewed about Black Saturday, and Zelma Gartner who recalled the Ash Wednesday bushfires of 1983. For many of them – especially those who lost family and friends, or

---

1   It is an indication of the difficulty and sensitivity of documenting catastrophic events that there are differing accounts of the number of fatalities in Strathewen on Black Saturday. The Royal Commission identified 22 deaths in Strathewen, counting both residents and non-residents (Bernard Teague et al, "2009 Victorian Bushfires Royal Commission Final Report," Melbourne: Parliament of Victoria, 2010, 83.) The memorial in Strathewen, however, lists 27 names, of whom the Strathewen Community Renewal Association nominates 23 as residents (http://www.strathewen.vic.au/ [Accessed 10 February 2014]). The discrepancy is due to differing definitions of the 'community' of Strathewen. The Royal Commission defined it by the location of the deaths, while the memorial includes people who, while not living within the settlement's official boundaries, were still part of Strathewen through their involvement in organisations like Strathewen Primary School. I have chosen the local interpretation.

PREFACE

whose stories do not follow accepted narratives – it was a difficult task.

In writing this book I have also drawn from the work of academics, medical practitioners, scientists, writers, historians and curators. For ease of reading I have kept footnotes and secondary references to a minimum, although there is a selective reading list at the end of the book. But I have, to use one of Al Thomson's favourite expressions, stood on the shoulders of giants, especially Tom Griffiths, Elaine Enarson, Stephen Pyne, Sandro Portelli, Judge Leonard Stretton and Al himself.

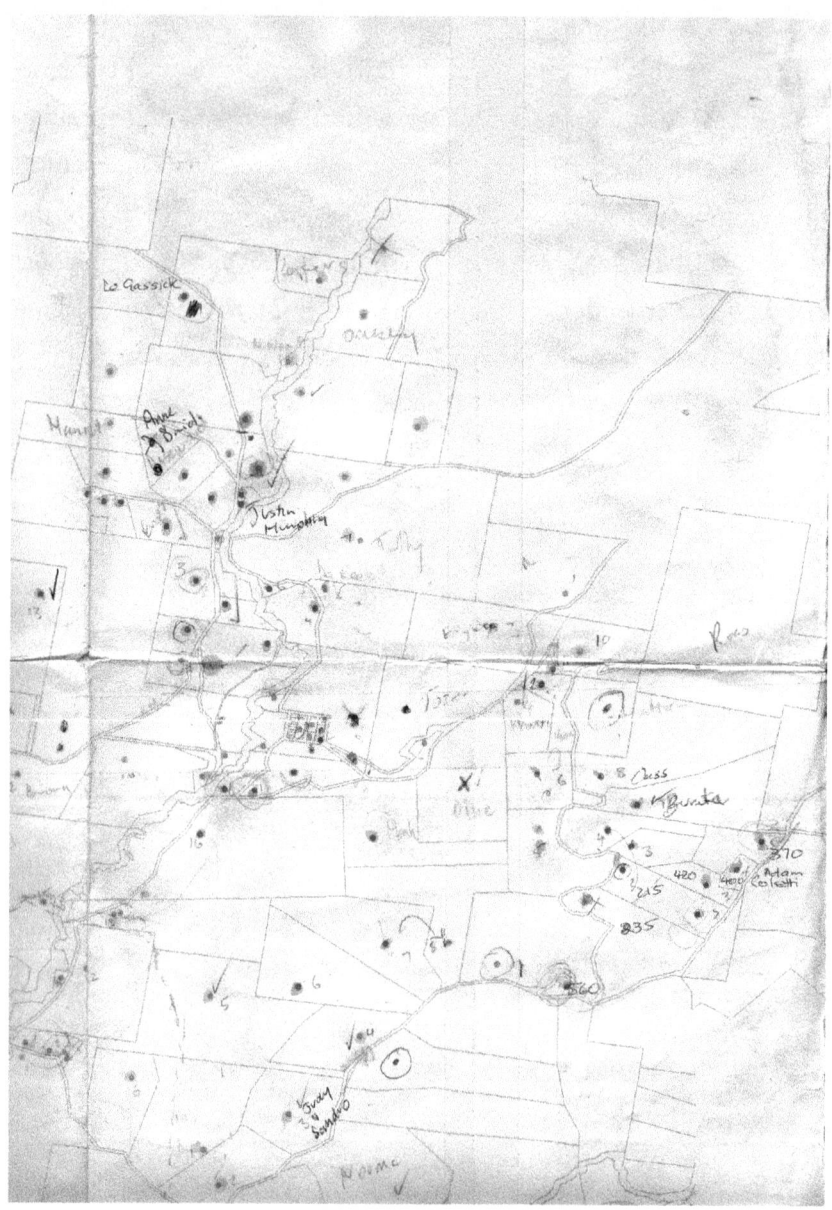

Figure 1. Map of Strathewen. Collection of Bronwyn Apted South.
Image: Peg Fraser

Chapter 1

THE MAP: BLACK SATURDAY IN STRATHEWEN

In the middle of the interview, Bronwyn flipped to the back of her notebook and carefully unfolded the paper glued there. It was a map of Strathewen. Originally intended as a plan for letterbox drops by the local Landcare group, the map bore a curious set of markings consisting of coloured dots and a wavering dotted line across the lower left quadrant.

It took a moment to realise that this was a picture of Strathewen immediately after the fire. The green dots were the houses that survived, the pink dots those that had been destroyed. Looking at the pattern, you can see that below the line all the dots are green and above the line they are mostly pink. The few green dots above the line are those on the outer edges, while the pink ones seem to flow like a river. They form a path through the settlement roughly following, on the left branch, the path of Arthurs Creek and, on the right hand, the route of Bowden Spur Road up to Kinglake.

The fire had started near Kilmore, about 40 km northwest of Strathewen, at 11:47 am on Saturday, 7 February; the cause was later determined to be a faulty power line brought down by the wind. Despite the fact that all of Victoria's emergency services were on high alert, the extreme weather conditions meant that the Kilmore fire was very quickly beyond the ability of the Country Fire Authority (CFA) even to monitor, much less control. The fire was soon throwing out embers 20 or more kilometres ahead, causing new fires to erupt in front of it. The CFA tanker crew stationed in Strathewen was called to fight a spot fire on the outskirts of the settlement.

The bulk of Mount Sugarloaf stood between Strathewen and the fire, blocking any sight of what was heading their way. Communications broke down and none of the communities in the path of the fire, including Strathewen, was warned. CFA captain David McGahy received a 'red flag' danger warning just moments before the fire's arrival and withdrew his crew in the face of overwhelming odds and certain death. The Kilmore East firefront broke around the flanks of Mount Sugarloaf and was suddenly in the middle of Strathewen. At the same time another front hit from the direction of Mittons Bridge. The firestorm engulfed parts of the settlement and was heading towards the outer-suburban towns of Hurstbridge and Wattle Glen (and beyond them, all of northeast Melbourne), when the wind changed.

The dotted line on the map marks, to the best of Bronwyn's knowledge at the time, the position of the fire at that moment, when the hot northerly wind gave way to a strong southwesterly that arrived with the cool change at about 5:40pm. This is where the fire stopped and then changed direction, just on the outskirts of Strathewen, on the boundary of the Apted orchards. It was as if a line had been drawn on the land as well as on the map; it was possible, in the weeks after the fire, to stand with one foot on ash and soot and the other on untouched vegetation.

THE MAP: BLACK SATURDAY IN STRATHEWEN

The eastern flank of the fire became, in the words of the Royal Commission, 'an extraordinarily wide fire front of increased intensity'.[1] The new wind drove the fire away from the outer suburbs of Melbourne, thereby saving tens of thousands of homes and lives, but it went straight back into the heart of Strathewen, through the valley and up the slopes to Flowerdale, Pheasant Creek, Kinglake and beyond. One hundred and thirteen people died in the Kilmore East fire.

Bronwyn lives on the edge of Strathewen, surrounded by the orchards of her family's business, and just beyond the reach of the fire. She and her neighbours created this map to help the police and emergency services search for missing persons. In the chaos immediately following the fire, they were able to significantly reduce the time that police needed to locate people in Strathewen. Bronwyn also kept a grim list of those who were known to have survived, and those who had not.

These little dots on the map reduce the story of Black Saturday to its essence: loss or survival. But even within such a small geographical area everyone experienced the fire and its aftermath differently. The stories of those who witnessed the fire do not add up to a single narrative in which people either win or lose. They show the ferocity of the fire but also its randomness, the wisdom of leaving but also the importance of being prepared to fight, and both the chaos and the calm resolve. The stories also show the way in which – even for the most competent and well-prepared – survival often came down to luck.

---

1   Ibid.

The chapters that follow this one provide the interpretation and analysis expected of written histories, placing the survivors' interviews in larger contexts, examining conflicting views and reflecting on how the structure and content of the stories are influenced by factors, both personal and social, that pre-date and follow the fires. But for the next few pages I want you, the reader, to forget analysis and interpretation and feel, in some very small degree, what the narrators felt.[2]

Before the fire

I'd said to my cousin a couple of months before, 'Rosemary, it's going to be a bad year, isn't it?' Because we were talking about what the conditions were actually like, and I said to her, 'Just promise me, if there's any problems up there, come to me. Please come out, please don't stay there.'[3]

The whole summer was a stinker.[4]

I'd been in the bush, I'd been riding my horses there for years and I had seen – I just didn't feel comfortable. It didn't feel right. The bush felt too dry. You walked in the bush and the grass crackled, everything crackled.[5]

---

[2] Elsewhere in this book I have used italics to indicate quotes from oral history interviews. For ease of reading I have dispensed with italics in the rest of this chapter, but all of the quotations are taken from the survivors' interviews. I have also identified the individual speakers only through footnotes rather than in the body of the text. This is a device which, although it may make it somewhat more difficult to follow individual stories, helps to evoke some of the chaos and confusion of the time. Like the flames did on Black Saturday, the voices come from all directions. I have arranged the excerpts roughly in chronological order, and there are two Darrens: Darren Thompson, who was on Ian McKimmie's property, and Darren Horne, who was with his parents on their property.

[3] Sylvia Shaw, Interview 15 September 2010.

[4] Darren Thompson, Interview 20 August 2013.

[5] Karen Gardam, Interview 15 September 2010.

THE MAP: BLACK SATURDAY IN STRATHEWEN

> The weather in the time before the actual fire was horrendous. It was dry, it was hot, everything was just crisp and burnt.[6]

I went to work and I saw three possums drop out of the tree, just on our drive, and I've never seen that before. And I called home and I said 'I think it's Armageddon.'[7]

> I didn't sleep very well that night and the next day I was just like a dog sniffing the air, waiting for smoke. The air was so dry, it was gritty. And the temperature was constantly going up.[8]

The bush was screaming out, you could smell it, you could sense it.[9]

> 49 degrees under my verandah, had a thermometer. I had never seen a day like it. [...] The birds had gone, there were no little animal noises. It was like it was waiting for drama.[10]

The colours of the manna gums along the creek and the air – there was something different, something I hadn't experienced. It was the dryness of the air. This whole spectrum of colour had changed almost, and there was a sense that you just didn't want to be there.[11]

> Oh, the wind. The wind was howling where I live, it was a funnel through the north and it was howling through there.[12]

---

6   Sylvia Shaw, Interview 15 September 2010.
7   Rosemary McKimmie Young, Interview 6 October 2010.
8   Barbara Joyce, Interview 31 August 2010.
9   Rosemary McKimmie Young, Interview 6 October 2010.
10 Robert Crisfield, Interview 7 August 2013.
11 Bronwyn Apted South, Interview 5 December 2012.
12 Robert Crisfield, Interview 7 August 2013.

Preparation

We were the best I'd ever been set up for fire. I had seventeen sprinklers just around my sheds and house all set up. I had fire pumps all set up, and I had two trailers. Me and the neighbour had a trailer each on the back of our four-wheel drives all set up with water.[13]

> We already had the weather reports it was going to be stinking hot and windy and we figured 'Well, if anything starts at least we can jump on it quick.' [...] We had it covered, we thought.[14]

Never thought of leaving that day, never entered our head to leave. We were looking after the place.[15]

> I tried to talk my mother into coming out of Strathewen on the day before the fires, but she was adamant that she was safe and that she'd already put her fire plan into action during the week. She'd been pumping water all round the house and keeping everything wet.[16]

I installed sprinklers all over the roof. Part of the roof and up to three metres outside was getting watered by the sprinklers, and that was fed from a tank which was up the hill so it didn't need power to really get it going. We had a pump on it but on that day the pump failed but the water still kept coming out. We had woollen clothing and boots and hats and all that in a bag ready.

---

13   Ian McKimmie, Interview 6 October 2010.
14   Darren Thompson, Interview 20 August 2013.
15   Laurie Nelson, Interview 7 September 2012.
16   Karen Gardam, Interview 15 September 2010.

We had galvanised garbage tins for the water, we had all the mops around.[17]

> I guess, personally, I have a preference for just going. You can always replace a house. I'd always have precious things that I'd put in storage, or in the back of my car, and I always intended to go. Being surrounded by bushland, very close, I just thought it would be unbelievable, the ember attack. And in fact a neighbour of mine, Marilyn, had said, 'If there was to be a bushfire, Barbara, you won't believe the ember attack. It will be constant, it will be relentless and it will exhaust you and, you know, it's just a house.'[18]

I'm proud to say that we had five or six different methods of putting out a fire. And if one failed I was down to the next one and if another failed I was down to the next one. So we used all that. We even got to buckets, getting water out of the swimming pool with buckets. You need to be able to have at least four able-bodied people, fit people, to defend your home because you can't be in all places at once.[19]

> We had a trailer with a 1000-gallon water tank on it. And we rang Rodney then, at Listerfield, and Rodney said yeah, he'd come. And Darren arrived in the afternoon and he and little Aidan and I filled up six buckets of water and I said, 'Now this is in case a spark comes we can put it out quick.' Oh, I wasn't that worried and there was nothing happening.[20]

---

17 Fred Bateman, Interview 27 June 2013.
18 Barbara Joyce, Interview 31 August 2010.
19 Barrie Tully, Interview 16 October 2013.
20 Joyce Horne, Interview 2 November 2012.

See, at that stage there was no wind, no smoke, and of course a lot of gum trees all round, and you couldn't see beyond the gum trees.[21]

Warning

I felt like a cat on a hot tin roof, I had to be outside looking, but it was very hot outside so you had to come inside. I'd got on the full clothing. [...] I went up and unlocked the dam paddock.[22]

> We all knew the smoke was coming – we could see the smoke over the back of the mountain. You could smell it.[23]

We were all out by the pool. Some of my kids had some of their mates up as well, we were just out in the pool. Knew something was up but we kept checking up with the CFA sites and ringing and that and they kept saying, 'No it's 45 kilometres away, 45 kilometres away.' And because we'd been evacuated previously quite a few times we just thought, 'No, it's going to be fine. Just don't want to go again, it's too hot.'[24]

> Things were dropping from the sky by 2:00 in the afternoon. There was no talk on television about any fires and that made me feel a bit isolated where I was, of getting no information where I was. I didn't have a radio so I didn't hear any CFA warnings, but in the distance the smoke was changing from white to black which indicates a forest fire. [...] Eventually I

---

21   Alan Horne, Interview 27 November 2012.
22   Bronwyn Apted South, Interview 5 December 2012.
23   Rosemary McKimmie Young, Interview 6 October 2010.
24   Angela McKenzie, Interview 20 August 2012.

THE MAP: BLACK SATURDAY IN STRATHEWEN

just said, 'I'm out of here, that's it.' I grabbed some clothes, personal photos that my parents had given me of me when I was young. I grabbed all them, luckily, and I just left, but I got a mile down the road and thought I was abandoning Strathewen.[25]

Within ten minutes, there was a second plume, a second fire and that's when I knew that things weren't right. And I rang my mother and asked her to leave and she was, like, "No, everything's fine here. I can't see anything". She said it was fine. […] Well, I hung up and then about half an hour later was when I decided to ring Mum again and I couldn't get her and I was really concerned.[26]

About half-past two, looking up and there's bits and pieces falling out of the sky. And they're bits of ember probably about two foot long, just black leaves and sticks.[27]

I went up to the top of a neighbour's hill, across the road, and what I thought was a dust storm coming, it was very clear to me that it was something worse than that. And there were embers falling and our neighbour Craig, who has been in the CFA, he said, 'Just go, get out. I reckon we've got about half an hour before it descends.'[28]

And I packed the cars and evacuated all the female neighbours and children, and my daughter and the three children that were here, and by the time that had happened, the fire was well and truly heading here. So I packed as

---

25   Robert Crisfield, Interview 4 August 2013.
26   Karen Gardam, Interview 15 September 2010.
27   Darren Thompson, Interview 20 August 2013.
28   Barbara Joyce, Interview 31 August 2010.

much as I could and left, after saying goodbye to Ian and another neighbour, and Bill, and thinking I'd never see them again.[29]

I was talking to the neighbour, Geoff, on the phone on and off and the neighbours, on and off regularly. And when Geoff on his side of the hill decided it was time to come over here, I rang the neighbours and said, 'Time to come here.'[30]

And I don't know, it must have been 4:30ish or something, I can't really remember the time, that I rang Vicki's house again and it was all good at her house and then about five, ten minutes later we get a phone call from one of Dylan's mates who lives in Arthurs Creek to say, 'I'm sitting on my verandah, it's jumped the hills, it's coming straight at your place. Get out.'[31]

Leslye was on the phone from Lake Boga saying 'Is there a sign of any fires?' and I said 'No, nothing,' and within five minutes of that it just hit like a bomb.[32]

Arrival

Then at quarter to five Thomas says, 'Look, there's smoke.' There was this column of smoke up at our other property, just straight up.[33]

---

29   Rosemary McKimmie Young, Interview 6 October 2010.
30   Rae Tully, Interview 16 October 2013.
31   Angela McKenzie, Interview 20 August 2012.
32   Fred Bateman, Interview 27 June 2013.
33   Joyce Horne, Interview 27 November 2012.

> I was monitoring all my sprinklers up the top and I had everything running and I noticed a fire start, just down on Chadds Creek Road.[34]

> Lynelle, Darren's wife, said 'What's that noise over there?' and it was the fire coming up that valley. And within five minutes the fire was here 'cause it travelled that quickly.'[35]

> Everyone else thought it came over from Mount Sugarloaf but ours come from the opposite direction, come from St Andrews and it came over a bit of a hill. It came over that and just dropped like a bomb on our place.[36]

> My husband was wanting to drive through. He was, 'I just need to get to your mother.'[37]

> You looked up and there was just like a big red cloud coming toward you. The sky was just red, a big red cloud moving toward you. And I looked at it and thought, 'There's not much you can do with that.'[38]

> And as I was driving up the hill, I saw the fire burst over the mountain on the north side and I saw fire coming around the mountain on the south-west side, so I knew the mountain was going to go. And so I tried to stand up the sprinklers in the wind – I'd never seen a wind like it. And the roar from the flames was just horrific. You just couldn't hear. There was no conversation, the roar was just deafening.

---

34 Ian McKimmie, Interview 6 October 2010.
35 Joyce Horne, Interview 27 November 2012.
36 Fred Bateman, Interview 27 June 2013.
37 Karen Gardam, Interview 15 September 2010.
38 Laurie Nelson, Interview 7 September 2010.

The roar, before the actual flames came, was probably more frightening than the flames.[39]

> My son-in-law came to the door and screamed out, 'You've got to come now, you've got to come out now!' [...] They were already in the swimming pool.[40]

Then all hell started breaking loose. We started getting spot fires around the houses. [...] It come from all directions, didn't matter where you were, started hitting you in the face.[41]

> I was in full firefighting gear and my back was that hot – it was facing the direction of the heat – it was that hot that I thought my back was on fire and I just dived off the tractor. I didn't jump, I dived.[42]

Lynelle said, 'I think we should pray,' and she said a short prayer asking God to be with us.[43]

> When the devil came over the mountain, God fucked off.[44]

Peak

So everyone got in the cars, we had five carloads of kids with us, and got down to the corner. Had a massive argument with my husband in the car 'cause he was saying, 'Go right,' and you couldn't go right 'cause it was already, like, the fire, the flames were like 40 foot in the

---

39   Ian McKimmie, Interview 6 October 2010.
40   Norma Nelson, Interview 7 September 2012.
41   Darren Thompson, Interview 20 August 2013.
42   Barrie Tully, Interview 16 October 2013.
43   Joyce Horne, Interview 27 November 2012.
44   Darren Thompson, Interview 20 August 2013.

air, it was coming up the back way. And so I turned left to go up the mountain. So he's screaming at me in the car, 'You're gonna kill us all, pull up and turn around,' but I just kept driving. […] And we got through – there was some fires on the way up, we got through those – got halfway up the cutting and saw the whole valley blow up like an atomic bomb.[45]

> One fireball from Mt Disappointment, the whole town – not town, the whole valley and side of the hill – exploded. The heat was so it just exploded and there was no – basically, there was no chance for anyone unless luck intervened and you had to have terrible good luck to come out.[46]

There was about three or four roadblocks, I just told them to get out of my way. And they were trying to stop me to begin with, they'd stop us and say, 'You can't go through.' And I'm, like, 'My mother's in there and you've got to get out of our way.'[47]

> I remember Laurie saying to me, 'Don't look, the house is going.'[48]

You couldn't see the fire as such. It was like a huge thick wall of grey and you couldn't see in it. It was so loud and the wind was so hot and just about blew you away.[49]

> I never panicked as such but it wasn't very nice either. I was outside most of the time and just with the hoses. We had

---

45   Angela McKenzie, Interview 20 August 2012.
46   Robert Crisfield, Interview 7 August 2012.
47   Karen Gardam, Interview 15 September 2010.
48   Norma Nelson, Interview 7 September 2012.
49   Karen Gardam, Interview 15 September 2010.

> four hoses all round the house but it just wasn't enough for me to go from one place to the other. One time I went down towards the back of the house and the hose had been up against a tree that caught fire, so that ruled that hose out. [...] All of a sudden part of the back of the house started and that was it. I was inside with buckets of water trying to slow it down but I had no hope once it started.[50]

Darren just drove like hell through the vegie garden and it was bump, bump, bump I felt, and I'm hanging on to him and round the corner and down to the dam. And of course there was all this smoke and dark and heat and fire raging. 'Get in the dam.' 'Oh, I can't get in the dam.' My legs weren't any good to do that. So we just sat there, he started up the motor and squirted us with water I suppose for an hour.[51]

> It was scary watching fire balls going overhead and take out houses and that sort of stuff. And it was scary listening to people screaming – kids, all that – but knowing you couldn't do anything was the hard part. Knowing they're out there screaming and there's not a damn thing you can do about it. If you had've left where you were you were dead.[52]

The hardest part for me and for those of us who did evacuate was the not knowing. I was convinced Bill was dead. When I evacuated, I got halfway down to Hurstbridge and I saw the fire coming from that

---

50   Fred Bateman, Interview 27 June 2013.
51   Joyce Horne, Interview 27 November 2012.
52   Darren Thompson, Interview 20 August 2013.

side, the other side of the mountain, which I knew no one had seen here. [...] So I thought, 'They're gone.'[53]

> I thought we might die. I thought, 'This is a strange way to die,' because we were just being pelted with embers. And I sat there with my head in my hands to cover my face and he'd squirt the water over us and that'd be cooling and the next moment you'd get a shower of hot pellets at you. And I had a nylon dress on and it all went in little knobs from the embers and I could feel it, little funny knobs.[54]

There was intermittent contact via mobile phone with my cousins that were still in there, and then that cut out and we just knew the place was burning down. We knew they were all trapped.[55]

> Things were just exploding before the flames hit them. They just exploded. And buildings were just igniting other buildings. There was no stopping it. The closest thing to hell I hope I ever see.[56]

I thought, 'This thing won't stop 'til it reaches St Kilda.'[57]

> The wind was blowing like jet planes, the teenagers are on the floor crying, children are over there, they're crying. The woman who was renting the house was in the lounge 'cause she cried the loudest. And I was handing out Coca-Cola at that stage to the kids because the power was off but

---

53   Rosemary McKimmie Young, Interview 6 October 2010.
54   Joyce Horne, Interview 27 November 2012.
55   Sylvia Shaw, Interview 15 September 2010.
56   Ian McKimmie, Interview 6 October 2010.
57   Jim Usher, Interview 289 October 2013.

> everything was still cold. [...] And then I got the face washers and put them in the freezer, giving them to the girls while they cried so everyone had nice cold face washers. And there was nothing else to do at that stage. [...] It was a very long hour.[58]

The last conversation I had with my mum was when I was at Mittons Bridge and I told her that I couldn't come through that way and I had to go round up Cottlesbridge Road and even then, she wasn't afraid. She didn't seem to – I don't know whether she was just being brave or she honestly didn't know what was coming at that stage.[59]

> In all the houses, while I was fighting the fire, just enormous explosions all the time. Either the gas bottles going up and/or the houses just collapsing, because every house in the Village just flattened and went to the ground.[60]

When the big ember attack started happening, it just sucked all the oxygen out of the house and you couldn't breathe. You couldn't breathe in and you had to hold your breath really hard to stop your lungs from getting sucked out. You could feel it.[61]

> The fire alarms were going screeching, the smoke was just black at head height, so we were all on the floor, on the cold tiles. They were lovely. And that was it. We just sat the hour out and ignored what was happening around us. Callum and Matt went out to see if the house was on fire and they

---

58   Rae Tully, Interview 16 October 2013.
59   Karen Gardam, Interview 15 September 2010.
60   Fred Bateman, Interview 27 June 2013.
61   Darren Thompson, Interview 20 August 2013.

couldn't breathe – there was no oxygen – so they were back in real quick. And the roof was making an awful noise when the roof was pulling off the beams, the screeching of the nails along with the wind and the noise of the fire, the roof was making an awful din, the nails screeching and then it started flapping so it was adding to the din. But we didn't know at that stage how bad the roof was until they came to replace it and they said, 'It's just sitting there.'[62]

We had to keep on taking breaths and going under the water to survive. And at one stage there you just felt as you came up – it just burned as you took a breath – and I thought, 'Oh, this is the end.'[63]

I ran down the street at Diamond Creek and saw the whole mountain burning, and I didn't think anyone would survive. I thought Ian was gone, everyone, my nephews and nieces – I thought everyone was dead. I thought nobody could possibly survive that fire.[64]

The wind change

Anyhow when the cool change, the southerly change, came, drove it up this way absolutely like a rocket.[65]

He says, 'I'm sorry, Mum, the house is gone.' I said, 'I know.' I knew it would have to be gone. And after a little while it went charging, the fire went charging down that creek bed.

---

62 Rae Tully, Interview 16 October 2013.
63 Norma Nelson, Interview 7 September 2012.
64 Rosemary McKimmie Young, Interview 6 October 2010.
65 Alan Horne, Interview 27 November 2012.

> And you know, it was just like a wild animal, the way the trees were leaning over and the heat and the smoke and the darkness and the noise and the violence. And I thought of the people further down the creek and thought, 'How are they going to manage?'[66]

It was chaos. And black. It was pitch black. The illumination was only from the flames. And the sparks, there was just a red illumination. You could see black shapes and eventually I saw Darren. He made a run for it in a lull and got in. We spent the rest of the time just inside the house waiting till the plaster fell out of the ceiling, and the whole house was on fire.[67]

> It was just – it wasn't a fire – it was just like a nuclear bomb what came through. And how we survived I don't know. I don't know how or why we're here but we are. It was just a miracle. We really lost oxygen at one stage and thought that was it.[68]

We only had a little thousand gallon tank with a little bit of water in it, which I knew the hose had already burnt off. So we took a whole heap of wet towels with us and jumped in behind the tank and dug a little trench, a little swamp there, and turned the tap on and just kept wetting towels and putting them over our heads until it stopped. And that was, like, three quarters of an hour or something. It seemed forever.[69]

---

66 Joyce Horne, Interview 27 November 2012.
67 Ian McKimmie, Interview 6 October 2010.
68 Vicki Mitchell, Interview 8 August 2012.
69 Ian McKimmie, Interview 6 October 2010.

I went under the water and the next time I came up it just wasn't quite so bad. And after that you got a little bit more air but it was a very hairy moment.[70]

Then it just went, as they said exactly, 'And then the wind changed,' and off it went up the hill. [...] It was just black and smoking, everything was smoking. Yes, quiet, but the most amazing thing is it was daylight again. It was so dark, pitch black, for that hour and then suddenly it was back to being in the middle of the afternoon and it started to get cool almost immediately.[71]

'Listen.' 'What? Listen to what?' 'It's quiet.' Yeah, it's quiet and it's still black, and all of a sudden I look around and it's daylight.[72]

Immediate Aftermath

Oh, it was such a relief when Lynelle came out of the dam with the two boys with her arms in the air. 'We're alive! We're alive!'[73]

My brother tried to get in after the fires to save my mum but he ended up having a massive heart attack and they were unable to get an ambulance in and he ended up dying.[74]

I got up and said, 'Oh, I need an ambulance.' And they said, 'You won't get an ambulance, Mum, nobody'll get through here.' And I thought, 'I'm going to die here.'[75]

---

70 Norma Nelson, Interview 7 September 2012.
71 Rae Tully, Interview 16 October 2013.
72 Darren Thompson, Interview 20 August 2013.
73 Joyce Horne, Interview 27 November 2012.
74 Karen Gardam, Interview 15 September 2010.
75 Joyce Horne, Interview 27 November 2012.

> My brother-in-law was – I thought we'd lost him, and the kids. I hadn't heard them leave. They'd gone down to the dam. […] After the lull came, I was sitting there, Darren said, 'Let's make a run for it.' But I said, 'Let's just sit here for a second and gather our thoughts.' Because the house had burnt down, it was still very hot, but I just felt that the worst of it had gone.[76]

When I knew I'd lost the house, I'd been fighting the fire for about an hour. I can remember I went out into our driveway which was fairly open and sat down and got my breath back. And when I saw the house really going then I decided to try and get out, so I walked out down towards the school and it took me three quarters of an hour to get down there. It wasn't a kilometre, it was so many trees were down everywhere. I had to crawl over them, under them, just to fight my way out. All the roads were blocked.[77]

> He managed to come through back paddocks and through people's paddocks and burnt-out orchards and trees across the road. He had a rotten trip because police didn't want him to come to Strathewen but he was determined to find us.[78]

Wes told me that they were going to go into Strathewen that night, at one or two o'clock in the morning that night. They were going to go in, they were going to try, a group of them, to walk in. And I'd asked him could he look for my mum, and he said he would.[79]

---

76   Ian McKimmie, Interview 6 October 2010.
77   Fred Bateman, Interview 27 June 2013.
78   Joyce Horne, Interview 27 November 2012.
79   Karen Gardam, Interview 15 September 2010.

THE MAP: BLACK SATURDAY IN STRATHEWEN

> My neighbour's husband and her son were on the CFA tanker and they'd got in to the first casualties. And they'd come out and just the look on their faces, the absolute horror on their faces.[80]

You knew that everything you possessed had gone. There was nothing, it was just wasteland, just black. Everything was black, there was no other colour.[81]

> David McGahy, Wes Stecher and Peter Jenkinson came walking up the track. [...] And their faces when they came up, they couldn't believe we were there. David said it was a very touching moment to see the little kids. He was like Father Christmas.[82]

The next morning coming up was something I'll never forget. There was [...] of course, all the deceased were still there – you knew – and I knew them. And hundreds and hundreds and hundreds of animals burning, still standing, burning, alive. I saw a horse with its face almost dropping off to its feet, hundreds of cattle blown up from the fire. Everywhere you looked there was something dead, burnt, those that hadn't turned to ash, because a lot of them were just ash.[83]

> Anything to show for the last 50 years' work, anything I've done, is gone. Your whole life's work, everything, just gone.[84]

---

80 Bronwyn Apted South, Interview 5 December 2010.
81 Norma Nelson, Interview 7 September 2012.
82 Rae Tully, Interview 16 October 2013.
83 Rosemary McKimmie Young, Interview 6 October 2010.
84 Laurie Nelson, Interview 7 September 2012.

BLACK SATURDAY

When you hear the house is gone, you just really, you just can't imagine it. You cannot imagine it. You don't feel anything really, it's just – you just can't sort of believe that it's happened to you. You see it on the news and all that, and then you sort of think, you know, 'We've got nothing.'[85]

> It was all black and grey, everything was all black and grey. Depending on where you walked you'd be nearly up to knee deep in ash, you just sunk like snow. I remember not being able to get my bearings in some places, coming up the roads and never realising the side of the road was so high and just the expanse of – you know, your perception of the area, it totally changed, all the boundaries were gone. You could see for miles, things you couldn't see before.[86]

I didn't quite know what it was I was looking at. Like, I knew what it was, but it wasn't in my experience so I couldn't relate the images. It was just hard to process, the black and white. That's why I thought, 'It looks like a snow scene,' because I'd seen a snow scene.[87]

> I had 25 burns, like ember burns, on each leg and […] they cut my clothes off me, they put me on this nice white bed and I said, 'Oh, but I'm so dirty.'[88]

The door downstairs had blown open and the door upstairs and the wire screens had filtered the particles of ash that came in the house, so the house was so black inside. Everything was covered with soot.

---

85 Leslye Chappelle, Interview 27 June 2013.
86 Angela McKenzie, Interview 20 August 2012.
87 Barbara Joyce, Interview 31 August 2010.
88 Joyce Horne, Interview 27 November 2012.

> It was ugly, it was really horrible. And I can't remember feeling pleased that the house was still standing. I remember feeling just overwhelmed by the blackness of it all.[89]

> And we got to a point on Eagles Nest Road and then: burnt-black grass. And then: untouched. [...] You could draw a line on it. And that's where the wind had changed.[90]

Later on

So I went to the Arthurs Creek hall and a lot of the Strathewen community were there and I got handed a box of tissues and then they told me Mum was gone. And then they just all hugged me.[91]

> Initially it was just touching, crying, talking, hugging. There were children arriving whose horses had died, there were children arriving who didn't have parents, or a parent. There were people just so, so hurt, and so worried, we still had so much news that we hadn't had confirmed. We were still hoping on a lot of fronts.[92]

They were searching for my body for three days, they went right over the property. I ended up in hospital and I registered with the Red Cross but that didn't get to the police. [...] So for three days, because our property was so big and our roof was so big, that for three days they were searching and searching.[93]

---

89 Barbara Joyce, Interview 31 August 2010.
90 Ian McKimmie, Interview 6 October 2010.
91 Karen Gardam, Interview 15 September 2010.
92 Jane Hayward, Interview 3 November 2010.
93 Fred Bateman, Interview 27 June 2013.

> We were, all of us, just looking for the people that we knew. Had they got out? Hearing deaths on a daily basis, and they were all pretty much people that we knew. It just went on and on. You looked and you looked and then if you were lucky, you found them.[94]

You'd hear, 'Oh, Peter Avola died.' 'Oh, Irma Winton died.' 'Oh, the Village got burnt out and the Paulkas died.' And you keep hearing all these people that died and it just – it was like a nightmare, it doesn't seem real, and we just kept hearing more and more.[95]

> I told [CFA captain David McGahy], 'If you had of had 20 tankers there, all those guys would have been dead. There's no point in saying sorry, you did what you could do. You would have just lost more lives.'[96]

Obliterated. Disintegrated. It hadn't even been blown up. It just disappeared. Things had just disappeared. There were ruins of houses, there were landmarks and things that had always been there, just disappeared. Gone.[97]

> Almost like they'd never existed.[98]

I knew it was gone, probably, when I went and first saw the house. It really sort of hit home that there was really nothing left, nothing. And the alpacas, they upset me. The alpacas, they were killed and

---

94 Sylvia Shaw, Interview 15 September 2010.
95 Joyce Horne, Interview 27 November 2012.
96 Darren Thompson, Interview 20 August 2013.
97 Karen Gardam, Interview 15 September 2012.
98 Sylvia Shaw, Interview 15 September 2010.

that really upset me. All I could see was their big brown eyes and they would have been so frightened.[99]

> The risky weather pattern continued, there were fires elsewhere, there were repeated flare-ups, there was smoke, for weeks. [...] We lived with the helicopters going over, and every time a chopper went over, the intake of breath in the classroom – you felt it, we felt it in the pit of our stomach, for all these kids.[100]

I found once I was here I didn't want to leave. It took me a while before I could even go shopping, to get food. It was like the outside world was not real any more. We were living in this black world that was like another planet. And those of us that were still here, and there was, what, five families, I think, in Strathewen then. There was no lights, no neighbours, at night time it was eerie.[101]

> Driving past, seeing people's cars still in the driveway, knowing they won't have survived, and day by day hearing of more and more people who didn't make it. And you didn't care about your house or belongings, it was so insignificant compared to the fact that all your children were alive.[102]

This is our second life, we're very grateful to still be here. [...] We know that we were a minute or two from death.[103]

---

99   Leslye Chappelle, Interview 27 June 2013.
100 Jane Hayward, Interview 3 November 2010.
101 Rosemary McKimmie Young, Interview 6 October 2010.
102 Angela McKenzie, Interview 20 August 2012.
103 Rae Tully, Interview 16 October 2013.

> I walked out with five cents and a torch, didn't even have a pocketknife. Walk a mile in another man's shoes? Try walking in his socks and jocks.[104]

Strathewen always seemed like this huge place and then after the fires went through, it was this tiny place. You could see every road, every – I just couldn't believe how small it was.[105]

> We stayed living elsewhere for a few months because it was just too ugly, and too filthy. Until we got electricity on, that seemed to take forever. We needed water as well. We needed a generator. It was too challenging to come back when we were already quite exhausted just by the trauma of the evacuation and what followed. And we were going to many funerals and memorials. So many.[106]

I knew that if I stopped and thought about it I could have really gone down in a big, bad way and no good to anyone, including myself.[107]

> Everything that was a given and a safety barrier and a safety net for these kids was destroyed. So school became that place where something was normal, as normal as we could make it. We weren't very normal. But we could pretend, and that is what we did.[108]

---

104 Darren Thompson, Interview 20 August 2013.
105 Karen Gardam, Interview 15 September 2010.
106 Barbara Joyce, Interview 31 August 2010.
107 Robert Crisfield, Interview 7 August 2013.
108 Jane Hayward, Interview 3 November 2010.

THE MAP: BLACK SATURDAY IN STRATHEWEN

You look at it and you say, well, really there is nothing left. The characteristics of that landscape have changed, probably forever. We're back to the bare bones. The backbones of the land.[109]

---

[109] Sylvia Shaw, Interview 15 September 2010.

Figure 2: Trewhella jack (bushfire-affected). Victorian Bushfires Collection, Museum Victoria, HT 27281.
Image: Taryn Ellis. Source: Museum Victoria.

Chapter 2

THE JACK: AN INTRODUCTION TO STRATHEWEN

Look closely at this photo, and you can see a long handle poking out of the mess of objects at the foot of a burned tree stump. It's a Trewhella jack, and the photo was taken in August 2011, eighteen months after the Black Saturday bushfires. The jack was used for many years in a sawmill in Strathewen, located on the Sparkes family farm. The mill, along with the family homestead and other buildings on the property, was destroyed in the February 2009 bushfires.

Let's back up a bit, to the time before the fires. Although for many of us Strathewen only came into existence when it appeared on television, radio, in the newspapers and online as a scene of death and disaster, it had been a place of European settlement for over 150 years. It is still there today – utterly changed, but not destroyed. The jack is one of many objects collected by the museum which place Black Saturday in a longer historical context, connecting Strathewen's present and past.

The sawmill in which the jack was used was a small affair, built to harvest and mill the eucalypts – mostly manna and sugar gums – that stretched up the flanks of Mount Sugarloaf. Kinglake National Park was created in 1928 and the gradual phasing out of commercial lumbering meant the eventual end of little farm timber operations like this one. The sawmill had been derelict for decades before it burned.

The Trewhella jack was an indispensable piece of timbering equipment. Invented by William Trewhella of West Trentham, Victoria, in 1888, the jack had a long lever and ratcheted hoist that made it possible for just one or two men to do a lot of the heavy lifting needed around a sawmill. William Trewhella developed the tool to lift logs in his own mill but it proved so useful for land clearing and stump pulling that Trewhella Brothers soon became a manufacturer of jacks and other farming equipment for both local and international trade.

This is a single-purchase 'Wallaby' jack, operated by one man, and it could lift 2.5 tons. It was part of the suite of equipment that made it possible for European settlers to move into the heart of the Victorian forests and set up sawmills and settlements in tiny clearings in the midst of the tall timber. The ability to mill timber on site before hauling it to market meant a great reduction in the transport infrastructure required, making it both easier and cheaper to deliver posts and planks where they were needed. It also meant that these little sawmill settlements were far from the cleared farmlands, surrounded by vast tracts of virgin forest and highly vulnerable to bushfire. This was brought home in terrifying fashion in 1939. Sixty-nine sawmills were destroyed in the Black Friday bushfires that year and, of the 71 fatalities on that day, most of them occurred in or near the deep-forest sawmills.

The Stretton Royal Commission into the 1939 fires recommended that such settlements should eventually be abandoned. The Commissioner, Judge Leonard Stretton, wrote, 'There are forest regions in Victoria which are particularly dangerous fire areas. Of these regions

THE JACK: AN INTRODUCTION TO STRATHEWEN

it can never be said that their mills are quite safe at all times or that, at some times, any mill is reasonably safe.'[1] His words were echoed seventy years later in the 2009 Royal Commission's controversial buyback scheme – although in 2009 they were talking about homes, not sawmills.

By the time of the 2009 fires, the jack had long been stored in the shed of the homestead, an object no longer in use but more trouble to throw away than to keep. It had been a significant labour-saving device in its day, but it doesn't strike us as one now. With the lever locked into position it's nearly two metres long and is made of solid steel, so heavy that it took three of us to lift it into the museum van. It has certainly lived up to the manufacturer's claim that it was 'proof against the weather and equal to any amount of rough usage'.[2] That an object like this could have been considered lightweight and portable shows us not only how much we have come to depend on modern materials like aluminium alloys, but also of what desperately hard work the early timber cutters and sawmillers had to do.

Tiny sawmills and woodworking operations go right back to the beginning of European settlement. One of the earliest operations in Strathewen was sited at Carseburn, a property settled by John Mann, to whom the Sparkes were related though marriage. When Joyce Horne's family bought Carseburn in 1944, it was a large house that had originally been a gracious home but had been allowed to decline over the years. *It was so green and beautiful with an old established garden and all the fruit trees we'd find tucked away on the flats amongst*

---

1   Judge Leonard Stretton, "Report of the Royal Commission to Inquire into the Causes of and Measures Taken to Prevent the Bush Fires of January 1939," (Melbourne: Government Printer, 1939), 34.
2   "Trewhella Grubbers & Jacks Etc.," ed. Trewhella Brothers (Melbourne1916), 28. Museum Victoria TL 012041.

the blackberries. It was funny: it had been neglected, the property had been neglected and you had all sorts of finds.[3] Surrounded by lilacs, roses and other European shrubs, the lush green surrounds were especially striking after Joyce's old home in Perry Bridge, Gippsland, which had been hit with drought and bushfire in previous years.

A diary from the Mann family recorded the cutting of timber at Carseburn for the new Strathewen community hall in October of 1901, which was built on land that another member of the Mann family had donated. Years later, the Sparkes' sawmill provided planks to repair the hall, as well as Strathewen Primary School, the guesthouse Singing Water, and the Country Fire Authority station in the nearby village of Arthurs Creek. It was originally sited near the creek, where the stream provided water for the steam-powered engine. In the early 1950s the sawmill equipment was put on the back of an old Bedford flatbed truck and moved to its final location just under Mount Sugarloaf's shoulder. The truck's engine was then used to power the belts that ran the saw and the track. All the structures in Strathewen built or repaired with timber from the sawmill were still standing in early 2009, but none survived Black Saturday.

Early settlement

Through its associations with timber cutting, the jack takes us back to the beginning of Strathewen's agricultural history. George McLelland, 'a thriving, industrious, and well-conducted settler,' was a squatter in the area in 1851.[4] Shortly after the Grants Land Act

---

3   Joyce Horne, Interview 27 November 2012. For ease of reading, I have used quotation marks to designate quotes from written sources, and italics to indicate quotes from oral histories.
4   *Argus*, 8 February 1851.

THE JACK: AN INTRODUCTION TO STRATHEWEN

of 1869 opened the area for selection, several selectors chose land in the Upper Arthurs Creek district, as the place was then known. The first were James and Duncan Smith and their selection (Allotment 1, Parish of Queenstown) in 1871 was named Glen Ard. They were soon followed by others, including John Mann at Carseburn and his brother James, who established Lang Fauld Farm nearby.

The location was attractive to selectors, situated in the upper reaches of Arthurs Creek just at the junction with Chadds Creek. The watercourses wind through a valley framed by timbered slopes, bordered on three sides by what is now the Kinglake National Park and overlooked by the distinctive presence of Mount Sugarloaf. Despite its promising aspect, James Mann found the area unrewarding for grain, reporting in 1876, 'The land is too poor for cultivation, scarcely producing the seed put on it.'[5] But the soil that failed to return a decent crop of grain proved good for orchards, especially apples and pears that benefited from the winter chill provided by the elevation and the encircling hills. *Because we were a stony-type ground [apples] kept well, had good flavour. An apple is suited to that type of ground*, according to Alan Horne, whose family took up land they called Hazelmead on the Arthurs Creek in the 1880s.

Orchards became the lifeblood of the area, supplying both the local market for fresh fruit and the pressing houses that cider manufacturer Paul Kitz established in nearby Diamond Creek and Hurstbridge. The main market, however, was the export trade to Britain, where Australian apples were sold in the northern hemisphere's spring, months before the English crop was ready. The names of the long-keeping varieties grown in Strathewen's thin soil

---

5   Lindsay Mann, *James and John Mann of Arthur's Creek: A Brief History* (Melbourne: self-published, c2004), 4.

are a paean to a forgotten diversity: Rome Beauty, Reinette, Sturmer, London Pippin, Democrat and Yates Statesman, along with better-known varieties like Jonathan, Delicious and Granny Smith.

At the turn of the twentieth century Strathewen acquired its name. An 1897 petition for a local post office proposed the name of Strathewen as a tribute to the veteran local politician, Ewen Cameron, MLA, JP. The petition was unsuccessful, but the name stuck. Strathewen was an amalgam of Cameron's first name and the Scottish word for valley, a reflection of both the topography of the area and the origin of many of the first settlers. Unlike many other parts of Victoria, Strathewen fitted into European ideas of what good country should look like: treed on the hillsides, waterways bubbling along the valley floor, the encircling hills offering protection from the sun and sometimes a dusting of snow on cold mornings. Even in the height of summer the valley was cool and green. To those first settlers it would have looked, if not exactly comfortable, at least comprehensible.

The name of Strathewen is also indicative of the extent to which European settlers brought with them a framework of attitudes to the land. Each selector was required to 'improve' – meaning to clear, plant and fence – a percentage of their property before they could obtain clear title. Undeveloped bush, often too steep for farming purposes, was regarded as 'useless' land, an expression used repeatedly over the years. Small landholdings were taken up and a scattering of homesteads established along the creek banks, moving up the hillsides as paddocks were gradually cleared. Their names were more declarations of European habitation: Glen Ard, Carseburn, Lang Fauld Farm, Hazelmead, Violet Glen.

Many of the settlers established English gardens as well as orchards. Carseburn was not the only paradise in Joyce Horne's memory; the

THE JACK: AN INTRODUCTION TO STRATHEWEN

home of her future parents-in-law *had a beautiful garden around it. I think Alan's father was very keen on gardening and they had a lot of ornamental plants like cypresses, but they were trimmed in fancy shapes, and hedges and camellias and those palm trees.*[6] The house was demolished in 1960 to make way for the power lines bringing electricity to Strathewen, but the palm trees that lined the drive from Chadds Creek Road still march across the paddock today.

Family members often selected land beside each other and created alliances that allowed them to meet the inevitable setbacks of early farming life. John and James Mann emigrated together from Scotland and took up adjoining selections in Upper Arthurs Creek, as did the Murphys and the Hornes. When John Mann died in 1875, leaving his widow Violet with 12 children, it was his brother David to whom Violet turned for help, later marrying him and having two more children.

Strathewen did eventually get its post office in 1909, followed by the school in 1917. Before this, children like Alan Horne's father Ray walked up the mountain to Kinglake three days a week to attend school there. These services, along with the community hall and the playing oval, formed the nucleus for the small community. The settlement never had a main street or a shop or even a pub.

Churches were permitted to hold services in the hall, including the Presbyterian Church's harvest festival each year. *Once a year they had Harvest Thanksgiving and all the locals would bring their fruit and vegies and flowers and make a beautiful display with different levels. They'd get a case of grapes from market and use that to decorate the shelves. There'd be boxes of apples and pears and potatoes and figs. And Alan's auntie grew*

---

6   Joyce Horne, Interview 27 November 2012.

the biggest dahlias, they were like prizewinners and they'd have dahlias everywhere. And then, on the Monday night, that was all auctioned and they'd bid for it, 'cause all the old bachelors would come, and the locals, and it was another social night.[7]

Strathewen started small and grew slowly, in part because of its isolation. Its position in the valley among the mountains was picturesque but difficult of access. From the time of its establishment as a farming community the settlement had been plagued by bad roads, and even today the state of the roads in Strathewen are a matter of half-joking frustration. (Alan Horne found that one of the few good things to come out of Black Saturday was that *they paved Chadds Creek Road: never thought I'd see that in my lifetime.*[8]) In 1923 the local paper complained that 'in wintertime the roads in these districts are one long course of deep heavy mud and slush, and in summertime one long course of blinding, choking dust'.[9] As late as 1941, when Lyn Lewis went to Strathewen to take up the first position in her teaching career, it was still considered remote and inaccessible. The only transport in and out of the place for those, like her, who didn't own a horse was a seat in the back of the butcher's cart.

The problems of getting increasingly large loads of fresh produce to market in such dismal conditions were believed to be holding back the development of the area. The Arthurs Creek Fruit and Progress Association was formed in 1917, on the initiative of disgruntled Strathewen orchardists, to bring pressure to bear on the decision-makers. Squabbles between the Association and local councillors over the cost and schedules for completion of roads, and

---

7   Joyce Horne, Interview 27 November 2012.
8   Alan Horne, Interview 27 November 2012.
9   *Hurstbridge Advertiser*, 18 May 1923.

accounts of deputations to the Minister to argue for the extension of the Hurstbridge train line through to Kinglake, enlivened the local papers for years. When an outsider complained in a letter to the editor that Strathewen was getting its share of government investment but 'that corner is always asking for more,' the residents of 'that corner' reacted with outrage: 'even with its present bad roads and rotten bridges, [Strathewen] produces more and better fruit, crops, vegetables and live stock yearly'.[10]

It would, however, be wrong to picture Strathewen as a community for which geographical distance meant social isolation. Despite the twisty dirt roads, narrow bridges and occasionally treacherous conditions, the people of Strathewen were part of a broad network beyond their own community that over the years included cricket teams, debating societies, tennis clubs, musical societies, agricultural shows, charities and church groups. Joyce Horne recalled arriving in the 1940s: *Well, when we first came to Strathewen there was a tennis club and a cricket club, and because the war was on they had fundraising events on a Saturday night for the war effort, and that was really good. All the locals would turn up and they'd raffle things and raise money. And socially they'd have a bit of a dance, somebody would be on the piano playing some dance tunes, and in the back room the old fellas would be playing cards. They'd have a big fire going and a big boiler for water for the supper and the ladies would all make a beautiful supper and it was just good fun on a Saturday night.*[11]

Local sports competitions, musical events and social nights attracted people from surrounding settlements like Arthurs Creek, Doreen, Whittlesea, Hurstbridge, St Andrews, Kinglake and Scrubby

---

10   Ibid.
11   Joyce Horne, Interview 27 November 2012.

Creek. The community hall repaired with the sawmill's timber was the site of musical performances, dances, card parties, recitations and fundraising concerts. In August of 1923 the *Hurstbridge Advertiser*'s correspondent reported that 'Strathewen functions have such a splendid reputation that in spite of a very dark, cold and wet night, people attended from the city, Kinglake, Arthurs Creek and Streamville, as well as the majority of local residents.' The entertainment that evening included music, cards, a shadow-dancing competition won by Miss Muriel Brain and a glorious array of refreshments. The finale was a confetti battle, after which 'the hall floor reminded one of the stately Sugarloaf mountain (which overlooks it like a fortress) after a heavy snowstorm'.[12]

The city and the bush

For some visitors Strathewen's relative isolation, which was such a disadvantage in taking produce to market, was part of its attraction. They liked the twisty dirt roads, narrow bridges and occasionally treacherous conditions. The area had a reputation as a beauty spot and was visited by walking parties, cyclists, motor clubs and groups on nature outings. R.H. Croll, journalist, naturalist and stalwart of the Melbourne Walking Club, exhorted his readers to take to the back roads and bush tracks of Victoria. Of a day walk in the Strathewen area, he wrote:

> It is a typical country track, and as it hugs the ridge it gives appetising glimpses, through the timber, of long slopes dropping to crop-green flats, varied by patches of bush, and rising

---

12   *Hurstbridge Advertiser*, 31 August 1923.

finally to form the everlasting hills. Mount Disappointment is there, and the Sugarloaf and the highlands of Kinglake.[13]

R.H. Croll was just one voice in a chorus that increasingly regarded the bush (or, as he wrote it, The Bush) as the inspiration for a distinctive Australian character. By the 1920s, when he was writing his popular column, the appeal of 'going bush' was no longer seen as an ambition of becoming a pastoralist or farmer but as an escape from the city. Increasingly the urban environment was pictured as one of dirt, disease and depravity. While Croll and others were extolling the virtues of The Bush, reformers like Oswald Barnett were campaigning against Melbourne's slums, bringing the public's attention to living conditions in neighbourhoods like Collingwood, Carlton and 'Little Lon'. Barnett lectured all over the state to raise funds for the Methodist Babies' Home, reinforcing the idea to many Victorians that the city was a dangerous and unhealthy place to be, especially for children.

The city was, however, where most of the writers and artists who embraced the ideal of The Bush spent the majority of their time. Croll's bush rambles with nothing more than a swag and a pack were written for an urban audience and were structured according to the city's schedule of weekends, long weekends and Christmas holidays. His description of the day walk near Strathewen is a depiction of wilderness tamed and shaped to northern hemisphere notions of the picturesque, with an inviting track, 'appetising' glimpses of farmland and a distant prospect of hills. The wild places have been reduced to unthreatening 'patches of bush'.

---

13   R.H. Croll, *The Open Road in Victoria* (Melbourne: Robertson and Mullens, 1928), 15.

This was the vision of the bush championed by urban Australians. It was defined as the antidote to the city, spiritually and emotionally as well as physically, but it was still defined within parameters that city dwellers could comprehend and accommodate. People yearned for The Bush, but not too much bush and not too far away.

As Melbourne's population increased and extended train lines put the mountains within reach of the city, tourism took hold in the hills and mountain valleys surrounding Melbourne. Guesthouses followed the trains, and places like the Yarra Valley and Yarra Ranges boomed in popularity as summer destinations, with their glory days falling between the wars. The Royal Hotel in Upper Ferntree Gully promised its guests in 1924, 'To sit on that beautiful balcony and breathe the pure mountain air will prolong your life and save doctors' bills.'[14]

In Strathewen, Eleanor Sparkes saw an opportunity. The train line from Eltham in Melbourne's north east was extended to Hurstbridge in 1909, something for which the local residents had been lobbying for more than 20 years, arguing, 'The district possessed air and scenery of the first quality, and it would be a grand outlet for Melbourne people to take a trip to view scenery that would compare favourably with many places now universally talked about.'[15] The Hurstbridge extension put Strathewen within twelve kilometres of the urban train service, and made it an attractive, if not exactly luxurious, weekend getaway. In April of 1917, a notice appeared in the Melbourne *Argus* for Mrs. Sparkes' guesthouse on the banks of Arthurs Creek, promoting its 'Artistic views, Shooting, Fish'. By 1921 it had a name: Singing Water Farm.

---

14   *Argus,* 8 November 1924.
15   *Evelyn Observer,* 29 March 1888.

THE JACK: AN INTRODUCTION TO STRATHEWEN

For the next 20 years Singing Water was a fixture of Strathewen, attracting visitors to the area with enticements in the *Argus* 'for jaded city folk' that included fresh fruit, milk and cream, fern gullies, mountain views and fresh eggs. One could enjoy the peace of the country from a spacious verandah, take advantage of the sketching opportunities in this 'Artist's Paradise' or go shooting and fishing. Singing Water never aspired to compete with the upmarket accommodation of places like Healesville which advertised such conveniences as sewered facilities and hot and cold water in all the bedrooms; it was quiet, homely and healthy. Its clientele was largely drawn from Melbourne's working class who could afford the train fare and accommodation, but not much more.

Singing Water was always 'Mrs. Sparkes' guesthouse', an indicator of the gendered life of the country, in which men ran the farm and women the house and barnyard, but it was also an assurance of respectability. (There was another guesthouse in Strathewen run by Miss Moody in O'Deas Road but, whispered Eleanor's great-granddaughter conspiratorially many decades after both women had died, *she wasn't as clean.*[16]) After Eleanor Sparkes' death in 1942, which coincided with both World War II and the shift in the holiday market from the mountains to the beach, the guesthouse stopped advertising. Eleanor's daughter Vera, however, continued to take guests until the 1950s. Vera's grand-daughter Sylvia remembered it as a beautiful old Tudor-style house enhanced by big pieces of furniture, some of which came from Parliament House in Melbourne, where her great-grandfather Frederick Sparkes was caretaker for many years. Singing Water was a Strathewen landmark until its destruction in

---

16   Rosemary McKimmie Young, Interview 18 June 2013.

the fire of February 2009. It remained, even after its destruction, a potent symbol of Strathewen's past, and you will find an echo of it in Barbara Joyce's poem that opens the next chapter.

In the records, the same names – Mann, Brain, Sparkes, McKimmie, Horne, Apted, Rankine and others – keep recurring in a complex network of marriages, community service committees, business interests and social connections. Many of Strathewen's current residents claim descent from one or more of these families with considerable pride. *We were the first*, said Rosemary McKimmie Young; *from the beginning*, declared Alan Horne.[17] But they were really thinking of Strathewen's settler beginning, when it began to be cleared for agriculture and homes and became, in the minds of Europeans, a 'real' place. In the stories of the old families there is only a faint echo of the time before that, when it was part of a squatter's sheep run, and the 'farmer's sons and other young men of the district [...] had very exciting times hunting kangaroo and the wild horses that frequented the country around what is now called Strathewen'.[18]

There is nothing at all of its Indigenous history as part of the territory of the Wurundjeri people of the Kulin nation, for whom the area retains cultural and spiritual importance. Their occupation of the land was seen by many as a mythic time, long finished and forgotten. *I think they found a few odd artefacts around the place. I remember Neville McKimmie came up with an axe they would have made, stone sharpened up, but no, I can't remember Aboriginals. They were out of the way, we spoke about them as in years gone by.*[19] Alan Horne's words echo

---

17 Rosemary McKimmie Young, Interview 6 October 2010; Alan Horne, Interview 27 November 2012.
18 *Hurstbridge Advertiser*, 16 May 1930.
19 Alan Horne, Interview 27 November 2012.

THE JACK: AN INTRODUCTION TO STRATHEWEN

Tom Griffiths' observation that 'some of the new sense of freedom felt by late nineteenth-century Europeans in the bush came from the knowledge that the Aborigines had been removed from it'.[20]

Comings and goings

With its quiet location and the ongoing presence of many of the original families, it might be imagined that Strathewen was a static, closed society. In fact, it was constantly changing and permeable, with people, livelihoods and environment shifting, adapting and being re-invented. Its position – both close enough to the city to be accessible and far enough away to be considered 'country' – meant that urban influences increased as the twentieth century progressed.

In the Great Depression, the community saw an influx of families from Melbourne looking for seasonal work in the orchards and market gardens. They found cheap accommodation in little shacks and cottages, sometimes the original homestead or workers' huts, on established properties. They rarely stayed long enough to become locals – a designation that needed, according to one story, at least 15 years' residence – but they established the pattern of a fluid population lapping against the bedrock of the old families.

Other people chose to leave the city for more rarefied reasons. Herbert Hewitt was the master of a private school preparing scholars for university matriculation. Despite his city-based profession, he bought land on the ridge between St Andrews and Strathewen, where today Hewitts Road meets Hildebrand Road. According to Hewitt's grand-daughter, his son-in-law frequently described him as *the first of the bohemians*, by which he meant someone who chose to

---

20   Tom Griffiths, *Hunters and Collectors: The Antiquarian Imagination in Australia* (Cambridge: Cambridge University Press, 2009), 119.

live in the bush for its aesthetic qualities rather than its ability to provide a livelihood.[21] In other words, he was not a farmer.

Three decades after Herbert Hewitt's arrival, Laurie and Norma Nelson were also city folk. Inspired by Norma's desire for a bit of garden, in the 1950s they found themselves 300 acres (121 hectares) on Eagles Nest Road in Strathewen. What had once been a viable peach orchard was, due to neglect and the loss of markets to Queensland peaches, in sad decline. Laurie and Norma re-established the property as a lemon farm, ending up with 3000 trees as well as commercial chicken and pig operations. Their presence in the area was welcomed, especially as their young children boosted school numbers and helped to keep it open, but they do not consider themselves to have been very involved in the community. They were working too hard trying to make a living from the farm.

And it was hard work. Alan Horne tells a story, handed down from the time before he was born, of Mrs. O'Dea who walked from Hurstbridge back to Strathewen (a distance of more than ten kilometres through rugged country) with a large sack of flour in one arm and a sack of sugar in the other. Even into the 1950s, Strathewen was not connected to the electricity grid and the simplest jobs around the farm and the home took time and effort. Joyce Horne remembers building a fire under the copper to do the household laundry, then rinsing the whites with bluing and putting them through a hand wringer. *When I look back, life was harder but that was all we were used to. We were really living, I felt, the same as my mother and probably my grandmother.*[22]

---

21   Bronwyn Apted South, Interview 21 November 2012.
22   Joyce Horne, Interview 27 November 2012.

THE JACK: AN INTRODUCTION TO STRATHEWEN

Yet there is in the stories of 'old Strathewen' a nostalgia for those times, for quiet days of hard work, simple entertainments and peaceful surroundings. 79-year-old Laurie Nelson remembered: *I enjoyed hard work, the lifestyle just suited me, I was happy. You know, I've got problems now, I guess, with my back and I've had knee replacements, but when you think about it I don't think I'd do anything different if I had my life over again.*[23]

Many of the people who grew up in Strathewen during the 1950s and '60s remember it as a place set apart. Rosemary McKimmie Young and Ian McKimmie were *bush kids, pretty feral. Didn't have electricity, we had an outside toilet, and kerosene lights, a kerosene fridge, an old copper that we used to heat up to boil our water for a bath.*[24] Their cousin Sylvia Skinner recalled an old-fashioned kind of life, in which the cricket club provided the main social outlet for the community and the big event was the Arthurs Creek Fire Brigade ball. Sylvia's best friend Karen Gardam, who had moved to Strathewen when her parents found work at Apteds Orchards, didn't share her love of school and domestic pursuits like sewing and baking; she was a tomboy who preferred riding her horse through the bush.

From today's perspective, Strathewen children had a remarkable amount of physical freedom. The McKimmies made their own fun, *little adventure parks and little log cabins in the bush. We swam in dams.*[25] Sylvia recalled walking on her own along the creek from the age of four, watching quietly as platypus played in the pools. Karen could shoot a gun before she was six and rode alone from the age of eight.

---

23 Laurie Nelson, Interview 7 September 2012.
24 Rosemary McKimmie Young, Interview 6 October 2010.
25 Ibid.

Although the word 'idyllic' comes to mind, it was also a hard upbringing. Children had little chance to see the world outside Strathewen. Girls in particular were strictly raised, with limited experience of society outside their own families and family friends. *Once a year into the city was by train, for Mum to buy our Christmas presents and some materials, 'cause she made most of our clothes, and some new clothes for herself. We'd see the Myer windows and ride on the Ferris wheel at Foy's, and we went to Coles Cafeteria for lunch.*[26]

All the children had jobs, including the Nelson children who worked in the family's commercial chicken operations after school. Rosemary and Ian did piecework, stuffing rags into mattresses and moth balls into bags, and Sylvia had her own vegetable garden from the age of six. Karen learned to handle a gun by tagging after her older brothers, who frequently were sent out to shoot rabbits for the family's supper. One year she *hand-reared a calf, then it was slaughtered right in front of us.*[27] It was an inevitable part of growing up in a rural community, especially one which depended on an increasingly marginal industry: apple-growing.

The entry of Britain into the European Common Market in 1973 is regarded as the death blow of Victoria's international apple exports. In reality the small apple orchard was in terminal decline by the 1950s, when Alan Horne was working the land that had been in his family for more than 70 years and the Nelsons had just arrived. The peak had been between 1870 and 1900, and the industry never really recovered after the First World War. In the 1920s and 1930s it faced increasing competition from Tasmanian apples, reduced demand during the Great Depression, greater government

---

26 Ibid.
27 Karen Gardam, Interview 14 March 2013.

regulation and significant damage from bushfire, especially in 1939. The Second World War, during which apple shipments to England were suspended, took its toll on the health of the remaining orchards. Apples rotted on the tree for lack of markets, and the trees suffered from lack of care. Joyce Horne's recollection of Carseburn in 1944 as neglected and overgrown reflected the condition of the Victorian apple export industry as a whole.

Perhaps more significant than the external changes and challenges to Strathewen's major industry was the weakening of many of the apple families' tight network of kinship, upon which much of their success had depended. The war of 1914–18, from which many men did not return and many more returned with injuries both physical and psychological, broke the line of generational succession in many of the original settler families. Alan Horne's father Ray inherited both his portion of the farm and that of an older brother killed in the war, but Ray himself had been badly wounded with gunshot wounds to the arms and abdomen. He returned to the farm but was of frail health and died in 1936, when Alan was five years old. His mother kept the place going but she and Alan moved to the city while he attended high school, hoping for a career in commerce. After the death of his only brother, however, there was no one else in the family to take up the farm, so Alan returned to the land to become an orchardist.

What is remarkable is not that he could not make the farm pay, but that he lasted so long in the attempt. Many of the old long-keeping varieties that grew so well in Strathewen's stony ground were not wanted in the local market. Small orchardists were particularly hard-hit by the changes in the industry, as new controlled-atmosphere technology required significant investment. A lot of orchards were uprooted to make room for cattle, but even then the small holdings lacked the economy of scale to make them viable. By the early 1960s, married and with a small child, Alan needed an income and went to work for the electricity company clearing paths for the new power lines coming through the Kinglake Ranges. Other people moved elsewhere to find employment and many of the little family farms became weekend residences or were abandoned altogether.

On the site of the original Glen Ard property is the last of the commercial apple operations. It belongs to the Apted family, who has owned the property since 1914 and through a complex network of marriages is related to half the district and has roots going well back into the nineteenth century. These connections are important, for through them the Apteds have been able to combine small orchard holdings into a single viable operation and to continue expanding. As early as 1916, the family had built a cool store that allowed them to provide the local market with the varieties it demanded. In the 1950s, structured as Leslie Apted and Sons, they built a dam for irrigation proudly reputed to be the largest dam in the southern hemisphere built on private land. By 1975, Apteds Orchard was the largest in southern Victoria.

Listening to Bronwyn Apted South, it is clear that the close family ties provided more than the opportunity to consolidate land and expand holdings. They provided energy and experience and a clear plan of succession – the legacy that Alan Horne needed and didn't receive. Apted and Sons became and still is the largest (and effectively the only) employer in Strathewen. Today, however, its employees largely come from the northern suburbs of Melbourne. Most of the locals are too young, too old or too educated to work in a packing shed.

THE JACK: AN INTRODUCTION TO STRATHEWEN

It was just a few years after Norma and Laurie Nelson moved to Strathewen in 1955 that the road into town was paved. There was now a school bus to take children to the new high school in Hurstbridge, and the city became accessible. Children who were used to a one-room school with a handful of other students were now negotiating the halls with several hundred strangers; to the Nelsons' daughter Vicki, it was terrifying at first. It also highlighted the differences between Strathewen and the larger world. Karen Gardam felt that *when you went to high school you realised you were a bit odd.*[28] When I told Karen that another Strathewen teenager had been advised to say she was from Arthurs Creek rather than Strathewen, Karen responded ruefully, *wish someone had told me that.*[29]

With the arrival of electricity in 1960 and the making of the road, Strathewen was increasingly accessible. In 1960 the Tully family moved their orcharding operations from Doncaster, where the suburbs were rapidly encroaching, to Strathewen. At the same time, the area began to attract a more diverse range of people. In an echo of her father's description of Herbert Hewitt, Bronwyn South described many of the new arrivals in the 1960s and 1970s as bohemians and artists. It was hardly surprising: Strathewen is, after all, in Eltham (now Nillumbik) shire, the epicentre of Melbourne's alternative lifestyle. It is the home of Alistair Knox's mudbrick houses, the artist's retreat Montsalvat and the St Andrews market. The artists' colony Dunmoochin, established by Clifton Pugh and inspired by John and Sunday Reed's property Heide, is just outside Strathewen at Cottlesbridge.

---

28 Karen Gardam, Interview 15 September 2010.
29 Karen Gardam, Interview 14 February 2013.

Along with the artists and back-to-the-land believers came drugs. Strathewen's combination of isolation and access – tucked, so to speak, into Melbourne's back pocket – and its agricultural heritage makes it attractive for the cultivation of crops that their owners try to keep below the official radar. More than one resident tells the story of an elderly farmer who discovered cannabis was a better cash crop than apples and grew it between his rows of fruit trees.

Depending on who you talk to, Strathewen is either a creative community free from outdated bourgeois notions of behaviour or it is a den of iniquity. The truth, of course, is far more complicated but drugs are part of Strathewen's life and image. Its reputation as a centre for growing, selling and using drugs is entwined, either openly or obliquely, with many of the stories I collected. Alan Horne identified drugs as one of the major changes he has witnessed in his 80-odd years of life in Strathewen.

The remaining orchardists and the alternative lifestylers of the 1960s and '70s were joined in the 1980s by the Perrys, who established an alpaca stud. Rae and Barrie Tully built their house in the family orchards in 1983. Shane Pugh, Clifton Pugh's son, and his partner moved in across the road from the Perrys in the 1990s. As Strathewen's isolation was further eroded by the expansion of outer Melbourne suburbs, more people followed – young families, retired couples and middle-class professionals. All of them chose Strathewen for reasons other than traditional agriculture: its beauty; its privacy; its proximity to the forests of the National Park, or the romance and affordability, compared to city real estate, of an old cottage in a neglected orchard.

Marginal orcharding enterprises largely gave way to lifestyle acreages, hobby farms and alternative agricultural pursuits like garlic, emus and alpacas. Like the Hornes, Barrie and Rae Tully uprooted their fruit trees in order to run cattle. *It's always tough when you see what you've been doing for the last 50 years being bulldozed over. We've seen it all before but it's always tough to see a good producing orchard being bulldozed over.*[30]

A real estate venture had had ambitions of establishing a town centre in Strathewen. 'The Village' never materialised, beyond the subdivision of part of the area along Arthurs Creek into smaller suburban-sized lots, but its name persisted for the handful of houses there. Modest houses were renovated or replaced with larger, more ambitious homes and Strathewen, for the very first time, was considered desirable real estate. Angela McKenzie and her family moved to Strathewen from nearby Wattle Glen, purchasing a large mud-brick home with paddocks *to give the kids a bit of space to grow up in, and have a horse and motorbikes.*[31] In an unconscious channelling of Oswald Barnett, she believed *the city isn't a good place to bring up kids.*[32]

There are echoes in all these motivations of Croll's writings about The Bush, but they are set within the framework of the twenty-first century. Strathewen is smack in the middle of what Stephen Pyne calls the 'bush-encrusted urban periphery' where it is possible to live an urban life in a forest environment.[33] City people were no longer just visiting for day walks or holidays but building houses, commuting to work and asking for the sort of infrastructure and services upon which contemporary urban life depends. At the same time,

---

30 Barrie Tully, Interview 16 October 2013.
31 Angela McKenzie, Interview 20 August 2012.
32 Ibid.
33 Stephen Pyne, *Still-Burning Bush* (Carlton VIC: Scribe, 2006), 110.

descendants of the older families found that working in the city enabled them to hold on to properties that otherwise they might have walked away from.

Many of Strathewen's residents, old and new alike, now worked outside the settlement and commuted to work. Angela's husband Dale worked hard running his own business and was rarely home. After the farm could no longer support them, the Hornes established a flooring business in one of Melbourne's northern suburbs. It was a long drive in and out (and the roads were still shocking in places) but they couldn't conceive of living anywhere else. And while some people were driving out, others were driving in. Strathewen Primary School began to attract students from nearby towns whose parents wanted the little-school-in-the-bush experience for their children and were willing to do a reverse commute.

Strathewen is a liminal place – close enough to the city, but also far enough away – where ideas and ways of life intersected and overlapped. So much of the debate around how to live in the bushfire zone polarises people according to whether they are 'city' or 'country' people. City people are generally characterised as romantic, inexperienced, educated but impractical, superficial in their love of the bush, more interested in defending aesthetics or politics than in defending properties, more affluent but less interested in investing in the land. Country people, on the other hand, are seen as capable, bushfire-savvy, committed to the long-term health of the country, focused on environmental values that promote earning a living rather than protecting native species, conservative and suspicious of change.

Bronwyn South is many of the things we associate with city-bred tree-changers: computer science graduate; professional manager; committed feminist and environmental advocate. But she's a fourth-generation Strathewen resident and a member of the Apted family, the last of the apple orcharding families. She attributes her assertive attitudes not to her university education but to her schooling at Strathewen Primary, her involvement in Landcare – an environmental advocacy group – to her maternal grandfather, Herbert Hewitt, the first of the bohemians. Joyce Horne calls herself a farmer's wife, but she loved her career before marriage when she was head of the custom-fitting services at Melbourne's stratospherically posh fashion establishment, Georges. Her husband found he couldn't make a living on a small selection, so started a suburban business whose success now supports three generations of his family.

Norma Nelson originally thought that the seaside suburb of Beaumaris was a long way from the city but she's spent the last 60 years farming on Eagles Nest Road in Strathewen. Barbara Joyce was a self-described city girl who fell in love with the bush nearly 30 years ago. In 2009 she left her home just minutes ahead of the fire and returned within weeks. In Strathewen – and I suspect in many communities – the city-country divide is often an unhelpful dichotomy that glosses over individual histories and the complicated ways in which 'city' and 'country' merge and are re-defined.

One thing, however, everyone does have in common. For a community perched within commuting distance of a large multicultural city, Strathewen is remarkably culturally homogenous. Everybody is white. This is not unexpected for the descendants of the settler families, but it is striking that there are no recent immigrant families, no one of Asian, Middle Eastern or African origin. It suggests that the desire to live in the bush is a European dream – or perhaps it is that the dream's dark opposite, the distaste for the city and the suburb, is not shared by a wider range of Australians.

Along with the people on the land, the land itself has changed. When Stretton wrote his famous report, he noted, 'When the early settlers came to what is now this State, they found for the greater part a clean forest.'[34] When Alan Horne's uncle went to school around 1910, *you could drive a wagon between the trees, there was no thick scrub.*[35] Rosemary McKimmie Young's ancestors *knew that this land was never thick bushland, it was open forest.*[36] In Stretton's time it was a matter of official belief that the park-like state of the bush at the beginning of European settlement was its 'natural state' and was due to the absence of fire. We are now aware that Aboriginal Australians used fire to shape the bush, employing a sophisticated regime of burning to create a landscape of benefit to them. Their displacement meant the end of land management through Indigenous use of fire.

Over time, European settlers cleared the areas near the water sources, and orchards and farms moved gradually up the lower slopes of the ranges. Where the paddocks stopped, the bush grew more dense and harder to penetrate. The creation of Kinglake National Park and the abolition of the small timber operations like the Sparkes' sawmill further increased the density of the bush. Many of the newcomers who moved in over the last 30 years craved a closer connection to nature and either built new houses in the midst of forest or allowed the bush to reclaim the paddocks. Nillumbik Council introduced stringent native vegetation protection regulations, limiting the degree to which property owners could clear their land or roadsides.

---

34 Stretton, "Report of the Royal Commission to Inquire into the Causes of and Measures Taken to Prevent the Bush Fires of January 1939," 11.
35 Alan Horne, Interview 27 November 2012.
36 Rosemary McKimmie Young, Interview 6 October 2010.

All of these changes have made the area more vulnerable to uncontrolled fire.

If there is a single symbol of Strathewen, it is the Sugarloaf, the mountain that overlooks the valley. It is a character in many of the stories old and new, including those of bushfire. Bronwyn Apted South said, *My father saw the mountain burn three times.*[37] It was in the shadow of Mount Sugarloaf that the Trewhella jack was used in the sawmill, and from its shoulders that the trees were harvested. Although you can't see it, the mountain forms the backdrop of the photograph at the start of this chapter. And it features in the most extreme of the interactions ever to take place between the people of Strathewen and their environment, on 7 February 2009.

Bushfire

And so we come to fire. It would almost be possible, up to this point, to place Strathewen in one of a number of places in the world. The pattern of clearing and settling the land, establishing European agriculture, experiencing both progress and decline, and then adapting to demographic change as people seek out a new kind of rural living is one that could happen in Canada or the United States – or, indeed, in other parts of Australia. Fire is what sets this place apart.

Stephen Pyne, the international expert on wildfire, has suggested that in southeastern Australia, including the mountain forests of Victoria, fire is the dominant force shaping the relationship between people and the land.[38] It brings into sharp focus the way in which

---

37   Bronwyn Apted South, Interview 5 December 2012.
38   Stephen Pyne, *Burning Bush: A Fire History of Australia*, 2nd ed. (Sydney: Allen & Unwin, 1992).

people, past and present, have engaged with the land, for bushfire has always been part of Strathewen's history.

We know that the pastoralist who lived in the area before settlement was George McLelland because his wife Bridget and their five children were killed in the Black Thursday bushfires of 1851, accounting for half of the deaths in all of Victoria. A shepherd working for McLelland reported that fires had been burning on the mountains around the property for three weeks, but that they had not come close until 6 February 'when, at about noon, in taking the sheep to the creek to drink, he suddenly found that the fire had reached the trees that were on the same side of the creek as the station'.[39] His attempts to reach the hut where Bridget McLelland and the children were trapped were unsuccessful. He found George, badly burned, in the creek. The records of 1851 described the location as in the Diamond Creek area, as the names Arthurs Creek and Strathewen did not exist at the time, but the location of the hut was at the edge of Strathewen, not far from where the Apted cool store now stands.

In November 1851 Rebecca Greaves wrote a letter to her uncle in England describing her life with her parents on the Plenty River, about 20 kilometres from Strathewen. Of the Black Thursday fires earlier in the year, she wrote:

> [W]hen it once begins all attempts to escape are in vain. [T]he fire last summer buried many Mothers and children and all the cattle on the stations where the fires raged. I myself saw [two] gentlemen that the heat of the sun as they were coming down the bush set fire to their coats they had on their backs so from that I leave you to guess how powerful

---

39   *Argus*, 11 February 1851.

the sun is here, the fire last summer got over the rivers so you see even water will not stay its rage.[40]

When she wrote about mothers and children she must surely have had in mind the McLelland family, whose station had been not far from the Plenty. Perhaps she had read the newspaper report detailing George's frantic efforts to save his family, his own injuries and the grisly account of the inquest in the Melbourne newspaper. The reporter wrote: 'When the boughs and few rugs which covered the bodies were removed, the spectacle was extremely harrowing'.[41]

In the Strathewen area, between 1885 and 1900 alone there were at least six major bushfires. In 1905, James Mann asked for a moratorium on the lease payments for his selection 'for my place has been all burned with the bush fire. It caused me a terrible lot of damage which has unabled me to meet the account at the present.'[42]

Most of the major bushfires of the early twentieth century passed through Strathewen or burned along its borders. In 1926, on Black Sunday, a bushfire started in nearby Flowerdale and burned as far as Strathewen, where it destroyed fencing and damaged orchards. In between the big fires smaller, localised fire outbreaks were a feature of every summer. The bushfire of 1913 did not take lives or destroy homes, but it caused great damage to the orchards. The *Argus* reported:

> A speaking illustration of the intense heat is to be seen at the orchard of Mr. David Mann, which was surrounded by the

---

40 Rebecca Sarah Greaves, 25 November 1851. Collection Museum Victoria HT 8270. http://museumvictoria.com.au/collections/items/1116482/letter-rebecca-sarah-greaves-plenty-river-victoria-25-nov-1851 [Accessed 27 July 2015].
41 *Argus*, 10 February 1851.
42 Mann, *James and John Mann of Arthur's Creek: A Brief History*, 5.

fires. The fruit was actually roasted on the trees and what in the morning was a green flourishing orchard out of which Mr Mann expected to export one thousand cases of fruit in a few hours was scorched and withered beyond recognition.[43]

It was followed by severe fires in 1914, 1923, 1925, 1926 and 1936. Then came the big one on 13 January 1939: Black Friday.

Stephen Pyne called it 'the superlative Australian holocaust'.[44] (That was written in 1992, after Ash Wednesday but long before Black Saturday.) Years of drought, weeks of soaring temperatures and a state that was tinder-dry combined to devastating effect. Fires that had been burning through December were fanned by hot northerly winds out of the desert and joined together in a week of burning that reached its crescendo on Black Friday. Most of the 71 lives lost were in the timber-mill areas of Gippsland, but over 2,000,000 hectares, more than one-tenth of the entire state, burned. Flames stretched from Omeo in the north east to the valleys and ranges on Melbourne's eastern fringe and also in the far west at Portland and the Otway and Grampians ranges.

It seems that everyone who writes about the 1939 fires returns to the words of Judge Leonard Stretton, who chaired the Royal Commission inquiry into the fires. No one has been able to surpass him for the majesty with which he described the devastation:

> Seventy-one lives were lost. Sixty-nine mills were burned. Millions of acres of fine forest, of almost incalculable value, were destroyed or badly damaged. Townships were obliterated in a few minutes. Mills, houses, bridges, tramways, machinery,

---

43 *Argus*, 6 February 1913.
44 Pyne, *Burning Bush: A Fire History of Australia*, 309.

were burned to the ground; men, cattle, horses, sheep, were devoured by the fires or asphyxiated by the scorching debilitated air. [...] The speed of the fires was appalling. They leaped from mountain peak to mountain peak, or far out into the lower country, lighting the forests 6 or 7 miles in advance of the main fires. Blown by a wind of great force, they roared as they travelled. Balls of cracking fire sped at a great pace in advance of the fires, consuming with a roaring explosive noise, all that they touched. Houses of brick were seen and heard to leap in a roar of flame before the fires had reached them. Men of science hold the view that the fires generated and were preceded by inflammable gases which became alight. Great pieces of burning bark were carried by the wind to set in raging flame regions not yet reached by the fires. Such was the force of the wind that, in many places, hundreds of trees of great size were blown clear of the earth, tons of soil, with embedded masses of rock, still adhering to the roots; for mile upon mile the former forest monarchs were laid in confusion, burnt, torn from the earth, and piled one upon the other as matches strewn by a giant hand.[45]

Against this, the men of Strathewen had wet hessian sacks and green tree branches to beat out the flames. As Alan Horne, who was eight years old at the time, dryly commented, *it was hard work*.[46]

Strathewen was relatively lucky. Fire had been burning since mid-December but because it was burning on 'useless' land, 'no one

---

45   Stretton, "Report of the Royal Commission to Inquire into the Causes of and Measures Taken to Prevent the Bush Fires of January 1939," 5.
46   Alan Horne, Interview 27 November 2012.

bothered to put it out in the early stages'.[47] Like almost all the fires of that summer, it was most likely started by a person – a careless farmer, labourer or traveller. By the time it reached the settlement it was too big to contain and burnt an unoccupied house and some fencing. In January, three days before Black Friday, two homes in Strathewen were threatened by fire and were saved by volunteers, but damage was done to outbuildings, fences and pasturage.

During a break in their efforts to move animals to safety, put out spot fires and patrol for embers, the workers came across 'a well-dressed young man in a smart sedan car with two young women' taking a photograph. They told the firefighters that they were there 'to see the fun'.[48] The *Hurstbridge Advertiser*, which reported the incident, was circumspect about the language the locals used in response.

By Friday the 13th – Black Friday – there were fires all over Mount Sugarloaf and the hot northerly was blowing out of the Kinglake Ranges. Local men were joined by volunteers from other areas, as well as Forest Commission employees and unemployed men, who gathered in their hundreds at Hurstbridge awaiting deployment to the various fire fronts. As the fire built strength in the wind and swept out of the hills from the north, they defended the homes as best they could. Fire burned up to the door of Alan Horne's family homestead before it was beaten away. In the end the cleared paddocks, the moist-leafed fruit trees and a wind change that slowed the advance of the fire gave Strathewen a fighting chance. Just as would happen in 2009, a cool change from the southwest blew the fire up the mountain. In 1939, however, the wind change saved the community.

---

47   *Hurstbridge Advertiser*, 22 December 1938.
48   Ibid.

THE JACK: AN INTRODUCTION TO STRATHEWEN

Rain extinguished the fires two days later, on Sunday 15 January. In Strathewen, one person had died, a few homes were lost, several men (including Alan's uncle Sid) were burned or injured, and extensive damage was done to orchards, fencing, outbuildings and stock. The single fatality was Albert Dudley Pentreath, a 53-year-old former journalist from Bendigo. He had suffered a nervous breakdown and was staying in a small hut on the Murdie property in Strathewen for a long rest. We can only imagine the effect on his fragile state of mind as the fire made its way down the mountain to the property. Although those fighting the fire tried to keep him safely in the creek, Pentreath panicked and ran for his hut. He fought off the men trying to restrain him and 'then he went inside the hut, which a moment later was enveloped in flames'. [49] His ashes were later found, identifiable only by a metal badge and a lucky penny he carried with him.

Compared to the toll in places like Fitzpatrick's Mill near Matlock in Gippsland, where 15 people died horrible deaths, it seems a blessed escape. Perhaps it seemed that way at the time as well, for amidst the roll call of damage and loss, the local paper found something for people to chuckle about:

> At Strathewen a group of volunteers from Northcote [a suburb of Melbourne] arrived at the Strathewen post office with the remains of two nine-gallon kegs of beer. Some of the men took the truck belonging to the mail contractor (Mr. Norris) and drove it down the road where it crashed into another truck, severely damaging both vehicles. Later, one of the men who took part in the exploit stopped a car going towards Melbourne, and asked for a lift to the city. He told the

---

49   Ibid.

occupants with great pride what fun they had had, and how they had taken the truck and was not sparing in detail. The two in the car listened politely, and even sympathetically. It was not until the car stopped at the Northcote police station that the passenger realised that he had "given the show away" to First Constables Brough and Grant, who were in plain clothes.[50]

The fires of 1939 spurred the creation of rural fire brigades in the district: Hurstbridge and St Andrews in 1939; Diamond Creek in 1940; Whittlesea in 1941. The Arthurs Creek and District Fire Brigade began at the end of 1941, with Lindsay Apted as captain. Their first action was to buy equipment with funds they had contributed themselves: six knapsacks, six fire beaters (shovel-like tools with a flexible fringed blade to 'slap' at the fire) and three rakes. A year later the Arthurs Creek brigade joined with three neighbours to form a fire brigade group, sharing training and resources.

Strathewen escaped the major fires of 1943 and 1944, which is why Joyce Horne found it so lush and green in 1944, unlike her old home in Gippsland. The frightening times were those in January of 1962. The fires were known, both at the time and later on, as the Dandenong fires, but the impact spread beyond the Dandenong Ranges on Melbourne's eastern flank into the Yarra and Kinglake Ranges. Half of Eltham shire, of which Strathewen was then part, was burned. In separate fires, Woori Yallock in Gippsland, Apollo Bay in the western districts and the outer Melbourne suburbs of Mitcham and Ringwood all suffered fire damage.

A dry spring had created ideal conditions for bushfire and, when fires started in a number of locations throughout Eltham shire,

---

50   *Hurstbridge Advertiser*, 20 January 1929.

there was a fear that they would join up and form an unstoppable inferno. Around Strathewen, there was 'a great arc of fire burning on a 17-mile [27 km] front through Kinglake National Park'.[51] The fires burned for three days and nights, running through nearly half the shire, destroying homes in the outer-urban communities of Eltham and Warrandyte and threatening Greensborough before they were quenched by rain. The day of greatest destruction was Tuesday, 16 January. According to *Age* columnist Claude Forell the following day, there was 'war in the smoke-filled bushland and hills near Melbourne yesterday – a relentless battle waged by a whole community against a dreaded common enemy, bushfire'.[52]

The rural fire brigades were in constant action. Men were going as long as 48 hours without sleep and up to 12 hours without food, all the while trying to beat back a 13-metre wall of fire with wet sacks, fire beaters and – if they were lucky – backpack water sprayers. Throughout the coverage of the fires in the newspapers was the recurring theme of how men were driven to the point of exhaustion and still kept going. Norma Nelson's husband Laurie was off fighting with the Arthurs Creek brigade. *He was gone overnight. We had no idea where he was, no information at all, and when he came back the next day he was black from head to toe, and he just fell into bed and slept for 24 hours.*[53]

Although she was a young child, Bronwyn Apted South remembered the 1962 fires. *My mother was beside herself. My father had gone out fighting and not come back again.*[54] Lindsay Apted had gone into Strathewen to help cut a fire break when he and two other men were

---

51   *Diamond Valley Mirror*, 24 January 1962.
52   *The Age*, 17 January 1962.
53   Norma Nelson, Interview 7 September 2012.
54   Bronwyn Apted South, Interview 5 December 2012.

caught by the fire coming off the mountain and had to take refuge in an old shed. Edith cut mountains of sandwiches for the CFA and kept the children busy with odd jobs while she waited to hear if he had survived. The fire changed direction and Lindsay returned safely. Rain on the third day quenched the flames, but not before the Dandenong fires had killed 32 people and destroyed more than 450 houses state-wide.

After 1962 there were small – and not so small – bushfires during most summers. In 1968 embers from a local bushfire threatened houses along Chadds Creek Road, including Singing Water, where *Uncle Clive put out the doorstep with some water.*[55] Rosemary McKimmie Young remembers *the black sky and the fear, and ash dropping around, and we put all of our possessions in the dam and put out embers that were falling with buckets of water.*[56] The Ash Wednesday fires of 1983 bypassed the Strathewen district and although fire in 2006 threatened to come down the mountain from Kinglake, it was never a serious danger.

For more than a generation, a time in which many new people had come to the district with new ideas about how to live in the bush, the residents of Strathewen had not experienced a major bushfire. This seemed like a blessing, but it was to have a devastating impact in 2009. Many people were prepared for bushfire but not for the kind of inferno that can happen, after a decade of drought, to homes built in and adjacent to native forest. Stretton's words still resound: 'They had not lived long enough.'[57]

---

55   Rosemary McKimmie Young, Interview 6 October 2010.
56   Ibid.
57   Stretton, "Report of the Royal Commission to Inquire into the Causes of and Measures Taken to Prevent the Bush Fires of January 1939," 5.

THE JACK: AN INTRODUCTION TO STRATHEWEN

Black Saturday had been coming for a long time. Victoria had had ten years of record low rainfall, during which water levels had dropped alarmingly and the forests had dried out. A heat wave hit the week before and deaths from heat exhaustion soared. Fires were already burning in various areas of the state. Six days before Black Saturday, Sam the Koala, who for many became the public face of the bushfires, was rescued from a fire at Mirboo North, 150 kilometres southeast of Melbourne.

Saturday, 7 February, was forecast to be the hottest day Victoria had ever seen. Strong northerlies were predicted until early evening, when they would be replaced by a fresh southwesterly change. Meteorologist David Karoly later reported: 'The FFDI [Forest Fire Danger Index] for a number of sites in Victoria on 7 February reached unprecedented levels, ranging from 120 to 190, much higher than the fire weather conditions on Black Friday or Ash Wednesday, and well above the "catastrophic" fire danger rating.'[58] The local CFA brigades held information meetings, warning residents of Strathewen and nearby communities that many of their homes were in particularly dangerous areas, built at the end of no-through roads or approached by heavily treed narrow lanes. The residents could not count on someone coming to save them.

On 6 February, with weather forecasts and fire predictions indicating the most serious threat in decades, Victorian Premier John Brumby took the unusual step of recording public announcements warning of the dangers; he called the coming Saturday 'the worst day in the history of the state'.[59] He was not wrong.

---

58   Karoly, David. 'Bushfires and extreme heat in south-east Australia.' http://www.realclimate.org/index.php/archives/2009/02/bushfires-and-climate/#more-654 [Accessed 25 July 2015].
59   *Sydney Morning Herald*, 6 February 2009.

> There's a summer bush requiem
> so silent it chills
> It's drifting on ashes
> through Strathewen hills.
>
> There's no song at 'Singing Waters'
> just an ashen lament
> and trees that stood straight
> are now blackened and bent.
>
> Strathewen's history
> is clouding the air
> with soft powdery ash
> and a wail of despair.
>
> There are spaces without traces
> of neighbours and friends
> We are missing their faces
> coming round the road bends.
>
> We're sooty and smudged
> and waitin' for rain
> As homeward we trudge
> we're nursing our pain.
>
> Our life's black & white
> no colour between
> just some sepia tree tops
> to colour the scene.
>
> We're drawn back to the place
> where we want to remain
> we're holding our friends
> and sharing the strain.
>
> 1/3/09   Barbara Joyce

Figure 3. 'Summer bush requiem'. Victorian Bushfires Collection, Museum Victoria HT 33723.

Image: Marita Dyson. Source: Museum Victoria.

Chapter 3

THE POETRY TREE: MEMORIALS

> There's a summer bush [requiem]
> so silent it chills
> It's drifting on ashes
> through Strathewen hills.

So begins this poem, one of the first to be pinned to the Poetry Tree in Strathewen.

The Poetry Tree is a manna gum situated in what many consider to be the entrance to Strathewen, where three roads meet and a small bridge crosses the Arthurs Creek. Located deep in the valley, even in the hottest summer the spot was usually cool and refreshing. In the weeks following Black Saturday, after John Brumby's 'worst day' had come to pass, it was a scene from hell.

From here you could see the remains of houses and burnt-out cars, the wreckage where the hall and the primary school had stood, great swathes of burned bush in every direction and the bare outlines of Mount Sugarloaf with a fringe of black and leafless trees, all of it a reminder of the terrible loss of human life. The tree itself was a blackened stump about three metres tall, on the edge of the road by the bridge.

Figure 4. The Poetry Tree, Strathewen, 2010.
Image: Rosemary Harris-Arnott.

THE POETRY TREE: MEMORIALS

On 22 February, Rosemary McKimmie Young wrote a brief poem and pinned it to the burned bark of the tree. 'Harder the tears / Sadder the pain / Inner the heartbreak / Loving our gain.' The date is significant, for reasons which I'll explain later. A second poem, by Rosemary's brother Ian McKimmie, appeared at the same time. Barbara Joyce recalled seeing the poems fluttering on the tree as she drove past to her home on the far side of the creek, and thinking they were coroner's notices. (Strathewen, like all bushfire-affected towns, had been declared a crime scene and the coroner's tape and signs marked the entrance to all properties where lives had been lost.) When she discovered that they were poems, she wrote one of her own – 'A summer bush requiem' – and posted it on the tree on 1 March, making it the third contribution to the tree. More poems from other Strathewen residents followed, along with flowers, pictures of deceased people, tributes to lost animals and declarations of resilience. The burned gum became known as the Poetry Tree.

As time went on, the tree began to put out new growth and the poems were joined by tributes to people who had not died in the bushfires, like Marilyn Langmead, who had been organising support for the community while fighting terminal cancer, and Henk Vreilunk, who survived the fire but took his own life months later. Testimonies appeared to the back-breaking and heartbreaking work of clearing and rebuilding. A big yellow ribbon marked the first anniversary of the fires and photos, poems and messages continued to accumulate on the tree. It had become, for many people, the visible heart of Strathewen's grief.

Part of the Poetry Tree's appeal is in the poems themselves, many of which draw on the beloved Australian bush ballad. Almost since the beginning of European settlement in Victoria, bushfire poems have been reshaping the Anglo-Celtic poetic tradition to the Australian continent and experience.

In March of 1851 the *Argus* published *The Bush Fire* by Charles Harpur (1813–1868), one of the first Australian-born poets of note. In the poem Harpur describes a major bushfire and the desperate efforts of men to beat it back from a homestead. His depiction of the fire's 'wild and lurid splendour' is part of the body of eighteenth- and nineteenth-century European poetry that found the sublime in the extremes of nature, but translated it to a new world. Even if today the language seems somewhat overblown, it is still gripping in its portrayal of the force of a 'fire / Huge as the world'. Harpur may well have witnessed the fires of Black Thursday earlier that summer, as he appended an author's note:

> The descriptive detail of the text may appear overcharged to all those persons who have only witnessed such Bush Fires as occur on our ordinary commons. [...] It has been my fortune, however, to have witnessed several very great ones, and I have thrown together in the poem the more striking aspects and circumstances of each and all of them.[1]

Just a few weeks earlier, the *Argus* had published a long poem by 'Spur' of Tyerock Vale, 'LINES Written on perusing the fearful destruction of property, and heart-rending loss of life, caused by the fire of the 6th January'. 'Spur' must surely have read the report of the inquest that appeared in the *Argus* in all its grim detail the preceding

---

[1] *Argus*, 31 March 1851.

week, as the central narrative of the poem is modelled directly on the deaths of the McLelland family in Strathewen:

> There was one, who on that eventful morn
> Possessed a loving wife, and children fair,
> Ere night closed in, they all from him were torn,
> And left him like a withered tree, all bare,
> Stripped of its scions! and who can declare
> The husband's feelings, and the father's woe,
> When he beheld his kindreds' dead forms, where
> He passed last night, with dear harmonious flow
> Of pleasing conversation, all by the ingle's glow.[2]

By the late nineteenth century, amid a growing sense of nationalism, poets found that the phenomenon of bushfire lent itself to a narrative of survival, against a unique and beautiful but harsh environment, that illustrated 'Australian' characteristics of courage, disdain of danger and persistence against overwhelming odds. Will Olgivie, who modelled his life and work on his hero Adam Lindsay Gordon, depicted bushfire as a red god of battle sending his mounted troops against the settlers: 'In the tall hollow trunk the red tongues roar, / Voicing their triumph and the lust of war.' The men's only weapons are cool heads, superb horsemanship and green boughs to beat out the flames:

> "Well, here's your ballroom!" says the overseer;
> "So take your partners and begin the dance!

---

2 *Argus*, 3 March 1851.

> She's burning on a five-mile frontage here,
> And if the wind gets up we've got no chance!"
> The men slip from their saddles one by one,
> Break boughs to beat with, and the fight's begun.[3]

In Henry Lawson's poem 'The Bush Fire', three anti-heroes rescue the cocky Pat '[a]nd his tough old wife, and his half-baked kids' from certain death, but do so with casual contempt of the risks and rewards. Alice Werner's 'Bannerman of the Dandenong' featured a laconic hero who sacrifices his own life so that his friend can escape. The bushfire is an enemy against which the qualities of courage, legendary riding and disregard for safety triumph, although at great personal cost.

What I find striking about these last three poems, written between 1890 and 1913, is the way in which they herald some of the most frequently asserted qualities of the Anzac myth: courage, sacrifice for another, mateship, heroism without heroics, coolness under threat and disdain for authority. The use of military metaphors is a recurring theme in twentieth-century bushfire literature but, in a circular fashion, the Anzac tradition itself built on an existing vocabulary of courage from the bushfire literature of the nineteenth century.

Ballad poetry declined in popularity after World War I, but bush poetry and the works of C.J. Dennis kept up the connection between ballad and bushfire (although Dennis was more concerned with man's stupidity than his courage). As an adult, Mona Farr wrote her own ballad to describe the fires of 1919 that she survived as a nine-year-old in Gippsland.

---

3 William Henry Ogilvie, *The Overlander and Other Verses* (Glasgow: Fraser, Asher & Co, Ltd, 1913), 17.

Through suffocating smoke and heat, we struggled to draw breath
And some while fighting for their homes, were trapped and burned to death.
Though the odds were great, all they had they gave, battling for all they were worth,
And many will carry the scars to their grave of that terrible hell on earth.[4]

In many ways the verses on the Poetry Tree draw on this heritage of story-telling through poetry. Many of the writers were, explicitly or unconsciously, referencing the tradition of the Australian bush ballad. But unlike the imaginative works of Ogilvie, Werner and the rest, many of whom witnessed but did not experience a major bushfire, the works on the Poetry Tree were, like Mona's poem, voices from the fire. These were people who were living in the ruins of their community, discovering the extent of the damage, beginning the task of clearing up and dealing with new setbacks and challenges. These experiences feed into not only the poems and the decisions of the authors to write and to share them but also into our experience of reading them. The Poetry Tree as a memorial reveals a lot about Strathewen, but also a lot about ourselves.

The process of memorialising death or disaster takes many forms, as it did in the weeks and months after Black Saturday, but I am using the term 'memorial' specifically to mean a construction that is built or assembled to remind the viewer of past events, especially deaths. In Australia, most historians' attention has been paid to

---

4   Mona Farr, 'The Nineteen-nineteen Fires', c.1929. In Interview with Liza Dale-Hallett, 22 July 2010. Victorian Bushfires Collection, Museum Victoria HT 27172.

formal memorials like monuments, sculptures, gardens and plaques and the vast majority of these have been erected to commemorate the war dead.

Over the last couple of decades, however, there has been rising academic interest, including in Australia, in informal assemblages – 'grassroots' or 'spontaneous' memorials – that spring up at sites of death and devastation. We are all familiar with the mountains of flowers, soft toys, signs, candles, flags and other offerings that appear at places of untimely death and are captured and broadcast repeatedly by the media. The Poetry Tree differs in some respects from these assemblages but it has this in common: memorials are never just about remembering the dead.

The tree is a many-layered installation in which the acknowledgement of death is only one purpose. In fact, the straightforward tributes to deceased people were significantly outnumbered by poems about many different aspects of the fire, but it took me a while to work that out. I expected a memorial to be concerned with death and grief and – in the beginning – that is what I saw.

I decided to unpack the Poetry Tree, looking for deeper meaning through examining it as an artifact. I considered where it was placed, who had created it and when, the different ways in which people both contributed and responded to the tree and – most importantly – its symbolic role in Strathewen. And here is what I found.

Unpacking the Poetry Tree

The Poetry Tree is located at the intersection of three roads and a creek; it's right beside the bridge over Arthurs Creek, practically on the verge of the road, and it is impossible to pass without seeing it. From the bridge the land rises in all directions, to Sugarloaf

THE POETRY TREE: MEMORIALS

Mountain and the Kinglake Ranges on three sides and to a more distant ridge of lower hills on the fourth. This is a highly public and significant place, the gateway to Strathewen. For many people who, like Rosemary and Ian, lived on the far side of the creek, crossing the bridge was a sign that they were home. For parents and children, this intersection was where the school came into view; in 2009 it was the beginning (or the end) of the only paved road.

Barbara described the spot as *the very entrance to Strathewen. There used to be a whole stand of trees there and it was like, you know, a beautiful colonnade of trees, but most of those had gone, or were burning and were being cleared away. But this one tree still stood there with a blackened trunk.*[5] It may not have been a conscious act by the first contributors to invoke ancient traditions, but crossroads and river crossings have always had symbolic significance in western culture. The Poetry Tree has echoes of the mythic guardians of such places; Barbara likened it to a sentinel standing guard over the bridge, *asking if I was strong enough to face what was on the other side.*[6]

The first poems went up in late February, when the area was still closed to the public and even residents were unable to return to the community. Unlike the grassroots memorials we are familiar with through media coverage of events like the destruction of the World Trade Centre towers in 2001, where thousands of strangers expressed sympathy and solidarity, participation in the Poetry Tree was initially limited to those who were directly impacted by the fires in Strathewen. Rosemary and Ian's poems were in place for ten days before Barbara's joined them. The sense that this was an action exclusive to those who had lived through Black Saturday continued even

---

5   Barbara Joyce, Interview 31 August 2010.
6   Ibid.

after the roads were opened and people came to Strathewen to help, to work or to sightsee. Almost the only messages from 'outsiders' were posted by working parties who came to help with land clearing and rebuilding fences, or by former residents. Visitors to Strathewen left flowers at the tree but rarely added their own messages. The tree was both public – positioned in the most exposed spot in Strathewen, and loaded with messages intended to be shared – and private, in its creation, maintenance and moral ownership by a relatively small group of people.

The purpose of the tree changed over time. The first poems, those posted by Rosemary and Ian, were not specifically tributes to lost friends or relations. They were declarations of solidarity and resilience. The first memorial notices were added later, when more people returned to Strathewen, and when the grim news of who had died became clear. These were dedicated to residents like Peter Avola, who lost his life on the Strathewen Oval nearby, and Joe Shepherd, who died in hospital nearly three weeks after he was injured on Black Saturday, and his son Danny. They were joined by more pictures and dedications, as well as flowers and plants, but it was still a local and individual response.

As people came to grips with the reality of rebuilding, and of new losses like Marilyn and Henk, the tree was used to express the changing lives of the contributors and of many of the people around them. Rosemary observed in 2010 that *some people feel their words aren't right now and they take them away and replace them.*[7] Among the ongoing messages of love and grief were writings that conveyed the effort of cleaning up. An unsigned poem says:

---

7 Rosemary McKimmie Young, Interview 6 October 2010.

> A stagger, a drag, a thump
> Dark sticks and branches moving
> Put 'em in a clump
> A dozen acres to go
> [...]
> Chop, cut, burr, hack
> Like ants before the rain we gather
> Build it all into a huge stack
> I want my trees back
> One more acre to go.
> [...]

It has the ring of a ploughing song or a sea shanty, a rhythm about doing things and getting on with the job, but this is a job filled with pain and longing.

Many contributors decided not to preserve or renew their poems as time and weather affected the originals. Words were allowed to fade, disintegrate and in some cases to blow away. Barbara saw this as a reflection of the sense of impermanence that she now felt: *so much has changed, a little more doesn't matter.*[8] When asked in 2010 about the future of the tree, the original contributors were content to let the future decide. *It will be what it will be and so let it be.*[9] The museum refrained from collecting any material that had been removed from the tree, choosing instead to photograph the tree and record interviews.

The words posted on the Poetry Tree follow familiar conventions, using free verse as well as the ballad style of poetry that is so much

---

8 Barbara Joyce, Interview 31 August 2010.
9 Ian McKimmie, Interview 6 October 2010.

a part of Australian bush mythology. They also embrace the conventions of our society about death, using euphemisms and avoiding distressing language. A family member who has died is 'in the arms of the angels'; the death of a teenage son is described as 'family ties are broken'. For Henk, there is only 'So many memories, love always.' There is nothing to suggest violent or untimely death. In fact, when you look carefully there is surprisingly little about death itself. Most of the texts are really concerned with life: a celebration of the life of the deceased, about the power of love over death, or a call to look forward and embrace life with renewed purpose and appreciation.

In this sense, the Poetry Tree projects a narrative of resilience that it shares with books, newspaper articles and speeches about the fires. By the time I first saw the tree in late 2009, there was a great deal in the poems about revival and continuity, but nothing of negative emotions like despair or anger.[10] Perhaps they had already been edited out (what Rosemary called the feeling that *their words aren't right now*) from respect for the survivors or a fear about releasing such raw emotions into a public forum inhabited by traumatised people.

It is part of the process of commemoration to edit the past, to decide what will be explicitly remembered and what is best 'forgotten'. Even in the first few days of the Poetry Tree's existence, a coherent narrative was beginning to emerge of grief, resilience, determination and a renewed commitment to both the people and the place of Strathewen. The contributors were beginning to compose a story to sustain them through the days ahead.

---

10   In 2013 someone posted a fierce poem on the tree about the death of Bill Putt, who successfully defended his home on Black Saturday but had recently died of a heart attack while clearing bushfire debris. Called 'It's a fucken' lottery', it showed that anger as well as resilience was considered a fit subject for both poetry and the Poetry Tree. By this time the public importance of the tree was waning but it remained, significantly, a site for subversive emotions.

THE POETRY TREE: MEMORIALS

Ian McKimmie lost his house as well as many friends, and survived only by digging a mud wallow against a water tank. His first poem read:

> The spirit of the Sugarloaf
> Protected us as it burned
> That is the gift which we [received]
> And will continue to [receive]
> As the spirit
> And the gifted ones
> Slowly heal together

In a significant departure from the nineteenth-century image of the bush as the enemy, in this poem and in several others on the tree the bush is as much a victim as its residents. In all of them, the environment's damage and its recovery are inextricably linked with the recovery of the people who live there, as they 'slowly heal together'.

Poems like this suggest a different approach to the environment than do memorials to earlier bushfires. Recent research into Australian memorials found little if any acknowledgement of what was called the 'landscapes lost to fire.'[11] Ian's poem, on the other hand, not only explicitly references the landscape but suggests that, far from being 'lost', the land will heal. This is echoed in other interviews from the bushfire zone: Ali Griffin, who lost her home in Yarra Glen, spoke not of destruction but of transformation; Barbara Joyce, who lives near the site of Ian's former home, said of Black Saturday that Indigenous people might have regarded it not as a disaster but as a

---

11 Paul Ashton, Paula Hamilton, and Rose Searby, *Places of the Heart: Memorials in Australia* (North Melbourne: Australian Scholarly Publishing, 2012), 75.

good clean-up of the bush.[12] It was this understanding of Strathewen, as a place changed but not destroyed, that set the Mitchell and Nelson families on the road to rebuilding even before the fires had stopped burning. *It is still our home.* [13]

Not everyone, however, agrees with the concept of a benevolent, even protective environment, or a continuing link with the land. Many people spoke of how Mount Sugarloaf blocked the view of the oncoming fire, contributing to their ignorance of what was headed their way. In their view, Mount Sugarloaf did not protect them; it added to the disaster. Even those who identified with the landscape still mourned, in addition to the people and animals killed in the fire, the loss of buildings and the material culture and memories they carried. No doubt there will be people in Strathewen who will find, as Zelma Gartner did after the Ash Wednesday bushfires in Mount Macedon, that the landscape of the community has changed beyond their capacity to accept. Zelma said, *It wasn't the same place at all.*[14]

The Tree's deeper meaning

Contributions to spontaneous memorials like the Poetry Tree do more than document or mourn what has happened: they become agents of change. In times of crisis, writing a poem is not a matter of art or aesthetics, but a political act. For Barbara, pinning her first poem on the tree was a commitment to Strathewen, *to let people know I was coming back.*[15] Although the poem itself mourns the loss of

---

12 Alison Griffin, Interview 12 August 2010; Barbara Joyce, Interview 31 August 2010.
13 Vicki Mitchell, Interview 8 August 2012.
14 Zelma Gartner, Interview 16 March 2011.
15 Barbara Joyce, Interview 31 August 2010.

so much in Strathewen, its creation was an act of resilience and an expression of solidarity.

The most revealing aspect of the Poetry Tree is why it was begun in the first place, and the earlier poems by Rosemary and Ian best illustrate the Poetry Tree as a place of symbolic action. The day on which they posted their first poems, 22 February 2009, was the date of the official memorial service for those killed by the fires. The service was held in the centre of Melbourne and was attended by the Prime Minister, the Governor-General, many senior politicians and religious figures, firefighters and emergency workers. Tens of thousands more people watched the televised service at home or in public squares.

This is how Rosemary explained why she and Ian chose this day to begin the Poetry Tree:

> *Because there were still road blocks then, Ian and I were here and some other people listening to it, and it was very distressing. And it was distressing for me also for the simple fact that that was happening in the city and we were here and we couldn't get there if we wanted to anyway and if we did, we probably wouldn't have been able to get back in. [...] And I know it was still very, very traumatic and we didn't deal with that day very well, either of us, because we've lost 17 very close friends, 43 people we knew. So we said, 'Let's make our own memorial. Let's go and put up a poem.' I'd written a poem, and we said, 'Let's go and put that up.' [...] So we decided to take it down to the corner of Strathewen, where the creek and the roads meet, and Ian found the tree that we now call the Poetry Tree and we nailed our poetry on it.*[16]

---

16 Rosemary McKimmie Young, Interview 6 October 2010.

So the Poetry Tree began not only as a reaction to the events of Black Saturday but also a protest against the authorities who planned this service without – as Rosemary and Ian saw it – consideration of the people most affected by Black Saturday. It was a declaration of defiance as much as of sorrow, and even anger: *bugger it,* said Rosemary, *we've got nothing else.*[17] The official memorial service held in the city shifted the Black Saturday narrative from the bushfire towns to a larger stage, where Australia as a nation could express its grief and solidarity and politicians could offer messages of reassurance and rebuilding. The creation of the Poetry Tree was a counter-action that reclaimed the bushfire zone as the centre of the event. By choosing a tree at the crossroads of Strathewen in the heart of the physical damage, rather than one on their own land, they were publicly staking a claim to the emotional territory of destruction.

This claim is reinforced in some of the later works on the Poetry Tree, which are self-referential. They were not only on the tree but about the tree and its poems. Barbara Joyce wrote:

> This tree becomes a monument
> A place for us to be
> A place where words are whispered
> In the arms of the "Poetry Tree"

She was binding the tree into the narrative as a character as well as a carrier, helping to consolidate the Poetry Tree's presence and influence.

---

17 Ian McKimmie, Interview 6 October 2010.

THE POETRY TREE: MEMORIALS

The texts and images on the tree created a narrative about the 'old' pre-Black-Saturday Strathewen as a place of beauty, peace and harmony. In doing so, it also provided a template for the new Strathewen. Michael Roth calls this a 'redemptive narrative', one in which the losses are either marginalised or mitigated by the gains – in this case, stronger community relationships.[18] To Barbara, *people who'd just been names before became friends. We became more closely knit, which was good. I think we needed that.*[19] This template was for a community in which the fire would be remembered but the individual horrors forgotten, in which disruptions like suicide would be gently transmuted into good memories and in which unity with both the environment and other residents would define the way of life. The Poetry Tree provided a moral foundation on which the new Strathewen could rest.

This is a vision in which people, through great difficulty, learn to care more deeply for each other and for the earth. It is a prospect that embodies hope rather than despair and a desire to create some good out of disaster. Searching for – or creating – meaning out of unexpected death is a powerful urge. Psychologist Rob Gordon, who has worked with many Australians in the aftermath of Black Saturday and other disasters, identifies it as an important survival mechanism.[20] But the Poetry Tree represents only one aspect of the fires and of Strathewen itself.

The Poetry Tree was such a dominant element in the physical and emotional landscape that it was easy to overlook the fact that it was

---

18   Michael S. Roth, *Memory, Trauma and History: Essays on Living with the Past* (New York: Columba University Press, 2012), 84.
19   Barbara Joyce, Interview 31 August 2010.
20   Rob Gordon, "Community Impact of Disaster and Community Recovery," *InPsych* (2009).

created and maintained by a small number of residents. Bronwyn South, who lives on the outskirts of Strathewen and does not cross the bridge every day, acknowledged its symbolic importance to others but did not have a strong connection to the poems. Joyce and Alan Horne respected the tree as an expression of other people's emotions but did not respond to it personally. They found their comfort in their faith and their religious community. Others did not share the importance of words, and they took part in creative projects that sprang up after Black Saturday – photography, artworks, sculpture – that gave a non-verbal outlet for emotions and thoughts. Still other people found sufficient outlets both physical and emotional in the challenges of rebuilding. They dealt with the damage by trying to repair it.

There were also people for whom the Poetry Tree represented a threat. As much as some people might be attracted and reassured by the message of the Poetry Tree, it distressed and alienated others. For Karen Gardam, the tree was a reminder of and a reproach for her inability to deal with the deaths of her mother and brother. *I can't write fucking poetry. I can't even get out of the bed in the morning.*[21] It was a further distancing from the community with which she had had a problematic relationship for many years.

For Vicki Mitchell, the tree's presence in the centre of Strathewen represented the domination of Strathewen's past and future by the people who created the poems, some of whom she considered bitter enemies. Bill Putt's poem read:

> In the valley of Ewen
> We are happy and free

---

21   Karen Gardam, Interview 15 September 2010.

THE POETRY TREE: MEMORIALS

> There's no other place
> I'd rather be
> Than Strathewen.

His words were heartfelt, but they contradicted and denied Vicki's memories of Strathewen as a place of conflict and anguish. After the fires she had a vision of a transformed community, one in which *good old-fashioned country values* were again in the ascendancy.[22] It could be debated what those values are and their role in shaping Strathewen, but that is beside the point. What is important is that the Poetry Tree, in failing to acknowledge the divisions and conflicts that characterised Vicki's experience before the fires, also created an emotional landscape after the fires in which there was no need of and no room for Vicki's reforms.

It is these negative reactions to the Poetry Tree that make clear that it is not a simple memorial, if indeed such a thing exists. Karen or Vicki might not have objected to the Poetry Tree so strenuously if its original and continuing purpose had been limited to expressions of loss and dedications to deceased residents. The Poetry Tree began with personal statements, posted in a public place of significance, of a vision that described a very different society to the one that the women had known, and expressed emotions and hopes they did not share. It was, perhaps inadvertently, an appropriation of the physical and metaphysical landscape of Strathewen and the women both resented and feared it.

This was made clear in 2010, when the museum started to digitise the Victorian Bushfires Collection and upload it to the museum's

---

22   Vicki Mitchell, Interview 8 August 2012.

Collections Online website.²³ Among the objects, images and stories made available to the public were photographs and some objects collected from the people who started the Poetry Tree. The museum's Discovery Centre was disconcerted to receive emotional phone calls from a small number of people, Karen and Vicki among them, who objected to the museum's decision to document the tree. Their reasons were different but the underlying motivation was the same: they both believed that the Poetry Tree, by offering a vision of a creative, harmonious Strathewen, invalidated their own understanding and experience of the place. In turn the museum, by documenting and publicising the tree, was considered to be privileging the narrative contained in the poetry and was therefore complicit in the suppression of alternative versions of the community's experience both before and after the fire.

It could have ended there, with angry phone calls, but both Karen and Vicki agreed to talk to me in detail about their concerns and their own experiences. Eventually they each agreed to do an oral history interview, although there were some topics and people that were still too sensitive to be discussed. What emerged was the complex, sometimes contradictory view of Strathewen on which this book is based, in which everyone tries to cope, with the infinitely variable combination of skills and resources that people possess, with what life throws at them.

I was grateful to the creators of the Poetry Tree for sharing their memories and experiences with me but I was also grateful to Karen and Vicki for challenging the vision of Strathewen that I had originally recorded. I could now see that Barbara was trying to build a positive foundation from which recovery could begin, but that the

---

23 Museum Victoria, 'Victorian Bushfires Collection.' http://museumvictoria.com.au/collections/themes/3032/victorian-bushfires-collection [Accessed 29 July 2015].

harmonising narrative of a united Strathewen also made it more difficult for some people to speak of unresolved conflict and anger. Vicki and Karen were distressed by the public attention given to positive interpretations of the Poetry Tree, but it was also apparent that their reactions were causing others distress. For me it was the beginning of a balancing act, trying to respect and understand each survivor's story without passing judgement on whether it was 'correct' or which is the 'right' story to tell, because there isn't one.

A permanent memorial

After the first anniversary of the fires in 2010, the Strathewen Community Renewal Association (SCRA) began to consider the creation of a permanent memorial. A survey of residents confirmed the view that the Poetry Tree should be allowed to age, unimpeded by efforts either to preserve or to dismantle it, and that a permanent memorial should be built elsewhere.

This was partly pragmatic, as the tree's location right beside the main road posed problems of parking and public safety, and partly political. The committee wanted a memorial that would, from its planning stages, offer everyone in Strathewen the chance to be involved. They also wanted a more secluded spot. 'The memorial should be nestled for a number of reasons; to allow people their privacy and not to be ogled by passers-by, to provide a degree of shelter and contemplation, and importantly to allow those living in the town not to be reminded of it every day. It is important to engage with the memorial rather than be confronted by it.'[24] Where the Poetry Tree was a

---

24 Strathewen Community Renewal Association, "The Memorial Development Process in Strathewen," http://www.strathewen.vic.au/we-remember/memorials/the-memorial-development-process-in-strathewen/ [Accessed 3 March 2014].

place of challenge and public declarations, the official memorial was intended to be a place of private reflection and consolation.

A memorials working group composed of members of SCRA, representatives of local council and the Red Cross began a 'long discussion' with residents, former residents and bereaved families through surveys, facilitated workshops and feedback to interim reports. A professional consultancy, Arterial Designs, was contracted to develop and build the memorial which opened in September 2012. In 2013, on the fourth anniversary of Black Saturday, the new memorial was the site of the community remembrance service. Despite the emphasis on privacy, it is like most community memorials a public place, and one that hosts public events.

It's a low-key, low-profile installation, spread out across an expanse of bush in a secluded spot, close to the road but well screened from both it and the cricket oval nearby. From above, it would resemble a series of water drops with ripples extending outwards, and at the centre of the largest is a low mound with the names of the 27 people who died in Strathewen. Each ripple is a red arc embedded in the ground in which are etched thousands of words drawn from the people who took part in the process. Some of the phrases have been borrowed from poems on the Poetry Tree. The words follow a chronology that describes Strathewen before the fires, the heat wave that preceded the fire, the conflagration itself and then the aftermath. Arranged in rows and columns that form a kind of de-constructed haiku, they can be read in a number of ways and the arcs offer different pathways through the memorial.

Like the Poetry Tree, the permanent memorial draws much of its power from words. It is in many ways reminiscent of the memorial in the Madrid train station to the 191 victims of the terrorist bombings there in 2004. In the days and months after the bombings, the train station at Atocha was the site of a grassroots memorial of flowers, candles and written messages, most notably inscribed on the walls and pillars of the station itself. The permanent memorial which replaced the original offerings incorporates some of the first messages along with condolences received from all over the world.

The Strathewen memorial is powerfully evocative but it is also problematic. Despite the almost infinite combinations of words, the many different voices and the many ways to navigate through the memorial, there is only one story. Like the Poetry Tree, the permanent memorial tells a harmonising narrative. Strathewen before the fires is depicted as an idyllic, close-knit rural community. In this version of the story, there is a premonition of disaster expressed through awareness of the heatwave and its effect on the bush. The experience of the fire and its immediate aftermath is powerfully conveyed through the broken, almost chaotic text, which is then superseded by reflections on both the past and the future and the hopes for rebuilding. The bush and the people of Strathewen are both depicted as victims of the bushfire, and as partners for the future. What is missing is the subversive text in which people did not get along, ignored the warning signs, made foolish decisions on the day of the fire or were overwhelmed in its aftermath and left Strathewen.

The problems surrounding memorialisation did not disappear with the completion of the new memorial. Vicki resisted the development process, refusing to become engaged with a narrative that did not reflect her own experience and in which she saw the influence of people with whom she did not want to be associated. Karen, who was also invited to be part of the consultation process, rejected the concept completely. Despite the fact that the names of her mother and brother are displayed on the central mound, she did not attend any of the ceremonies held there.

The trouble is that the permanent memorial does what many official memorials do – indeed, what most people want official memorials to do. Like the Poetry Tree before it, it provides a single unproblematic story around which people can build a sense of unity and common purpose and a continuing conviction that death has not been in vain. There is no room for counter-narratives that are messy and conflicted.

Part of Karen's unhappiness was related to the nature of the memorial and its dominant narrative, but it was also concerned with the principle of a memorial. She worried that the only place in Strathewen where her mother's name appears will forever link Irma to a horrific death. *I'm not going to let the fires define me [...] and I didn't want that to happen to my mother. These were people way before the fires and they had lives, they had wonderful lives.*[25] Her words echo the concerns of Holocaust historian James Young that Holocaust museums do not document Jewish culture and civilisation but their destruction, and that Jewish lives are known only by images of death.[26] Karen looked for alternatives to create a permanent reminder of her family's presence, in the naming of a road or a building, to place Irma firmly in the everyday world of the living. *I don't want my mother to be remembered for her death; I want her to be remembered for her life.*[27]

Karen's concern that Irma's accomplishments in life are overwhelmed by the circumstances of her death is echoed in how the ordinary tragedies of life in Strathewen have been overshadowed

---

25 Karen Gardam, Interview 27 March 2013.
26 James Young, *The Texture of Memory: Holocaust Memorials and Meaning* (New Haven: Yale University Press, 1993), 133.
27 Karen Gardam, Interview 14 March 2013.

by the events of Black Saturday. Edith and Lindsay Apted were important people in the community through their social positions as Strathewen's largest employers but also because of their personal contributions. The list of the organisations in which they were involved – church, school, CFA, Landcare, Rural Shire Action, Orchards and Cool Stores Association and the Australian Apple and Pear Growers Association – is a reminder of the many roles that prominent people in small communities often fill. They were both almost universally admired and in happier times their deaths, in 2008 and 2010 respectively, would have sparked discussions about how to recognise their contributions. The fires of early 2009, however, disrupted the process of grieving and memorialising 'normal' death and established Black Saturday as the only event for which it was appropriate to mourn. Edith and Lindsay's daughter Bronwyn noted the eclipse of her parents' lives and deaths not with resentment but with sadness. To her it was an indication of the degree to which Strathewen had been shaped by the fire.

The Poetry Tree today

You might have noticed that, despite our decision not to solicit donations from the Poetry Tree's creators, the photo with which this chapter begins is captioned 'Victorian Bushfires Collection, Museum Victoria.' That is because in 2013, shortly after the permanent memorial was completed, Barbara removed her poem from the tree and donated it to the museum. *It had done its job and it was time.*[28] This was a change from her position three years earlier, but for her the tree had become an historical artifact, a symbol of the past – still

---

28   Barbara Joyce, Interview 13 February 2013.

significant, but lacking its previous ability to challenge and console. In the same way that SCRA envisioned the Strathewen memorial as taking on the burden of remembering, relieving people (at least for a while) of the pain of remembering the past, for people like Barbara the museum collection is taking on part of the memory-work of the bushfires.

Barbara now visits the permanent memorial to reflect on Black Saturday. The Poetry Tree still has poems on it, and someone still brings flowers occasionally, but the number of poems and visitors has diminished. The contributions are looking worn and shabby. Other people have changed as well. Karen Gardam, who objected so strenuously to the Poetry Tree in 2010, looked back on her reactions in 2013. She saw that her anger and distress were caused in part by the poems' preoccupations with life at a time when she was consumed by grief and death, and she now accepts that the authors of the Poetry Tree were finding their own way through the destruction. The irony is not lost on her that she now objects to the permanent memorial's emphasis on death when she wants to focus on her mother's life.

The tree itself has regenerated and has a thick green canopy of leaves. Manna gums have evolved to survive Australian bushfire, sometimes even those as severe as Black Saturday, and an arbourist's report gives it at least another 30 years of life. The thick layer of burned bark, the tree's protection against fire, is slowly peeling to expose new skin beneath it. When the bark falls away, so do the poems that are fixed to it. Every time I pass it, another poem is gone. The tree will soon appear almost normal, an ordinary tree at the side of the road.

So what do I call the Poetry Tree? A memorial or an art installation, or even a manifesto? It has elements of all of these, but none of them expresses the complexity of either the emotions it contains or the reactions it has evoked. Dacia Viejo-Rose has described memorial places in Spain as palimpsests, social documents that have layers of new meaning added to them but through which the original message can still be perceived.[29] In the same way the Poetry Tree is a palimpsest, in which the original motivations for its creation – the assertion of life in a place of death – have been overlaid with memorial declarations that have, in the public understanding, become its primary purpose. Added to this is the evocation of the Australian bush ballad and the qualities we associate with that tradition, the declarations of commitment to staying and rebuilding, the emotional links to the land, the tug of power relations within Strathewen and the negative reactions of some residents. The result is not a tree but a tangled thicket of concepts and emotions: defiance, grief, hope, anger, resilience, exhaustion, patriotism, fear and determination.

---

29   Dacia Viejo-Rose, "Memorial Functions: Intent, Impact and the Right to Remember," *Memory Studies* 4, no. 4 (2011): 467.

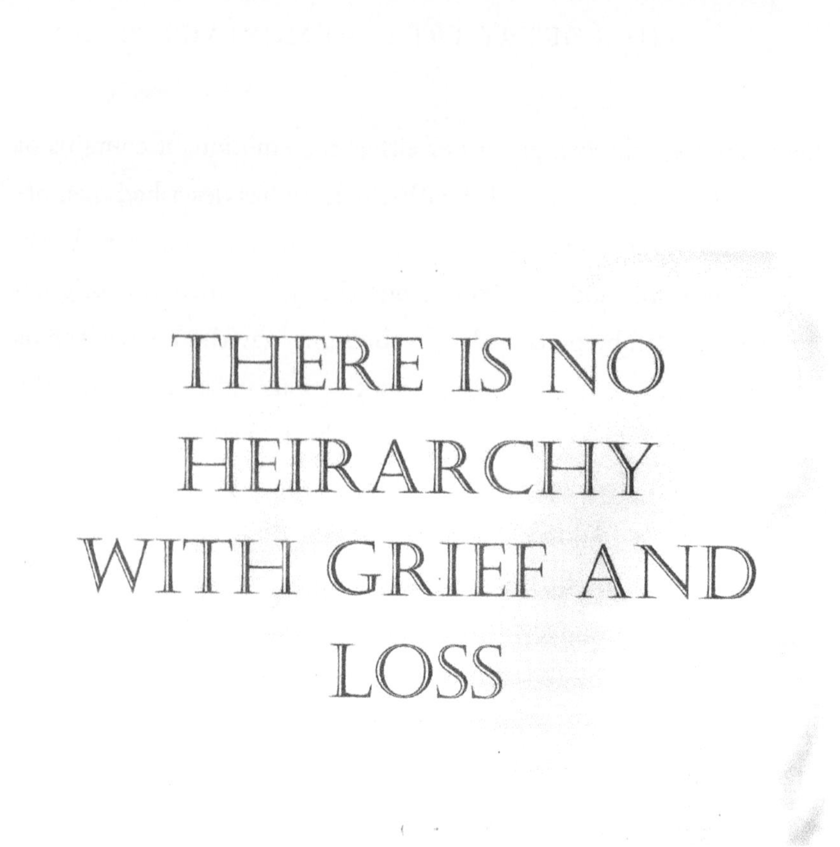

THERE IS NO HEIRARCHY WITH GRIEF AND LOSS

Figure 5. Sign, Hurstbridge Bushfire Relief Centre. Victorian Bushfires Collection, Museum Victoria, HT 48472.

Image: Peg Fraser. Source: Museum Victoria.

Chapter 4

THE POSTERS: LOSS, ANGER AND OPPORTUNITY

It was a simple sign produced on a home computer, laminated and stuck up on a wall with a couple of thumb tacks. The choice of a monumental font emphasised the importance of the message, the common spelling mistake the speed with which it was created. Helen Legg, who made it, thought it was a quote from a psychologist or grief counsellor, but she wasn't sure.

The sign hung in an unofficial relief centre in Hurstbridge, a small town at the end of the suburban railway line and the service centre closest to Strathewen. It was opened and operated by a group of local volunteers headed by Helen Legg, a resident of the area whose house was not affected by the fire. 'Unofficial' refers to the fact that it was not part of any government or charitable structure but purely a local grassroots response from neighbours and acquaintances. Initially called the Hurstbridge Bushfire Relief Centre, then the Hurstbridge Bushfire Support Centre, it was best-known as Helen's Place.

The centre opened within a couple of weeks of Black Saturday in an empty shopfront, the use of which was contributed by the property owners. Initially starting with local donations, the centre soon was inundated with gifts from all over Victoria and further afield:

clothing, toys, kitchen items, computers, books, food, and furniture. The women who started and ran it became expert in sourcing what individuals or families needed, often just ringing companies or organisations out of the phone book to ask for help. They held raffles to give away special donations, like a family holiday. Tens of thousands of dollars' worth of white goods alone were distributed to bushfire-affected families.

In many ways Helen's Place closely resembled the Kingston Voluntary Relief Organisation (KVRO), the informal relief system set up in the aftermath of the 1967 Tasmanian bushfires that killed 62 people and penetrated into Hobart's inner suburbs. Founded by 'Miss C. Atkinson and another woman' along with help 'from about 20 other local housewives', the KVRO was informal, highly flexible, long-term and personalised; they were reputed 'to be able to supply anything from a handkerchief to a toilet, a teaspoon to a house'.[1] Like Miss Atkinson and her co-workers, the women who ran Helen's Place were answerable only to their clients and their own consciences, allowing them a freedom and flexibility unavailable to official emergency responses. Only eventually – as they began to access government funding for programs – did Helen's Place become subject to regulations.

Although providing material aid was the most visible of the centre's functions, its real value lay in the emotional support it gave to bushfire survivors. *It wasn't just the material things, it was being able to see and speak to those ladies and I think [it was] because you knew that they were so involved in everything, they knew what was going on. They*

---

1   R.L. Wettenhall, *Bushfire Disaster: An Australian Community in Crisis*, ed. Grant Harman, Studies in Australian Society (Cremorne NSW: Angus and Robertson, 1975), 160–61.

cared, they really cared and they knew what you were going through.[2] For very nearly two years after Black Saturday the women provided food, coffee and down-to-earth sympathy. They set up programs for people to get away for a break, to talk things over or to enjoy a family day. Most of all they listened, encouraged and gave people space to express any and all emotions. *They were easy to talk to, there was no pressure, they didn't follow you around to say 'how you going' and they didn't tell me once that I needed help. They were just there.*[3]

This poster set the rule – essentially the only rule – by which the centre operated. Everyone who walked in would be treated equally and no one would be judged by what they had lost, how much stuff they took or how long they continued to need support. Significantly, the women thought it necessary to make this statement. By repudiating a hierarchy of grief and loss, they were acknowledging its existence.

Hierarchies of loss

After extreme events, an administrative hierarchical order kicks into action, especially when it comes to delivering services and dispensing public funds. This helps to ensure minimum standards of transparency and accountability and in the case of Black Saturday, when hundreds of millions of dollars were donated through public appeals, transparency and accountability became even more important. Helen's sign was referring to something quite different, to the effects on the survivors of social hierarchies of loss.

Rob Gordon, one of the leading Australians in the field of disaster psychology, called it 'social comparison.'

---

2   Vicki Mitchell, Interview 8 August 2012.
3   Robert Crisfield, Interview 7 August 2013.

As time passes, the recovery environment tends to identify more severely affected people as benchmarks against which other losses are judged and disenfranchises those with less obvious impacts. Tensions begin to develop because people increasingly feel the need for recognition of their unique problems, but feel unable to communicate them. As recovery proceeds, the complexity of the situation develops. Issues affect people differently and divide the group's unity. The uninsured become envious of those who are, the insured become angry when the uninsured receive appeal funds.[4]

It is inevitable and necessary, in the attempt to retrieve order from chaos, to develop a system that sorts out the relative experiences and losses that occur from living through an extreme event. But in an attempt to understand what has happened, a complex situation is sometimes reduced to a simple dichotomy like 'burnt' and 'not burnt'. There are many such orderings in the bushfire zone: those who lost their home and those who did not; those who evacuated and those who stayed through the fire; those who rebuilt and those who moved away; those who owned their homes and those who were renting. The underlying assumption is that some people, who can be identified by such parameters, have lost more and therefore need more – more assistance, more sympathy, more compensation – than others. The Hierarchy sign was a challenge to this social comparison.

No dichotomy can capture the multitude of experiences and reactions of such an event. It is impossible to compare the relative losses, especially the emotional and psychological ones, without someone being left out. Rae and Barrie Tully, whose house sheltered 19 people

---

4   Gordon, "Community Impact of Disaster and Community Recovery". n.p.

THE POSTERS: LOSS, ANGER AND OPPORTUNITY

during the fires, appeared to be lucky – Rae herself said that theirs was the happy story – but their farm and livelihood were destroyed. She tried to explain the complicated relationship between their own situation and those of people who lost their homes but still had a job in the city. *This was our work, our life, our everything. So when the farm went and left the house – it's hard to explain, really, that [other people have] still got a life except they don't have a house, whereas we didn't have a life but we had a house.*[5]

Barbara Joyce, whose house survived the fires, experienced a similar reaction. *A lot of people after the fire said we were lucky, and it took me by surprise to be called lucky. When I was feeling so grief-stricken when such a disaster surrounded me, I didn't really feel a sense of luck at all.*[6] There are people in Strathewen who did not lose a house but who endured the worst of the firestorm and will remember it for the rest of their lives. There are those who lived below the fire line but lost close friends or family members. Some CFA volunteers may not have had family or property losses but they experienced horrific things, including discovering the remains of friends. Some people lost less in the way of material assets, but they had little to start with. Others were emotionally vulnerable before the bushfire and increasingly unable to cope after it. The sign at Helen's Place repudiated the idea that people's experiences could be measured against each other – or against anything other than the individual's own ability to cope.

The sign was also a response to perceptions both within and outside the bushfire-affected community that some people were benefiting unfairly from the flow of goods and money donated to the

---

5   Rae Tully, Interview 16 October 2013.
6   Barbara Joyce, Interview 31 August 2010.

relief effort: *just little whispers, little comments in the community about how so-and-so had got lots of money, or had taken more than he needed, or that someone else was still taking free groceries.*[7] Complaints about 'professional fire victims,' people who were turning their own and others' misfortunes into social or financial profit, were not uncommon in my conversations with survivors. One of the reasons that Darren Thompson relied so much on Helen's Place was that he felt the machinery of the official recovery effort unfairly rewarded those who could navigate bureaucracy, those survivors who were *switched on with the reading and writing. They come up with stuff I could only dream of.*[8] There were also angry observations that people unaffected by the fires were helping themselves to material aid.

There probably were people who took unfair advantage of Helen's Place, but the volunteers at the centre decided that the damage caused by questioning people's motives and actions, especially at such a vulnerable period of their lives, outweighed the risk of the occasional 'undeserving' recipient. *When people came in, we didn't ask questions. They might have been collecting stuff for other families, or taking it to a local centre, or maybe they were just trying to fill the big hole left in their lives. As far as we were concerned, if they asked for it, then they needed it and they could have it. If they were still collecting groceries 18 months after the fires – well, there were lots of people even then who were still too traumatised to write a shopping list. We weren't going to question them.*[9] The women at the relief centre also understood that, often, the need for 'stuff' wasn't about stuff at all, that a cry for emotional and psychological support often underlay a request for material assistance.

---

7   Helen Legg, Interview 25 June 2013.
8   Darren Thompson, Interview 22 August 2013.
9   Helen Legg, Interview 25 June 2013.

THE POSTERS: LOSS, ANGER AND OPPORTUNITY

They were a security blanket, a huge security blanket down there that you just didn't want to let go of.[10]

Helen and her co-workers also realised that public expectations of 'recovery' often failed to acknowledge the size and complexity of the difficulties faced by survivors and the length of time needed to come to terms with the fires. These unrealistic expectations were partly driven by the well-intentioned efforts of government and the media to focus on rebuilding and, later on, good-news stories of recovery. The repeated promises from government to rebuild bushfire communities 'brick by brick' implied that replacing homes and physical infrastructure was the solution to all the problems, and that recovery was just a matter of a couple of years and a lot of money. Under the glaring light of media attention, survivors carried the additional burden of living up to these expectations. *The biggest question that I found hard to deal with is 'Have you finished your rebuilding yet?' Like, as if we only needed to replace a house, without the understanding there's much more.*[11]

The emphasis on rebuilding and its importance to 'recovery' meant that support services were often perceived to be linked to rebuilding. Fred Bateman and Leslye Chappelle rarely attended Strathewen social events after the bushfires, even though they had lost their home on Black Saturday. *We thought that because we were leaving Strathewen we didn't want to take in some of those things. We thought [attending them] was unfair, that they were meant for the people living in Strathewen.*[12] Bronwyn South described another Strathewen family trying to cope with the effects of extreme trauma on their young

---

10   Vicki Mitchell, Interview 8 August 2012.
11   Ian McKimmie, Interview 18 June 2013.
12   Fred Bateman, Interview 27 June 2013.

adult children: *I know that despite what that family went through they were challenged with why they were attending fire recovery things, why were they involved. They weren't [considered] fire-affected because they hadn't lost their house.*[13]

And yet, under the tensions of who was more in need or who was more deserving of material aid or emotional support, ran a counter-theme. Bronwyn South watched the fire come to the boundary of her property, then turn on the wind change. On Black Saturday she lost close friends, the community she had grown up in and an environment she was passionate about, *but the people who were faced by flame on the day have had an experience that [I] have not and cannot presume to have had.*[14] Despite bitterness over his own losses, Darren Thompson said *it took a lot more from other people. It took their families, their friends.*[15] Fred Bateman endured two hours of the firestorm on his own, lost his house and everything in it and made his way, with serious injuries, through a devastated landscape, but he said *we're lucky. We're both fairly strong people, so mentally it didn't affect us as greatly as it has other people, 'cause a lot of people just didn't cope.*[16] On the scale of comparison that really counted – that of emotional and psychological loss – nearly everyone I spoke to, while acknowledging and mourning their own losses, also privileged the greater losses of others.

So perhaps the issue wasn't about where you fit in the hierarchy or even, despite Helen's sign, the existence of a hierarchy. Perhaps what counted was who made the call. It was the perception that someone

---

13 Bronwyn Apted South, Interview 5 December 2012.
14 Ibid.
15 Darren Thompson, Interview 22 August 2013.
16 Fred Bateman, Interview 27 June 2013.

else was judging – through money, material aid or media attention – the extent and depth of one's own loss that people objected to. Helen had translated into psychological terms the warning that one narrator gave me as the greatest lesson that outsiders could learn about bushfire survivors: *Don't tell me what I have lost.*[17]

Yet even as I write this, I am not so sure. The sign struck me as a powerful artefact and there is an undoubted synergy between it and Bronwyn's statement but I wonder if, in looking for evidence and meaning of a hierarchy of loss, I have missed something more important. I realised that sometimes objects can point the way to greater understanding, but sometimes they can obscure it.

Perhaps in placing themselves lower in the 'hierarchy of loss' the narrators were just attempting to convince themselves that their own losses were more bearable because they were less extreme than others'. Perhaps, aware that the interview was being recorded and deposited with a public institution, they worried about being misinterpreted as selfish complainers. They might have been using a disclaimer much as women involved in the war effort said they 'didn't do anything important' as a way to defuse conflict with social expectations. Or perhaps they were unsettled by revealing the extent of their troubles and this was one way to reassert their control and authority over their circumstances.

Or maybe the real significance of these stories is the intense pressure we, as a public, put on survivors to be resilient, to be gracious and generous even under such difficult circumstances – in other words to be better than, we suspect, we would be ourselves. And perhaps my own interpretation of these statements as evidence of a

---

17   Bronwyn Apted South, Interview 5 December 2012.

hierarchy of suffering was driven in equal parts by a desire to believe that someone who had experienced extreme losses could still feel empathy for others, and a far more selfish and less admirable desire to promote a particular academic conceit – trawling through the oral histories for testimony to support an idea that wrapped things up in a neat package.

I have, for instance, not mentioned a narrator who challenged the pattern of privileging others' losses over her own. Angela McKenzie defied the expected norms of behaviour when she said of some Strathewen residents who lost their lives on Black Saturday that *I know you shouldn't speak ill of the dead but they weren't nice people.*[18] Not only did Angela acknowledge that she was challenging the discourse about suffering (*I know you shouldn't*), she was also placing herself completely outside of the conversation (*you shouldn't*, not *I shouldn't*). Throughout our interview Angela frequently positioned herself as an iconoclast, one who was not afraid to say shocking things and disrupt the accepted narrative of community. Although I have in other places in this book quoted from her interview, among others, to complicate public narratives of community resilience and solidarity, I avoided her testimony with regard to my personal interpretation of hierarchies, aside from those weaselly words five paragraphs back: 'nearly everyone'.

This doesn't mean that narrators were not genuine in their acknowledgement of other people's losses. I do not find it contradictory to believe in the sincerity of statements of empathy while at the same time exploring what has inspired them. Nor do I think that my perception of hierarchies of loss is incorrect. It does mean that not only is

---

18   Angela McKenzie, Interview 20 August 2012.

THE POSTERS: LOSS, ANGER AND OPPORTUNITY

the relationship between survivors' narratives and public narratives messy and complicated, but so is the relationship between what they say and what I hear.

The other posters

At some point, the 'Hierarchy' poster at Helen's Place was joined by two others. One has been lost, but the remaining one was donated to the museum. On it are some of the comments made to bushfire survivors by people unaffected by the fires. 'This bushfire has been very good to you.' 'I might start a fire and see what I can get.' The missing poster had more of the same. 'I'd like a bushfire so I can get a new house.' 'At least you still have your children.'

In Helen's words:

> *I remember this particular day. What seemed to be a common thread facing a lot of survivors were these terribly unhelpful comments that society and friends and family would throw at these people who had been through such devastation. [...] I said, 'We're going to make a poster today of the most unhelpful comments that people have had to endure in this bushfire. Let's make a list now.' So I just had a couple of big sheets of paper and survivors started throwing at me all the comments that had come their way. [...] Someone said to me, 'They came up to visit my block the other day and we're still in the caravan, you know. They came up and said, "Oh gee, this is nice, this is cosy, it's just like camping, isn't it?"' Or someone else had endured a comment from, I think, a relative of hers. 'I might start a bushfire and see what I can get.' 'Well, it's OK, you've still got your children. At least your children are still alive.' And that was said to someone who lost their husband. And the list went on*

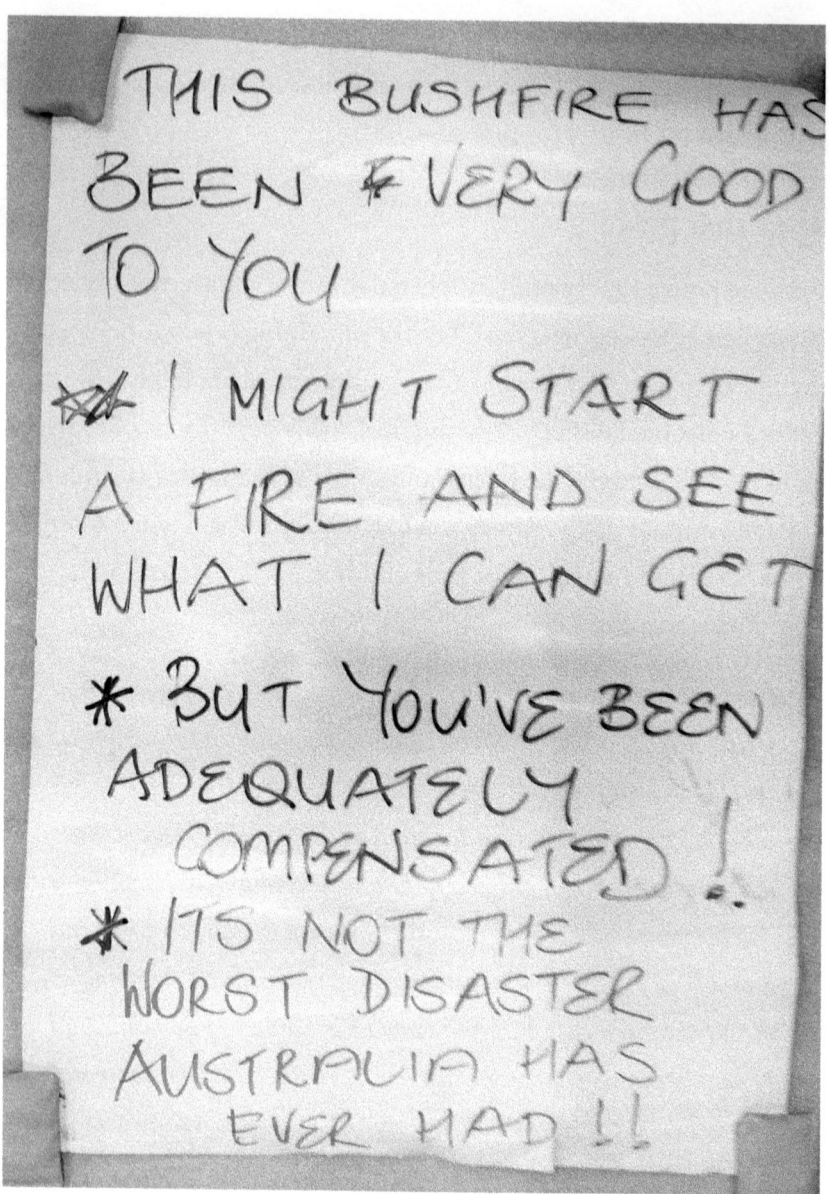

Figure 6. Poster, Hurstbridge Bushfire Relief Centre. Victorian Bushfires Collection, Museum Victoria, HT48439.

Image: Marita Dyson. Source: Museum Victoria.

THE POSTERS: LOSS, ANGER AND OPPORTUNITY

and on, the most unhelpful comments. [...] They had no concept of the absolute devastation and loss and the journey that these people were on to try and re-establish themselves. Otherwise they wouldn't say that.

It wasn't that people didn't care. The Victorian Bushfires Relief Fund was the largest fundraising effort in Australian history, attracting more than $300,000,000. Relief centres everywhere were overwhelmed with donations of goods and labour. Everyone had stories of the kindness of others, often strangers. People donated thousands of hours to Strathewen survivors alone to clear the destruction, set up a temporary school, rescue animals or help put down those too injured to survive, organise social events, provide a break for a little while, or help with the interminable job of replacing untold kilometres of fencing. The list is endless. In the face of such generosity, the poster of unkind statements might be read as an insignificant element, evidence of a lack of charity that a tiny minority of people, even in the face of such an event, might display. I think it tells us something more.

These posters expose the deep discomfort that many people feel about acknowledging others' loss. Some of the remarks captured on them, such as 'You still have your children', minimise the severity of the loss. Especially in a country where stoicism and self-reliance are part of the national myth and whingeing is frowned upon, many people don't know how to respond to survivors' stories of loss and hardship. Denial is often one of the reactions of listeners to catastrophic events, a sort of protective mechanism to discourage survivors from sharing stories that will cause distress in their audience. The attempts to deny the reality of a devastating experience keep the listener from having to confront their own nightmares, but the result is often awkward and appears insensitive.

Many of the other remarks, Helen noted, have to do with money. Public assistance, compensation, grants and donations carry with them the expectation that they will fix the problem. The implication is that people who receive public assistance have an obligation to recover and that not to do so, or not to do so in a timely fashion, is somehow cheating the public, a bit like fare evasion or dole bludging.

But I think the significance of these posters lies not only in the nature of the comments they recorded, but also in the simple fact that they were created. By writing down the comments and displaying them in the centre, the bushfire survivors were not just documenting these responses. With Helen's help, they were creating an alternate narrative that rejected outsiders' judgement of their situations – that, in fact, passed its own judgement on those outsiders. They turned individual negative experiences into a sense of shared hardship and a statement of solidarity in the face of a public audience who did not understand what they had been through.

The closing of ranks against the outside world is not an uncommon reaction after an extreme event. Carolyn Mears, in her oral history work after the shootings in 1999 at Columbine High School, described it as 'a feeling of being separated from those who have not experienced the event. [...] A protective boundary seems to form as those who are affected seek to avoid further violation. Sharing a catastrophic event leaves people feeling separated from those outside of the event who, it is thought, cannot understand a reality that common language cannot express.'[19] In 2013 Rosemary McKimmie Young

---

19 Carolyn Lunsford Mears, "A Columbine Study: Giving Voice, Hearing Meaning," *Oral History Review* 35, no. 2 (2008): 160.

said that, even in the social services sector in which she worked, she discussed Black Saturday only with other survivors. *I try not to even talk about it outside of that community now, because people are going, 'She's still on about that Black Saturday. That's five years ago, isn't it?' You know, you're doing training on trauma and you're [thinking], 'Oh, that's everyone, that's everyone I know. That's us exactly, what we're still going through.' And it can take years and years and years, post-traumatic stress and trauma, but you dare not mention it outside of your own community who have experienced it because they think you're meant to get over it.*[20]

Earlier in this book I suggested that the creation of the Poetry Tree was a political action which not only memorialised the destruction and deaths of Black Saturday but also described a vision for Strathewen's future. The creation of these posters was also a political act and can be seen not only as a defensive reaction but also as an affirmative one. Helen said that writing the posters was itself a cathartic experience but that many more survivors read them, recounted similar experiences of their own and then laughed. Sharing these comments exposed them as insensitive but also held them up to ridicule and destroyed their power to hurt. The posters reinforced people's sense of agency and control, and their feeling of community in the aftermath of the fire. They gave the narrative back to the survivors.

The Cricket Pavilion

Throughout this project I have been intrigued by contradictions, by someone whose story doesn't follow an accepted narrative arc or things that do not follow an established pattern. Such a contradiction

---

20   Rosemary McKimmie Young, Interview 18 June 2013.

is the story of the Peter Avola Memorial Cricket Pavilion, and it too is concerned with agency, action and control.

On 7 February Peter Avola and his wife Mary were fleeing their property in Chadds Creek Road when fire overtook them. While Mary escaped in her car, Peter lost control of his and left the road not far from the cricket oval located deep in the centre of Strathewen. He sought refuge in the clearing of the oval but was overcome by the fire and died there. Because the entire bushfire zone was quickly declared a crime scene, police officers did not touch the body or alter the scene in any way. Peter's body remained in clear sight of anyone driving past; I saw him in the video that Geoff Raftery shot as he and Barrie Tully drove out through Strathewen the next morning, and I heard the shock in Geoff's voice.[21] At 11:30 the next morning, David McGahy, Strathewen farmer, captain of the local fire brigade and Peter's old friend, requested the police 'as a mark of respect to cover body because very visible from the road'.[22] When they refused to do so, David and his son Andrew cut a section from the cricket matting and covered Peter's body themselves.

In 2012, the new pavilion on the Strathewen Oval was christened the Peter Avola Memorial Cricket Pavilion. This does not initially seem surprising, as Peter was deeply involved not only in the maintenance of the cricket oval but also in its establishment many years ago. His death on a piece of land in which he had invested so much of his time and effort added poignancy to the tribute. But this is the only public place in Strathewen to be named after a specific victim

---

21 Geoff Raftery, 'Black Saturday.' Viewed at the home of Rae and Barrie Tully, 16 October 2013.
22 Arthurs Creek CFA Captain's Log, 8 February 2009. Quoted in Jim Usher and Mac Gudgeon, *Footsteps in the Ash: The Story of St Andrews and Strathewen in the 2009 Bushfires* (Melbourne: Usher and Gudgeon, 2010), 47.

THE POSTERS: LOSS, ANGER AND OPPORTUNITY

of the 2009 bushfires. Of the 27 people named on the Strathewen memorial (23 of them residents), Peter is the only person to be individually and publicly memorialised.

It is not for lack of other candidates. Karen Gardam campaigned to rename the street on which her mother, Irma Winton, had her home and in which she died on Black Saturday. She wanted Gregorys Lane, named after the mudbrick builder Drew Gregory who hand-built his own home there (and which was also destroyed), to become Winton's Way. One of Karen's arguments for the case was the naming of the pavilion after Peter Avola.

SCRA initially advised Nillumbik Council against changing the name of Gregorys Lane, pointing out that to do so would erase the history embedded in the original name and privilege the day of the fire over every other facet of Strathewen's history. You can also imagine that such an action would set a grim and difficult precedent. Should there be a street named after every fire victim? There are probably not enough streets in Strathewen to do so. Should recognition be extended to every person who died in Strathewen, or only those who were residents? There were concerns about the effect on current residents, who would confront the names of dead friends and neighbours every day. The association emphasised that the permanent memorial, on which was inscribed the name of everyone who died in Strathewen, should carry the burden of memory for the community.

These considerations add to the singularity of the naming of the pavilion. They suggest that there was a hierarchy of loss at work and that Peter was in some way a more valued member of the community than the rest of the victims, but I think there is another explanation. I think that forces in addition to grief and memorialisation inspired the naming of the pavilion.

BLACK SATURDAY

Throughout the bushfire stories that I heard – in recorded interviews, in preliminary meetings and in casual conversations – three particular narratives resonated time and again. One was the moment of the wind change; the second was the saga of 'Tullys' place', where 19 people were found alive and safe; the third was the story of Peter's death. In every version, Peter's death was related not only with sorrow but also with anger. I think that the pavilion was named after Peter not for what he did during his life but for what happened to him after his death.

In refusing to cover Peter's body, the police posted on the Strathewen Oval were following established protocols that prohibit tampering with a crime scene. But to the people of Strathewen, they were denying Peter a deeply embedded cultural tradition: that of respect and privacy for a deceased person. Leaving his body exposed on the oval, a painfully public site, for an extended period of time was for many people a denial of basic humanity. It took a member of their own community, who was a close and long-time friend of Peter's, to extend to him the courtesy owed to that humanity.

This incident was interpreted by many people as a message that 'outsiders' – authorities such as the police – did not understand the level of pain and loss experienced in Strathewen and could not be counted on to do what was right. The naming of the pavilion was, I think, a deliberate reminder of that pain and a repudiation of outside authority. It was a declaration that Strathewen looked after its own.

Peter Avola's widow, Mary, agreed to do an oral history interview with me. During the course of it, I had the temerity to suggest such an interpretation. She fixed me with a death stare worthy of Julie Bishop, and mentally I began to pack my belongings in advance of being asked to leave. After a long, uncomfortable moment she finally

THE POSTERS: LOSS, ANGER AND OPPORTUNITY

said that naming the pavilion *was a way of making up for [what happened to Peter's body]. That's why, you know, why we took on our own recovery, because* we *knew what was best for us. [...] We just took it on ourselves to drive our own recovery.*[23]

The naming of the pavilion after Peter Avola reinforced and embedded a course of action and way of thinking that, from the initial aftermath of Black Saturday, had guided Strathewen's journey after Black Saturday: that of self-determination. When I suggested to Mary that the naming of the pavilion after her late husband had been a significant statement about Strathewen, I had been thinking in symbolic terms. In her reply, however, she immediately linked it to the reality of the recovery efforts. Both Mary Avola and Bronwyn Apted South, who have been deeply involved in post-fire community work, identified independence and self-determination as central to its success.

The Strathewen Community Renewal Association (SCRA) began to be formed within a few weeks of Black Saturday. Anne Leadbeater noted that 'community-led recovery' had since Ash Wednesday in 1983 been part of the official response to bushfire, but that specific models for this kind of recovery effort did not exist. Leadbeater's 2011 study of SCRA echoes Wettenhall's case history of Tasmanian responses to the 1967 bushfires, although it is more focused on social recovery than on physical recovery. She identified that SCRA provided:

> an important contrast to the experiences of some other bushfire-affected areas. With communication, transparency, self-determination and accountability as its hallmarks, the SCRA

---

23 Mary Avola, Interview 29 October 2013.

has served as a critical link between the area's remaining residents, those who have returned, those who have permanently relocated, and those still displaced. [...] The work of the SCRA was recognised nationally in 2010, winning the volunteer section of the Australian Safer Communities Awards and is acknowledged as a best practice example of 'bottom-up', community-led recovery.[24]

I do not intend (and, indeed, am not able) to replicate Leadbeater's work. Not everyone I interviewed would agree with her uncritical endorsement of SCRA's work. There were still people who felt disenfranchised, unsupported or deliberately excluded from the renewal efforts. I mention this not to criticise SCRA but to point out the enormous difficulties under which they worked, and the impossible task of serving everyone's needs. Read the minutes of just one of their meetings and you are overwhelmed by the size of the job the committee took on. From managing donations and facilitating rebuilding through to residents' support, environmental issues and memorial plans, SCRA's work reflects on a community level the monumental task that so many residents, including many of the committee members themselves, faced on a personal basis: that of rebuilding, from almost nothing, all the physical, social, financial and emotional infrastructure of life.

Throughout their efforts runs the herculean task of balancing competing hierarchies, of allocating resources according to who is 'fire-affected', how and to what degree. Bronwyn Apted South was part of SCRA from before its constitution as a community recovery

---

24 Anne Leadbeater, "Community Leadership in Disaster Recovery: A Case Study," *Australian Journal of Emergency Management* 28, no. 3 (2013): 43.

committee to its winding-up in 2014. In her interview she spoke of the many different ways in which the fires affected people both above and below the fire line, but also within neighbourhoods and even within families, and the difficulties of recognising and accommodating those losses. *Even within the fire line, you have so many and so varied experiences and losses and traumas. If you explore all these stories, you can't [...] you'd be terrified to embark on a community-based recovery if you thought that you were going to create a set of rules that kept everybody happy. [...] We've just tried so hard in the Renewal Association to ensure that we don't create any rigid lines and don't create a sense of exclusion.*[25]

In the same interview, however, she sent a strong message to the audience beyond the interview – not just the general public as represented by the museum, but also to those people involved in the official recovery efforts. At one point, with careful deliberation, she stopped speaking to me, turned her head and for the first time spoke directly to the audio recorder to say that all the people she knew who were not materially affected by the fires *have never come seeking inappropriate financial or material support.*[26] On the one hand, Bronwyn attempted to erase a hierarchy; on the other, she offered reassurance that a hierarchy of 'appropriate' need had been maintained. This was the unenviable job of SCRA.

Opportunities

In the bushfire zone, the balance to loss is not profit – hence the bitter references to professional victims – but opportunity. It is not its opposite but its partner, and exists only because the loss also exists.

---

25 Bronwyn Apted South, Interview 5 December 2012.
26 Ibid.

The idea of opportunity surfaced surprisingly often in the bushfire interviews. Many people felt lucky to be alive. *This is our second life. We're very grateful to still be here. [...] We know that we were a minute or two from death.*[27] After Black Saturday Rae Tully started to do many of the things – ballet, concerts, evenings in the city – that she had wanted to do but never made time for before. Helen Legg found that the effort of caring for bushfire survivors developed skills that she never imagined she possessed and started to see a future in public service.

Some of those who lost family and friends reflected not only on their sadness but also on the chance they had to help others in the same situation. Mary Avola joined a support group for bereaved persons and found that listening to others helped with her own grieving process for her husband. *They were the friends you never wanted to have. [...] Only people that had gone through it knew what it was all about and how to communicate with each other, because they had that bond. [...] It helped me with my own difficulties.*[28]

The theme of strengthening personal and community bonds resonated in a number of narrators' stories, especially those of women. Barbara Joyce spoke passionately of the many ways in which bushfire survivors came together: community meals; choirs; rebuilding projects; art classes, and much more. Bronwyn Apted South said, *I've lost friends. I've lost my assumptions of growing old with my friends. [But] I've gained friends, and it's early days yet but I am beginning to gain confidence in the security of growing old with new friends.* New friends do not replace or compensate for the loss of old, any more than community meals or art projects wipe out what happened during the fires,

---

27   Rae Tully, Interview 16 October 2013.
28   Mary Avola, Interview 29 October 2013.

THE POSTERS: LOSS, ANGER AND OPPORTUNITY

but they do offer the chance to defy the losses and salvage something from the ruins.

Many of the oral histories collected after Black Saturday demonstrate what the oral historian Michael Frisch referred to as 'multivalence', a concept he described as a contrast to the uncertainty of ambivalence. It embodies 'many values, the holding of different values at the same time without implying confusion, contradiction, or paradox'.[29] Multivalence is present in almost all the oral histories of Black Saturday. A bushfire survivor could be both embarrassed by sympathy and distressed by its absence; insistent on their rights to assistance but also fiercely independent of charity; devastated by the fires but also grateful for the opportunities they presented; mourning for lost friends but also appreciating new ones. There was no contradiction between wishing Black Saturday had never happened, and understanding that positive, meaningful consequences might be created from it.

Of course, not everyone saw opportunity in the same place, or shared a positive narrative of resilience. Where Barbara saw a stronger, closer community, Joyce Horne felt more isolated, due in part to her age but also to the influx of people who lived in the settlement but worked elsewhere. After more than 60 years of knowing everyone in Strathewen, *new people have come into the district, like these two houses just over the creek from us. We've never met them, we don't know anything about them so there's no friendship, not even a name.*[30] Vicki

---

29 For a country that makes heroes out of losers (Burke and Wills, Gallipoli and the jolly swagman all come to mind), this is a familiar idea. It also applies as much to historians as to their narrators. Michael Frisch, "Working-Class Public History in the Context of Deindustrialization: Dilemmas of Authority and the Possibilities of Dialogue," *Labour / Le Travail* 51(2003): 159.

30 Joyce Horne, Interview 27 November 2012.

Mitchell, who saw a chance for a different kind of community rising from the wreck, was discouraged to see the same patterns of drug-related behaviour emerging after the fire. For some people there was no ambivalence *or* multivalence, just continuing distress. Three years after the fires Angela McKenzie was still dealing with the destructive effects of the fire on the family's finances and on the emotions of her young adult children. And Darren Thompson, still locked deep in the misery of the day and its effect on his life, could not comprehend even the concept of opportunity.

Of course, oral history is itself an opportunity, an idea I will explore further in the next chapter. As Rhys Isaac said, 'History writing is a political, and so a moral act. It is a shaping not of the past, but of its own present; and so it is an intervention toward shaping of the future.'[31] I am conscious that a seemingly neutral action by the museum – that of collecting, documenting and interpreting the oral histories – is a decision as politically charged as any of the actions described here, and so, therefore, is this book.

---

31 Rhys Isaac, "Stories Historians Make out of the Stories They Find," in *Quaderno 6* (Milan: The Milan Group, n.d.), 1.

Chapter 5

THE MOBILE PHONE: NARRATIVES, TESTIMONY AND HISTORY

Without the title of this chapter, it might be difficult to place this object very easily. It looks familiar yet foreign, something ordinary that has been transformed by fire into a thing of mystery. It is a mobile phone, a flip-open model manufactured by Samsung. It is damaged, but on the reverse it just possible to make out the lettering 'samsungmobile.com'. Many people who have seen it are intrigued by how it has been changed and compare it to their own mobile phone, something they use every day but are often not aware of as a material object in its own right.

There are many mobile phones in the museum's collection, but this one is both catalogued and stored differently. It is in quarantine out of concern for toxic substances that may leach from it at some point and is recorded as part of the Victorian Bushfires Collection rather than the Information Technology Collection. Its significance still lies in its purpose as a communication device, although in this case the device leads down unexpected paths.

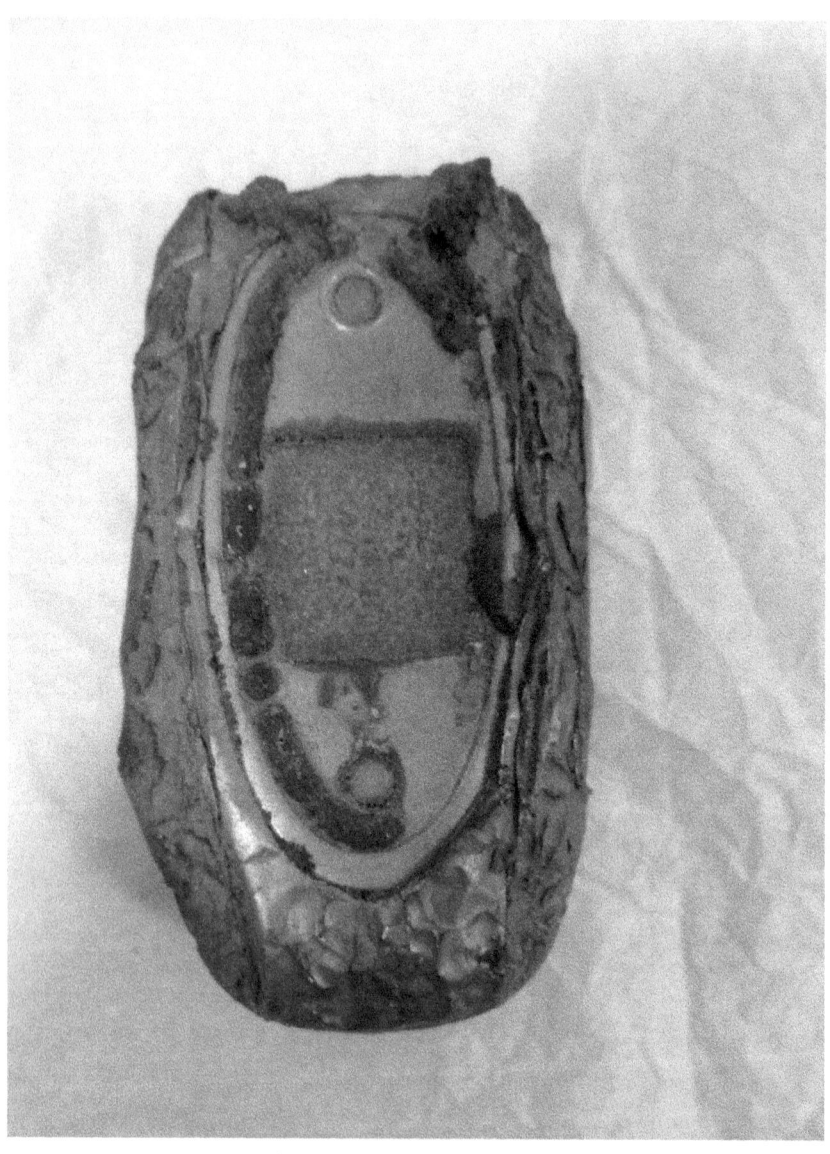

Figure 7: Samsung mobile phone (bushfire-affected). Victorian Bushfires Collection, Museum Victoria, HT32669.

Image: Marita Dyson. Source: Museum Victoria.

THE MOBILE PHONE: NARRATIVES, TESTIMONY & HISTORY

The phone belonged to Vicki Mitchell, who spoke to her friend Angela McKenzie just seconds before the fire arrived at Vicki's home on Eagles Nest Road in Strathewen. *We're jumping in the pool now. Get out of here.*[1] Angela, her husband Dale and their extended family and friends took a convoy of cars up Bowden Spur Road to Kinglake, where they sheltered in the café on the main street until the fire front passed. Looking back down the mountain to Strathewen, Angela found it hard to believe that anyone, including Vicki and her family, could survive the firestorm. Vicki, sheltering in the family swimming pool, was convinced that Angela had not made it out in time.

After the fire passed Vicki, her parents and her family emerged from the water to find their homes destroyed. One of the few recognisable objects was the phone, lying beside the pool. It was in bad shape but its position on the concrete pool deck and its proximity to the water meant that it suffered much less damage than the rest of Vicki's possessions. If it had been in the house, it would have been ash.

It was late that evening, while sheltering in a neighbour's house, that Vicki was examining her phone. Aside from the clothes she was wearing, it was the only possession she had left. *I was just fiddling with the phone, trying to open it, trying to get my fingers inside.*[2] The casing had fused shut, but Vicki must have hit something inside it and there was just enough life left to send a signal to the last number to which it had been connected: Angela's. When Angela saw the 'missed call' signal from Vicki, she began to hope that the Nelsons and Mitchells had survived. The friends met again several days later.

---

1 Angela McKenzie, Interview 20 August 2012.
2 Vicki Mitchell, Interview 20 August 2012.

Vicki kept the phone and in 2012 donated it to the museum. She was slightly puzzled about why she had kept it for so long and said she just didn't get around to throwing it out, yet she spoke of it with affection and wonder. It was a reminder both of her own survival and of Angela's.

Like all the objects in the Bushfires Collection, this is a rich artefact that tells many varied and complex stories. It is, for example, a witness to the physical force of the fire. The polycarbonate plastic from which the phone's casing is made begins to soften and flow at 147°C, so temperatures must have been higher than this although not high enough to melt the magnesium antenna, which becomes liquid at 650°C. This is hot, but bushfires and house fires burn much hotter; the CSIRO calculated that a house in a fire front would experience temperatures in the vicinity of 900°C. In that sense, the damage to the phone demonstrates the severity of the conditions, but its survival is testament to the same things that saved Vicki and her family: an area clear of flammable materials and the presence of a significant body of water.

Information like this is valuable to bushfire researchers in a number of areas, including how to prevent future bushfire fatalities, but I think that, to me, the real value of an object like this is that it speaks to us of communication, story-telling and relationships. The mobile phone – the intimate and indispensable tool of contemporary life – is an ideal entry point into narratives of bushfire.

One of the recurring themes in the stories that survivors, including Vicki and Angela, tell of Black Saturday is the lack of warning from official agencies. In many of the oral histories in the Bushfires Collection, narrators tell of being unable to get through on bushfire information lines, or of monitoring emergency websites and radio channels and being falsely reassured by notices that were either incorrect or dangerously out-of-date. Karen Kissane has documented to devastating effect 'the repeated failures of the Country Fire Authority to respond effectively to the speed and ferocity of [the Kilmore] fire by at least warning communities in its path'.[3] Strathewen was one of those places that received no warning and Kissane's dissection of the system failures and the human inadequacies is chilling reading.

Many people attribute their survival to telephone calls from friends warning them of approaching fire. Vicki lived just below the shoulder of Mount Sugarloaf, and her property was one of the first in the path of the fire. As the phone's damaged circuitry attests, her last act before jumping in the pool was to warn a friend whose property was further down the valley. In Yarra Glen, on the far side of the Kinglake Ranges from Strathewen, Bill Chisholm received a call from a friend higher up the mountain: *Mate, it's headed your way. Get out of there now.*[4] By the time Bill, with his daughter and dog in the car, was driving away from the house, he could see flames in the rear-view mirror. In Strathewen itself, Barbara Joyce had received an alert call through the fire phone tree – a network of residents who keep each other informed of fire emergencies – but it was the phone call from a neighbour that convinced her partner Shane. *[Craig] said, 'Just go, get out. I reckon we've got half an hour before it descends.'*[5] They evacuated just as the fire entered their property.

This object could be the starting point for any number of ways of investigating the intersections of bushfire, technology and people,

---

3   Karen Kissane, *Worst of Days: Inside the Black Saturday Firestorm* (Sydney: Hachette, 2010), 38.
4   Bill Chisholm, Interview 12 August 2010.
5   Barbara Joyce, Interview 31 August 2010.

from an analysis of organisational failure to an investigation of informal channels of communication within communities. But what really interests me is the path that leads from it to a small collection of videos that Strathewen survivors created in the days and weeks after Black Saturday to reflect on and interpret what happened to them on that day. Each of them arises from different perspectives and experiences but they explore common themes and each of them uses multi-media technology to tell their story, for this was the bushfire in which almost everyone had a camera in their back pocket.

The videos

The trail starts with Angela. Acting on Vicki's advice she, according to her husband Dale, 'got 12 people and three dogs out in five cars in five minutes, two minutes before the fire engulfed our home and still managed to stop and rescue 3 neighbours trapped on the mountain on the way out'.[6] One of the twelve people was a young friend, a teenager, who took video footage on her mobile phone as the convoy drove as fast as they could up the steep rough road to Kinglake.[7] In a few jerky, erratic and badly focused minutes she caught the confusion and urgency of the evacuation: the line of cars; the sounds of stopping to pick up three more people; the billows of smoke filling the whole sky, and – overwhelmingly – the sight and sounds of the firestorm coming up very fast behind and beside them. A second segment was taken inside the café in Kinglake, where they took refuge while the town burned around them.

---

6   Dale McKenzie, "Black Saturday Escape," http://www.youtube.com/watch?v=f9qeN_ouvnk, uploaded 9 June 2009 [Accessed 14 January 2013].
7   Anonymous, "Trying to escape the Strathewen King Lake fires,"http://www.youtube.com/watch?v=iQEYPdlhySc, uploaded 17 February 2009 [Accessed 14 January 2013].

I first saw this video at Vicki's house on the day I spoke to Vicki and Angela about the mobile phone. In the midst of describing the phone call and Angela's subsequent evacuation on Black Saturday, Vicki leapt up and, turning on the video player, said, 'You want to know what it was really like? *This* is what it was really like.' We watched silently as images of the firestorm filled the screen.

The young woman who had taken the footage uploaded it to Youtube ten days after Black Saturday, where it joined dozens of similar videos documenting every conceivable aspect of the fires from their approach to their aftermath, as well as the emergency response, the TV coverage and messages of grief and sympathy.[8] Born into a generation for whom digital communication seems as natural as breathing, she captured the immediacy of the threat and shared it with the world.

At the time that she was filming the climb to Kinglake, in the valley immediately below her Geoff Raftery was documenting the fire from the home of Barrie and Rae Tully, where he was one of four men defending the house designated as a safe haven. His video, also on Youtube, showed the advance of the fire as it came over Mount Sugarloaf and destroyed nearby houses.[9] Several short segments have been edited together and bracketed with stills showing the hills, paddocks and nearby bush both before and after the fire. It is this central section – just over two minutes of video from Black Saturday – that is both riveting and revealing.

---

[8] 'Plush Princess', "Black Saturday Strathewen," https://www.youtube.com/watch?v=Yp7Aucd4jJ8&list=PLkjxEUnx2QQiyeFKOy09OHx6BcR3LZxCu&index=12, uploaded 9 March 2009 [Accessed 20 November 2012].

[9] Geoff Raftery, "Black Saturday, Strathewen, Melbourne," http://www.youtube.com/watch?v=nXf-gBSAbXQ, uploaded 17 March 2009 [Accessed 14 January 2013].

Although Geoff's piece shared a number of traits with the other video – the pace, the rough camera work and the sheer enormity of the fire – as a narrative it has a vital difference. From the very beginning, Geoff was deliberately creating an historical record. In 2011 he explained on his Youtube site, 'My intent was to capture as much as possible to help understand as much of events like this as possible.'[10] It is clear in the video that he was intensely conscious of the significance of the event. History was breathing down his neck; even before the fire reached him, he asked his future audience, 'What will they call this? Black Saturday? Ash Saturday?'

This awareness of a purpose and audience has shaped the video. From the opening moments, Geoff spoke to his audience as he filmed, setting an epic tone: 'February 7, 2009, and the Sugarloaf Range is on fire.' He described the progress of the fire as it crossed roads and houses went up in flames. In the background we can hear the wind, Barrie Tully talking about their firefighting preparations and the roar of the fire itself. Despite the danger of the situation and the destruction taking place in front of him, Geoff maintained an understated, laconic commentary that distances both him and us from the scene. When a neighbour's house went up in flames, he said, 'I really liked that house. Never mind, too late now.'

Geoff's dispassionate tone is in stark contrast to another video of the same fire, taken at roughly the same time just a few kilometres away in St Andrews.[11] There, the unidentified cameraman was overwhelmed by the scale of the inferno heading towards him and can barely be heard whispering to himself as it approaches: 'It's coming

---

10   Ibid.
11   Anonymous, "Black Saturday Bushfires St Andrews Vic Australia," http://www.youtube.com/watch?v=F3dPlVvkIZ8, uploaded 16 February 2009 [Accessed 16 January 2013].

towards me ... God ... shit ... shit ... it's beside me.' The video ended abruptly as large embers started to land just a few metres in front of the camera. According to the video's caption, its anonymous maker survived in a home-built bunker as the fire swept through his property.

It is perhaps not surprising to learn that Geoff was not only a member of the local CFA but served in the military for many years, including time in the Special Air Service (SAS) and in Afghanistan. His training doubtless was the source of his calm manner but it also gave him a useful framework within which to describe the experience. There is no battle rhetoric in this video but a military analogy underpins every moment of it. As he noted the position of the fire, described the way it advanced across the country and matter-of-factly reported on the conflagration of a neighbour's house, we can hear in Geoff's voice the discipline required to keep calm in the face of a rapidly advancing threat. His style is that of the military observer rather than combatant, and it displays a dispassionate and restrained approach.[12] Geoff ended his Youtube video with stills of the fire's aftermath and did not include the video footage he took as he and Barrie Tully drove through Strathewen the morning after the fire, and which I saw in Rae and Barrie's home years later. In that footage he sounded exhausted and shattered as the extent of the destruction and the human toll began to sink in, but on Youtube there is no hint of emotion.

Emotion, however, is what Dale McKenzie's video is all about. Shortly after Black Saturday, Angela McKenzie's husband Dale was

---

12   Geoff Raftery, "Black Saturday Strathewen photos, Strathewen," http://www.youtube.com/watch?v=1opDnosREgk&list=UUtGRKaK_AZZbQXuty-i0RNw, uploaded 8 November 2009 [Accessed 20 January 2013].

given a copy of their friend's video of their flight up the mountain and refuge in the café – the same one that I saw at Vicki's house. He is not visible in the video but he was there. Dale re-worked the original video, adding titles, music and material of his own that documented the effects of the fire and images of the house before it was destroyed.[13] Creating his own response to the fire became a focus of his energy; according to Angela *we didn't even see Dale for the first six weeks [after the fire]. He went to work and came home and turned on the computer to work on it. [...] He had to make sense of [what had happened], get some control over it.*[14]

Where the original work was an in-the-moment story of fear and urgency, Dale created a narrative that built on the adrenalin of the original video but extended it to convey the complicated emotions of the immediate aftermath. He juxtaposed the footage of the flight up the mountain and the shelter in Kinglake with a pop anthem by Robbie Williams, reflecting the gratitude and elation they all felt in having survived. Dale's own footage that followed documented their return to the site of their house, where nothing was left standing but a few mudbrick walls. The camera panned around the ruins of their home, then circled the perimeter of the property. There was a windless stillness and everything – absolutely everything – was the black and white of ash and char. It was devastating but also, said Angela, *it was just mysteriously beautiful at the same time. It was just amazing, just the colours and all the shades of grey and black and white. It was amazing but it was also horrid.*[15] The soundtrack switches to a classic from the Rolling Stones, 'Painted Black'. The words are appropriate

---

13 Dale McKenzie, "Black Saturday Escape".
14 Angela McKenzie, Interview 20 August 2012.
15 Ibid.

but it is the rhythm that sets the tone, a raw, driving drumbeat that conveys anger and energy rather than defeat. The energy is a common response to disaster; Rob Gordon refers to it as 'rebound'.[16] It is the start of doing what you have to do, of getting on with the job of survival.

After the emotional highs of the preceding segments, the end of the video is eerie and sorrowful. It finishes silently with the photos, supplied by friends, of the house and garden before the fire. Seen with the knowledge of what was to come, the images are an elegy for something irretrievably lost. Angela and Dale did not return to live in Strathewen and, four years later, the shell of their house was still standing on the hillside above the creek.

An elegy of a different kind is given in Bill Putt's 'Rosewood'. Bill, best-known as the bassist for Australian prog-rock band Spectrum, was also a songwriter, sound engineer and producer. He stayed to defend the house while his partner, Rosemary McKimmie Young, evacuated with her daughter and grandchildren. The house survived but the property was heavily damaged and they lost many friends and neighbours. In the three months after the fire, Bill created a video that set a suite of photographs of their property to Bill's original music. A copy was given to the museum in 2010, but it can also be seen on his website.[17]

Bill opened with images of Rosewood before the fire set to an original piece of music he had composed for Rosemary's birthday the year before, a warm, engaging melody that brings to mind a lazy afternoon in the country. The images changed abruptly to the

---

16   Gordon, "Community Impact of Disaster and Community Recovery".
17   Bill Putt, "Rosewood," http://www.mikeruddbillputt.com/home/Demos/Videos.htm, uploaded 2 May 2009 [Accessed 21 January 2013].

photographs they took in the immediate aftermath of the fire, with their house damaged but still standing and surrounded by blackened bush, destroyed outbuildings and burnt-out vehicles. The music deepened as a melancholy bass line was introduced; it was the musical expression of grief. The video concluded with a shot of the entrance sign to Rosewood, fire-damaged but still legible.

As in Dale's video, Bill's narrative contains a before-and-after storyline, but it differs in important ways. Dale's depicts a cataclysmic interruption to their lives in which the past is irrecoverable, expressed not only through the visual images he started with but also through abrupt music changes, the hard-driving tempo of the Stones' song and the sudden silence as the house is viewed for the last time. It already appears a distant, lost world.

Bill's interpretation, in contrast, stresses continuity and promises recovery. The fire, it implies, is part of the natural order rather than a violation of it; life will go on. There is grief but not anger and the final shot of Rosewood's sign is a metaphor for survival. Over the next three years Bill made two more videos about Rosewood and the closing moments of the final part of his trilogy, entitled 'We Start Again', show Bill in front of the restored Rosewood with his arms raised – not in victory, but in celebration and welcome.[18]

Dale and Bill created radically different emotional landscapes from the same event. In his story of Strathewen before and after Black Saturday, Bill placed the fire as part of a much larger cycle of life, loss and renewal, while Dale's story resounds with a permanent, painful disjuncture. Part of the contrast can be attributed to the difference in their experiences – Bill kept his home while Dale lost his – but I

---

18   Bill Putt, "We Start Again," http://www.mikeruddbillputt.com/home/Demos/Videos.htm, uploaded 4 February 2011 [Accessed 21 January 2013].

think it goes deeper than that. After all, many people who lost their homes decided to rebuild, while others who kept theirs decided to leave. A person's relationship with a place, especially after a catastrophic bushfire, is influenced by factors far more complicated than simply the bricks and mortar of a building.

I think the contrast between Dale's and Bill's approaches shows a corresponding difference in their engagement with Strathewen before Black Saturday. Angela and Dale had lived in Strathewen for 13 years but they felt unsettled in the community. Long working hours, conflict with neighbours, differences in lifestyle and worry for their children all contributed to a sense of disengagement with where they lived; Angela felt it was not a welcoming place. Black Saturday, when it arrived, was a disjuncture that was not welcome but was somehow appropriate. This was catastrophe on a biblical scale, *a kind of cleansing*.[19] Angela recalled looking at her home in the rear-view mirror as she drove up the ridge to Kinglake and thinking, almost with relief, that an unalterable decision had been made for her and she would not be returning to Strathewen. Dale's narrative, that includes no chance for return or rebuilding, not only reflects their unhappy sense of place but also supports their decision to leave.

Rosemary and Bill, in contrast, had a strong commitment to Strathewen nurtured not only by their own years there but also their awareness of Rosemary's family's history that goes back almost to the beginning of European settlement. That history includes a long engagement with the environment, including other fires, but also farming, tourism and appreciation of its natural beauty. A story that emphasises continuity and regards bushfire as a natural part of a long

---

19   Angela McKenzie, Interview 20 August 2012.

cycle of repeating events ('We Start Again') reflects their heritage but also, like Dale's, documents and affirms the decisions they made after the fire.

A strong attachment to Strathewen doesn't depend on having generations of ancestors live and die there. Norma and Laurie Nelson have been there 'only' since the 1950s yet they were convinced that, despite losing two family homes, their orchard and their children's inheritance, Strathewen was where they belonged. Their grandson Philip was an emerging film-maker and in the weeks after the fire he made a short film in which the members of his family took turns narrating what had happened to them.[20] Despite the chaos of the fire, and the six different narrators involved, the film conveyed a single storyline handed from person to person in a cohesive and linear fashion. So smooth is the transition that they appear to be finishing each others' sentences, emphasising the impression that there is only one story to be told.

That story is one of catastrophe but not trauma, of hardship but also – remarkably – humour. The Nelsons and Mitchells live up to the popular understanding of Australian farming families as stoic, resilient, short of words but able to make a wry joke in the midst of calamity, and utterly devoted to the family and the land. Vicki appears more concerned about getting her neighbour's house dirty when they are taken in for the night than for the loss of her own home. Norma tells, with perfect understanding of the irony, of her efforts to save her account books because her accountant said, 'If you lose those books I'll kill you.' It is through relating these events to the

---

20   Philip Mitchell, "07/02/09," http://diamond-valley-leader.whereilive.com.au/news/story/film-students-family-focus-on-black-saturday/, uploaded 21 July 2010 [Accessed 24 January 2013].

small details of a former reality that the narrators mediate the enormity of what has happened to them, bringing the fire into the context of ordinary life and making the incomprehensible at least partially conceivable for both themselves and their audience. The film also protects the narrators through leaving out intimate details that do not support the narrative of resilience. They tell briefly of losing their livestock, but not of Laurie's reaction when he realised he no longer had a gun with which to put down Vicki's mortally injured horse. It was the first time Vicki saw her father cry.

Each narrator re-affirms their commitment to Strathewen as their home, now and into the future. The video ends with Philip's father Mitch talking about rebuilding the houses and re-establishing the farm: 'Everyone will be home all together again. I'm looking forward to that day. It may take a while but we're gonna do it.' His words give additional resonance to the way in which Philip chose a single story line delivered by six people, as the structure of the film echoes the dominant message of survival through sticking together.

The final shot is an Australian flag blowing in the breeze and the caption, 'There's no place on Earth like Australia.' Although viewers might find a grim irony in the expression, Philip is explicitly linking his family's survival with national pride. It brings to mind the Australian flags that were raised on makeshift flagpoles in the ruins of many houses in the bushfire zone. When he was interviewed by the local paper about his film, Philip said, 'We are now part of the history of the event so I felt it was important to document it.'[21] He does more than document his family's survival; he celebrates it.

---

21 Elizabeth Allen, "Bushfire Horror Caught on Film," *Whittlesea Leader*, 2 August 2010.

Stories and meaning

These videos are just a handful of the many that were created in the years after the bushfires of 2009. In Strathewen alone, there were a number of other media productions, especially Celeste Geer's award-winning film 'Then the Wind Changed' and the 'Big Stories, Small Towns' project. I have selected the ones described here because they were created by people who lived in Strathewen and had direct experience with the fires and their immediate aftermath. The wide availability of multi-media technology meant that they could be created quickly and shared with a very large public audience, without the intervening presence of a reporter, editor, film-maker or publisher (or historian, for that matter). These stories have bypassed the usual media channels of reportage, editing, publication or broadcast by third parties but they are not unmediated experiences – 'raw material', so to speak. They are in fact carefully constructed narratives, but the difference is that the narrators themselves have crafted the storyline, choosing what to say and how to present it.

This is where the language gets tricky, with talk of 'crafted stories', 'composed memories', 'constructed narratives', and 'cultural scripts'. We tend to assume that stories can be imagined, that memories are unreliable, that scripts are made up, and that a constructed narrative must by definition be fictional. If faced with conflicting accounts, we believe that only one can be right. We want the hard facts, the real story – in Vicki's words, *what really happened*. But every story, no matter how faithful and accurate in detail, is an edited version of reality. No narrative can contain everything that happened; choices must be made about what events or actions to describe, what to emphasise and what to pass over. Each story tells a piece of the truth from the perspective of the narrator. All the narratives in this book were true for the people who told them, at the time they were told, but it was not the truth for everyone, or for all time.

The videos tell us some of the facts of what happened on Black Saturday, but they tell us much more than that. Decisions made about what to include in (or leave out of) a story, the interpretation of one's own or other actions, the words used to describe an event, the emotions hinted at in music or silence, the pacing of images and the links to historical, political or social themes are just a few of the ways in which these narratives tell a complex story of how their authors see the world. When the structure of a narrative follows the trajectory of a well-known story of the past, it is using a 'cultural script' to organise the events but also to evoke deep emotions and connect to a particular understanding of human experience.

Angela and Dale's story is one of an unrecoverable past that resonates with biblical parallels of being driven from Eden. The decision to move from Strathewen was not, it implies, a matter of choice but a matter of fate. Geoff framed his story in a way that echoes reports from war zones, portraying the bushfire as a conflict between people and nature and suggesting that he will continue the fight. Bill's video is a narrative of continuity and identification with the cycle of death and rebirth in the environment; Philip affirms the same continuity and commitment, although in his story the environment itself is a threat to survival. Even though Philip's is the only one of these works to explicitly reference the future, all of these videos are as concerned with what lies ahead as they are with the events of the past. Whether the decision is to leave, to rebuild or to repair, the events of Black Saturday are filtered through the lens of present and future needs.

By using established themes such as exile, regeneration and resilience, cultural scripts allow the narrator to put boundaries around a traumatic experience, much like containment lines around a bushfire. The narrative structure becomes a container that holds memory safely confined and survivors can focus on the story – the container – rather than confronting once again the fear and grief within it. They can revisit the past without having to relive it. The oral historian Alistair Thomson calls these 'composed memories', meaning both the process of composing a story that places difficult experiences in the framework of an accepted cultural narrative and the striving for personal composure, creating 'a safe and necessary personal coherence out of the unresolved, risky and painful pieces of past lives'.[22]

Rosemary McKimmie Young observed this effect when she wrote and read poems on the Poetry Tree: she said the process of shaping a story about the fire *puts it into a compartment that you can go away and return to.*[23] Norma Nelson's humorous story of worrying about her account books so that she wouldn't get into trouble (implying that sheltering in a swimming pool while your house burns down doesn't count as trouble) provided a tool for both her and her audience to contextualise her experience but it also deflected a more serious discussion of what it felt like to be close to death; it contained the experience. The strategy was so useful that she repeated the story, almost word for word, in the oral history she recorded for the museum nearly three years later.

These narratives, which use familiar themes that most of us can identify with, ally the narrators with accepted social beliefs.

---

22 Alistair Thomson, *Anzac Memories: Living with the Legend* (Melbourne: Oxford University Press, 1994), 10.
23 Rosemary McKimmie Young, Interview 18 June 2013.

Sometimes, however, there is conflict between the ideal and the reality, between what we feel and what we believe we are expected to feel. I am interested in how these scripts have been used in a sophisticated and, I believe, deliberate way to resolve tensions between individual memory and socially acceptable attitudes.

If someone were to look only at Dale's video, without the background provided by Angela's interview, the immediate assumption would be that they remembered Strathewen as an idyllic place and that they were devastated to leave it. Angela, however, described their time in Strathewen as unhappy despite the beautiful house and surroundings, and the decision to leave was accompanied as much by relief as by loss. (I am also aware that Angela's oral history interview in 2012 was itself a crafted narrative, and that the three years' absence from Strathewen may have given her the freedom to emphasise negative aspects of the community, which in turn reinforced their decision not to return.) But the acknowledgment of the McKenzies' conflict with other people in Strathewen, and how that influenced their decision not to rebuild, gives Dale's story a subtext that is not accessible from the video itself. The sense of unreality that I observed in the closing moments of the film, with silent images of the house before its destruction, takes on a new significance. The video, I believe, records the loss of a dream rather than the loss of the reality, and it does so in a way that accommodates the McKenzies' ambivalence about Strathewen while keeping them safely within the limits of socially acceptable behaviour. Dale subverted a powerful cultural narrative to express grief not for a paradise that they had and lost, but for a paradise that never was.

In the same way, I think that Philip used an important cultural narrative, that of the stoic Australian farming family, to deflect other tensions. He connected his family's resilience to his understanding of a national character, expressed through the image of the flag and his caption, 'There's no place on Earth like Australia.' This follows a well-accepted narrative so familiar and obvious that its significance only becomes apparent when viewed in the context of other survivors' tales.

Many of these other stories mention the importance of the local community in their recovery efforts, a theme that was repeatedly emphasised through popular culture and official channels but is markedly lacking in Philip's film. The reason for this difference is explained, I believe, in his mother's and his grandparents' oral history interviews. They describe a decades-old distance from most of Strathewen's residents, ranging from Norma and Laurie's careful statement that they were not very involved in the community to Vicki's belief that she had been ostracised and vilified for many things, including her outspoken criticism of certain activities in Strathewen. Philip could not portray his family as part of a close-knit local community, so linked them to the larger community of rural Australians. In identifying his family with a beloved national narrative, Philip neatly leap-frogged over the problems of connection with people in Strathewen and did so in a way that is not only hard to detect but is also impossible to criticise.

Both of these examples suggest to me that, although the structure of a story may be culturally influenced, its use and significance can be far more subtle and individual than we often recognise. Stories don't always mean what we think they mean. Both Dale and Philip have re-worked major cultural narratives – the expulsion from Eden and the importance of community – to their own needs and in the process have subverted the commonly ascribed meanings into something far more complicated, while still keeping the protective colouration of the original story.

The use of established cultural narratives is not, of course, limited to new media, a circumstance made clear to me when Mary Avola agreed to an oral history interview. Mary's husband Peter died on Black Saturday and she did not want to relive those moments by telling me the story. This was not an uncommon reaction among survivors, for whom the retelling of what happened on Black Saturday can be deeply distressing, and the account of Peter's death had been covered extensively in the Royal Commission hearings, the local media and books about Black Saturday. But I was a little surprised when, at the start of the interview, she handed me a printout of a story she had written describing the events surrounding Peter's death. It was, she insisted, the true, complete story of what had happened and I needed nothing more.

The account is a heartfelt tribute to her husband, whom she believed saved her life at the price of his own. We stuck to our deal about not discussing Black Saturday but during the course of the interview Mary began to talk about memory and the importance to her of making a permanent record soon after Peter's death. *You do things quickly, because you hear other things and you start changing stories and adding things to them that you shouldn't. You start finding out things perhaps you don't want to hear.*[24] It seemed to me that Mary's reliance on a written account was in part because of her reluctance to re-engage with distressing emotions but also because she feared that, in the retelling, she would change the story. In the narrative she had written, Peter's sacrifice – yet another powerful cultural script – gave

---

24 Mary Avola, Interview 29 October 2013.

meaning to his death and gave her a reason to continue with her own life. It kept her from despair, and she could not permit the alteration of a single word.

For Mary, the immutability of her account of Black Saturday was a fiercely defended mechanism for coping with the impact of the bushfires. She was aware of how memories change, not only because of time and distance but also through intervening experience. Throughout this work I have been continually revisiting and adding to what I have written, as narrators' interpretations of their experiences have altered. Over the course of 18 months, Karen Gardam moved from being critical of the Poetry Tree's celebration of life in the face of death to criticising the permanent memorial for being concerned with death in the midst of life. Two narrators, both of whom declared soon after Black Saturday their total commitment to remaining in Strathewen, have since talked separately with me about their growing concern about environmental and social changes and the possibility of leaving the area. The narrators' process of revisiting the past and constructing new interpretations of it, as well as decisions for the future based on those interpretations, will continue long after this book is finished.

Selected memories, assembled into narratives, can provide explicit support and justification for decisions made during and after the fire, and provide a mechanism for negotiating the future. They also allow people to accommodate and reconcile the events of their past by creating meanings that offset the pain. Angela's words about Dale – *He had to make sense of it, get some control over it* – communicate the need, shared by many people, to regain agency in a place they could no longer control or even recognise. The method Dale chose to contain and make sense of what happened was to turn it into a story and tell the world. It was not a happy story, but happiness seems to be secondary to understanding. The American historian Jerome Bruner observed that narratives can console, but not necessarily by resolving difficulties; they offer 'not the comfort of a happy ending but the comprehension of plight that, by being made interpretable, becomes bearable'.[25]

Testimony

I had originally been attracted to the videos about Strathewen because I thought that one of the ways in which the bushfires of 2009 were fundamentally different from earlier disasters was the use of media technology to convey information, create connections and express emotions. Black Saturday as an event dominated mass media and social media outlets in Australia and echoed around the world. Digital technology gave people unprecedented opportunity both to communicate and to receive support. The critical difference, however, was not the use of digital tools but the purpose to which they, as well as more conventional media, were put: the rise of testimony.

The narratives of survivors' individual experiences and the effect upon their internal and external lives have become so important to the way in which we try to grasp major events like natural disasters, war or genocide that it is sometimes hard to remember that 'witnessing' was not always a part of the historical record. Historian Annette Wieviorka coined the term 'the era of the witness' and traced the emergence of witnessing back to the Eichmann trial after World War II when, for the first time, survivor testimonies were a central focus of the evidence given against a Nazi war criminal.[26]

---

25 Jerome Bruner, "The Narrative Construction of Reality," *Critical Inquiry* 18, no. 1 (1991): 16.
26 Annette Wieviorka, *The Era of the Witness* (Ithaca, N.Y.: Cornell University Press 2006).

The degree to which testimony has become the dominant channel for our understanding of bushfire is sharply illustrated in the differences between the Royal Commissions of 1939 and 2009. The Stretton Report is written on a grand scale, describing the sweep of events and their impact, but it does not recount personal stories of either victims or survivors. The transcripts of the oral proceedings were made available online in 2009 and even in them there is little detail about personal experiences through the fire.[27] Despite Stretton's frequently expressed sympathy and concern for those who lost their lives, homes and livelihoods in the fire, his hearings focused on obtaining facts about the causes and progress of the fire, the means of preventing fires and protecting people, and the politics and governance of the responsible bodies. Farmers, forestry officers and timber workers were called upon to give information and opinions, not to tell stories. It is disconcerting today to read of the way in which events like the loss of a house or the death of a person were so quickly noted and passed over as the Commission moved on to deal with technical or administrative questions.

This is very different from the decision by the 2009 Royal Commission to provide the opportunity for public testimony: 'as much as possible, the people who were most directly affected by the fires were given a voice and their stories and views were heard'.[28] From the beginning the Commission took as one of its objectives 'to contribute to community healing' and that contribution had two parts: a supportive and safe environment in which difficult testimonies could be told, and the public dissemination of those testimonies.

---

27   Judge Leonard Stretton, "1939 Bushfires Royal Commission: Report and Transcript of Evidence," University of Melbourne Archives.
28   Teague et al, "2009 Victorian Bushfires Royal Commission Final Report," 1.

The stories of victims and survivors, families of the deceased, emergency workers and others directly impacted by the fires occupied much of the Commission's hearings and form a good part of the final report.

There was no Royal Commission for the Ash Wednesday bushfires in which 47 Victorians died, but one can imagine that it would have resembled the Stretton Report more closely than the 2009 Commission's final documents. In 1983 the concept of post-traumatic stress disorder was just beginning to enter the public consciousness and trauma psychology was in its infancy. Many people would probably have agreed with the advice that Zelma Gartner received from her husband: *he said, 'It's over and there's nothing we can do. We'll put it behind us.'*[29] She didn't talk about the fire again until 2011 when she decided it was time to tell her story. She attributed her change of mind to the stirring of memories after Black Saturday, but perhaps she was also influenced by changes in social attitudes. Far from John's advice to put everything behind them, a perceived wisdom today is that it is unhealthy not to talk about bad experiences. This, according to psychologist Rob Gordon, is an established precept in trauma counselling although it is one that, after more than 30 years in the field, he has begun to question.

The Royal Commission was concerned with the causes of and responses to Black Saturday and how those could inform future planning and prevention, particularly of loss of life. As sympathetic and sensitively conducted as the hearings were, they were formal investigations into causes of death and the policy and procedural issues arising from them. They did not – nor could they be expected to

---

29   Zelma Gartner, Interview 24 March 2011.

– reflect all the ways in which people were affected by the fires, nor provide a forum in which people could engage in what has become a profoundly important part of coming to terms with disaster: the search for meaning.

In developed countries like settler Australia, where death has been largely restricted to the elderly or the unfortunate, there is an increasing conviction that premature death is unacceptable. In this society, unexpected death can become tolerable only if it is perceived as meaningful. The search for meaning is at work in many of the Black Saturday narratives, expressing the belief that the deaths, injuries and traumas are somehow more bearable if they are not in vain. Meaning can be extracted from death if it leads to a greater appreciation and protection of life; from destruction if it leads to building new social relationships; from terror if it leads to new resolve.

Many people after Black Saturday found comfort in the idea that testifying about their own losses might help to change attitudes and behaviours. Many interviews contained variations on the hope that, by telling their story, they might somehow prevent it happening to someone else. In speaking to the museum, people emphasised the stories that they thought the public record should preserve, from messages of a hopeful future to dire predictions of future disasters, from blaming 'greenies' to emphasising the importance of managing the landscape. The narrators were acutely aware of the public audience of the museum, and these were the people to whom they were really speaking.

There was jostling for the definitive narrative. Vicki's cry of '*This is what it was really like*' was in protest at what she saw as the public's desire to skip over the horrors and focus on feel-good stories. Some people presented a narrative of Strathewen as close-knit, community-minded and resilient while others focused on a counter-narrative of dysfunction and division. There were attempts to cancel out conflicting stories. I received carefully coded warnings from some residents about the unreliability of other narrators in this study, and one interview stopped abruptly when I brought up the name of a community 'trouble-maker'. There was a lot at stake in Strathewen, in both psychological and material terms. The community was held up as a model of bushfire recovery, making it more susceptible to scrutiny and more vulnerable to criticism.

Narrators wanted to share their stories, to believe that by testifying about their experiences they could influence the future. But despite their commitment to documenting Black Saturday, most people were pessimistic about how long, even with oral history projects like this one, the public memory of the fire would persist. Rosemary McKimmie Young said that Ash Wednesday had been forgotten and that Black Saturday will be as well. Laurie Nelson thought that memory would not outlive him: *In a few years I'll be gone, so the memory of that fire will be gone.*[30] He believed that over the course of time new people would not only be unaware of what had happened, but would not believe that it was possible. He and his wife Norma appreciated that *the record will be kept, our thoughts and that*, but he doubted the ability of testimony to convey the impact of the day*: unless you've seen it you can't appreciate it. [...] You just can't convey [what it was like]*.[31] The extremity of the event both guaranteed that it would be remembered in the public record, but also that a record could not capture the reality of what it was like. Words could be no

---

30 Laurie Nelson, Interview 7 September 2012.
31 Ibid.

substitute for the experience, public documentation no substitute for personal memory.

For many narrators, the changes in the landscape reflected the forgetting they perceived in the public. The resurgence of 'scrub' (uncontrolled regrowth of native and exotic vegetation) in the years after Black Saturday has hidden the effects of the bushfire, at least to the uninitiated eye, but has increased the risk of bushfire recurring. This loss of bushfire memory from both individual memory and from the perception of the land is preparing the way not only for another catastrophic bushfire but for another 'unprecedented' catastrophic bushfire. *I've got a sad vision of Strathewen as I knew it. [...] I do feel that there is going to be a danger in another 30, 40, 50 years of bushfires again. People will just repeat the same pattern, probably worse. I think [the memory] softens.*[32]

Some historians have worried that the personal, individual scale of testimony has replaced the broad perspectives of history, hindering our understanding of the past. I am unconvinced that the move to testimony has harmed historical narrative. Testimony – one person's story, told in their own words – is narrative in its finest grain and most intimate detail, and gives us an insight into a personal reality that may support or challenge a larger historical narrative. Both Geoff Raftery and Philip Mitchell are explicit in positioning their Black Saturday videos as historical records. Geoff's work was triggered by the size and inevitable impact of the event, and by his own awareness of the history of bushfire in Victoria. Philip was responding to the initial media coverage of Black Saturday; if he and his family were to be 'part of history', they would do it their way. But it

---

32   Rosemary McKimmie Young, Interview 18 June 2013.

could be said that all of the videos I have discussed are historical in nature. Choices made about structure and content reveal connections with established historical themes, both positive and negative: exile, conflict, regeneration, continuity.

The eminent oral historian Sandro Portelli, back in 1992, made a distinction between traditional story-telling and what he called 'history-telling'.[33] For him, the distinguishing features of history-telling were the presence of an outsider who helped to shape the narrative through asking questions and proposing alternative views, the purpose of the narrative in contributing to historical understanding, and the presence of a distant audience represented through the process of recording the interview. The videos created by Geoff, Dale, Bill and Philip lie somewhere between story-telling and history-telling. They were created for the purpose of documenting events for a wider audience – Geoff and Philip in particular were self-consciously historical in their framing and presentation of the story – but they lack the awareness of multiple dimensions that full-on history brings with it.

'Real' history, meaning complicated, multi-dimensional history, takes account of many different viewpoints, acknowledges conflicting or complicating evidence, can be justified through inquiry and analysis, and does not subordinate the narrative to a pre-set agenda. Dale's and Philip's videos in particular serve their creators' purposes – the first to justify leaving Strathewen in the aftermath of disaster, the second to justify staying after the same disaster – and to bring in conflicting evidence is, for them, not only unnecessary but counter-productive.

---

33 Alessandro Portelli, "History-Telling and Time: An Example from Kentucky," *The Oral History Review* 20, no. 1/2 (1992): 51.

As listeners we need these stories, but we need more than just these stories. Through the analysis and juxtaposition of differing views (the differences between Dale and Bill, or between Bill and Philip, for instance, or how in the oral histories the same event is told by different narrators at different times to different audiences) we can begin to understand the many ways in which people attempted to come to terms with what happened to them, and how it changed their understanding of themselves, their community and their home. At that point, testimony becomes history. Testimony moves us and connects us to another's reality but history allows us to learn.

Testimony is by definition intensely personal but it is, also by definition, highly public. The kind of testimony – of danger, loss and trauma, but also of hope and regeneration – that filled the newspapers, internet and commemorative books after Black Saturday were stories that people needed to tell, but most of the time they were also the stories that we, the people outside the bushfire zone, wanted to hear. Just as they supported decisions, reinforced positions and provided comfort for the people who told them, they satisfied our own desires.

Listening to bushfire stories

There has been for a number of years concern about the responsible portrayal of bushfire in the media, especially about portrayals of bushfire that feed into an appetite for vicarious excitement. After Black Saturday, the focus intensified with research into the ethical behaviour of the media. These studies were worried about stories of horror, loss and crisis that satisfied the public taste for drama and danger but exploited survivors and obscured important discussions of policy and decision-making. They echo playwright and performance artist Julie Salverson's critique of the 'erotics of suffering' that underlie our fascination with disaster, suggesting that identification with suffering is often self-indulgent and exploitative.[34]

I share these concerns about the manipulation of emotions through retelling dramatic stories from Black Saturday, or from any catastrophic event. I remember the moment when Jim Usher told me his 'favourite' bushfire story, in which a mother defended her children, cowering under a table, with a hose trained on the fire, all the while screaming 'You will not take my children.'[35] Jim is a good storyteller and I was thrilled by the tale of the woman's desperation and determination in the face of extreme danger, imagining the scene with flames licking through the ceiling and the courageous mother fighting to save her family. It was only later, when the second-hand adrenalin had subsided, that I was appalled at my reaction. Those children were exposed to terror of the most extreme and damaging kind, within minutes of facing a horrific death, and I was treating the story like a scene from a disaster movie. It was then that I began to question both the circumstances that had led to such danger and our vicarious experience – and enjoyment – of that danger.

The realisation of my own visceral reaction to a horror story involving young children led me to consider something more subtle but equally exploitative, and even though I wrote 'our own desires' in the previous section, this is really an exploration of my own motives. To do that, I will have go back to the beginning of my research and even further back to 1983, and Zelma Gartner's story of Ash Wednesday.[36]

---

34 Julie Salverson, "Change on Whose Terms? Testimony and an Erotics of Injury," *Theater* 31, no. 3 (2001): 123.
35 Jim Usher, Interview 29 October 2013.
36 The following section is based on Zelma's recorded oral history interview on 24 March 2011, but I have summarised it rather than building quotes from it into a narrative or historical analysis. The purpose is not to analyse her history but to explore the mistakes I made in our relationship and what I learned from them.

Zelma's story

Zelma Rowley was born in country Victoria and came to Melbourne in the early 1950s. She finished school at 14 and when she was 18 she started to work for John Gartner, who owned a successful printing business but who was best-known as a collector and international authority in the fields of numismatics, philately and letter-press printing. Zelma was young, beautiful and clever, and John was wealthy, cultured and sophisticated. It was perhaps inevitable that they would eventually fall in love and marry.

Zelma's life was transformed. She delighted in telling me of their life travelling the world (first-class, she emphasised), and returning home to their magnificent property in Mount Macedon called Viewfield. She learned about coins and stamps, met artists, experienced foreign cultures and developed collections of her own. They had no children and were almost inseparable. To many people it must have seemed like a life out of a fairytale – until Ash Wednesday.

On the night of 16 February 1983, Zelma and John were home in Mount Macedon. At about 10:00pm, Zelma noticed large embers falling from the sky. By the time she and John opened the front door, their way was blocked by a wall of fire. Wrapping themselves in blankets, they ran for the swimming pool where they spent the next three hours, struggling to breathe and watching their home and all their possessions burn.

When they finally emerged, they walked out through a devastated landscape. They were picked up along the road and taken off the mountain for medical treatment but they were determined to return as soon as possible. Within weeks they had established themselves in a borrowed caravan in the midst of the ruins and were sifting through the ashes for remnants of their belongings. Everything was gone, or charred or melted almost beyond recognition.

They decided to rebuild the house exactly as it had been and in 1986 the new Viewfield was opened to great celebration. Within a few years, however, they had sold up and moved to a property in another area. John died in 1996 and in 2010, Zelma decided to record her story for the Victorian Bushfires Collection, and to donate some objects connected to her bushfire experience. It was in early 2011, just as I had completed a year of work on the collection, that I met Zelma.

At early meetings, Zelma told me what had happened to her and John on Ash Wednesday. She said she had not discussed it with anyone in the intervening 28 years, but I was struck by the detail in her story, right down to what she had been wearing and where the blankets were kept. When we recorded the interview, she told the story again, almost word for word. I was curious, and tried to get past the set storyline, asking questions from different directions and perspectives. She became irritated with me, saying, 'Why are you asking these questions? I have told you what happened.'

As well as being rigid, her account, especially of the emergency response and the recovery efforts, was relentlessly critical. Everybody, except for herself and John, was a fool or a crook, or both. The police were incompetent, the charities were naïve, the local council was corrupt, the builders were dishonest, the other bushfire survivors were greedy and the general public was crass and insensitive. I found out through later research that some of her stories were incorrect or at least incomplete but when even her own account contradicted this view of the world as venal and stupid, she ignored the inconsistencies and created a narrative where everything was against them and she and John had only each other.

I found I was compensating for this unrelieved negativity by asking questions about positive outcomes, or leaving openings in the conversation that could lead to more gentle reflection, but she was having none of it. When I asked Zelma what lessons she had learned from Ash Wednesday, she leaned forward and hissed, 'Trust nobody!' I found this constant negativity more depressing than many of the heartbreaking narratives from Black Saturday. After our sessions I would drag myself back to the museum and one of my colleagues would look at me and say, 'You've been to see Zelma again, haven't you?'

And then we began to argue. Zelma disapproved of the narrative I had written for the collection, and wanted me to change substantial parts of it – for instance, to include her criticisms of the official agencies. Some of our discussions resulted in changes for the better, as I came to understand the differences between her experience and those of Black Saturday, but she wasn't happy that I refused to write that the Red Cross and the Salvation Army were idiots. She also objected to the naming protocols the museum uses to identify objects. I could see that the museum – and I especially – was about to be added to Zelma's list of fools. When for the third time she returned the donation form unsigned, with minute changes to the wording, one of our collection managers said, 'What's going on here? What is this woman's problem?' And in that moment I realised that Zelma didn't have a problem; she had a mission.

John Gartner had been Zelma's lodestar. He had taken her from a modest background to a life of privilege, had opened her mind to new worlds and ideas and had guided and protected her every step of the way. Even when I met her, fifteen years after his death, I could see how greatly he still influenced her. For Zelma, this project wasn't about contributing to the state collection or preserving the past or reflecting upon questions for the future. It was a memorial to John, and Zelma was utterly determined to get it right. She was also aware of her own increasingly frail health; when I interviewed her in 2011, she could barely speak above a whisper, a legacy of those three hours 28 years ago, breathing super-heated air and smoke as her house burned.

So John's version of events had to stand exactly as it was, without question or elaboration. He had to be the hero, and therefore everybody else had to be cast to some degree as a villain. Every story she told pointed to John's wisdom and integrity, or to other people's lack of the same qualities. And every word in the catalogue mattered because John was knowledgeable and precise and he would have cared about every word. And because I also care about every word, I resented her incursions into what I believed to be my territory.

Once I was able to see Zelma's story and my own actions in this light, my simmering resentment dropped away and I was able to complete the project with a good grace. I didn't write everything she wanted me to but I did make some changes. I have a feeling that she still thinks I am an idiot, but we parted on good terms. And more importantly, the museum acquired an extremely valuable account – the only one in our collection – of what it was like to experience Ash Wednesday firsthand. There are some aspects of it we will have to treat with great care but it is still an important addition to the Bushfires Collection. But for me the most important aspect of working with Zelma was what I learned about myself, because Zelma was not the only person who came to this project with an agenda.

I have mentioned previously the links between extreme events and the search for meaning. For many people, both those who are directly involved in catastrophic situations and those of us who are merely onlookers, the search for meaning takes the form of personal transformation. Great losses – even greater than Zelma's, such as many people experienced on Black Saturday – are somehow more bearable if the survivors feel a renewed gratitude for life, a greater appreciation of family bonds, a stronger sense of community and a determination to leave the world a better place. This is the narrative of redeeming some good from great evil and it is what usually appears in newspaper accounts, books and oral history interviews. It is what most of us want to hear, because it gives us hope for the world and for ourselves.

And that is what I wanted to hear from Zelma. I struggled with her negative interpretation because it didn't fit the redemptive narrative. I wanted her to find at least some little morsel of positive wisdom she could share, but she rejected it all. She had built a bastion of negativity and she refused to be dislodged from it. She had good reason to be there: Ash Wednesday destroyed a beloved home and many rare and precious objects; it shortened her husband's life; it left her with lifelong health problems, and it robbed her of a peaceful and financially secure old age.

So in the end, the problem was with me, and with what I was trying to accomplish. By refusing to enter into a narrative of positive transformation, Zelma showed me that I was bringing into the oral history process a whole heap of expectations about how bushfire survivors ought to think and feel. I began to wonder whether I was really very different from those people whose comments were recorded in the Hurstbridge posters.

Zelma taught me to leave behind those assumptions and look for the complicated, the confronting and the hidden stories, as well as those that I originally set out to find. And if she had followed my lead into a positive ending to her story, I would have missed seeing how all her memories of Ash Wednesday – the direct ones, the borrowed ones and the invented ones – had been used by her to support the story of her life, and to continue to give her strength long after the fires, and long after John's death.

I think the kind of exploitation of which I was guilty (or would have been, except for Zelma's stubbornness) is more insidious and in some ways more damaging than outright sensationalism. Julie Salverson wrote of dramatic productions about trauma that 'If we write a play that presents an uncomplicated portrayal of victims, villains, and heroes, what choices do we give an audience about how to relate?'[37] And if we write a history that presents an uncomplicated portrayal of victims, villains and heroes, what choices do we give survivors about how to live? By trying to position Zelma as a heroic figure able to find good in the worst of situations, I was denying her both agency and individuality, and placing on her shoulders the burden of my own discomfort of the unfairness of life. It is a burden that bushfire survivors do not need to carry for the rest of us.

---

37 Salverson, "Change on Whose Terms? Testimony and an Erotics of Injury," 124.

Figure 8. Bushfire chook drawing by Jesse. Victorian Bushfires Collection, Museum Victoria, HT 26895.

Image: Peg Fraser. Source: Museum Victoria.

Chapter 6

THE CHOOK: BUSHFIRE AND GENDER

Strathewen resident Barbara Joyce had a longstanding interest in handcrafts and in 2004 was delighted with a gift from her neighbour, Libby Perry, of fibre from one of her alpacas, Cocoa. Barbara handspun the dark brown fibre and knitted it into a large cushion in the shape of a stylised chicken.

On Black Saturday Libby and her husband Phil were killed; they perished while sheltering in the kitchen of their home in Chadds Creek Road. Their herd of alpacas also died in the fire. For reasons that she could not explain – perhaps a needed connection with Libby and with life before the fire – Barbara thought of taking the chook cushion to Libby's funeral. *So I did, and when we are all having a cup of tea afterwards, and people asked me, 'How did you get to know Libby and Phil?' I pulled out the chook and told them the story. And Libby's mum and sister recognised Cocoa's fleece immediately and wanted to talk to me and it just created a stir and created smiles on people's faces. Something I thought we'd never see again.*[1]

Barbara subsequently made another chicken cushion as a gift for a young girl from Strathewen who was the only surviving member of her family and who had suffered severe burns on Black Saturday.

---

1   Barbara Joyce, Interview 31 August 2010.

Based on the reactions to the chicken cushions, Barbara decided to make a chook for everyone in Strathewen, child or adult, who wanted one. The children at Strathewen Primary School, located in temporary quarters in Wattle Glen Primary School, were given the outline of a chicken to colour in. Volunteer knitters then created a cushion for each child, faithfully reproducing each design. The chooks were presented to the children at a special assembly in November 2009.

The volunteers continued to meet, talk and make more chooks. The project became a social and therapeutic process for the makers as well as for the recipients: *we did it for the kids. And I think we did it because we enjoyed getting together and talking. [...] The knitting was just an excuse, I think, just something that glued us all together and I think deep down we were all trying to re-weave, re-knit the fabric of the community together.*[2] Cushions were displayed at memorial events like the community gathering at Museum Victoria on the fourth anniversary of Black Saturday. It also inspired a spin-off project in neighbouring St Andrews, where fourteen people had been killed on Black Saturday.

The 'Chook Project' was one of many creative responses that emerged from fire-affected communities after Black Saturday, along with art exhibitions, photographic displays and publications, public art installations, private art projects, films and books. They were largely generated within the affected regions, by people who had been directly impacted, and were often begun in an astonishingly short space of time. Film-maker Celeste Geer, whose house in Strathewen survived the fires, began to record the aftermath within days of Black Saturday. The Three Stories Gallery in Healesville held

---

2   Ibid.

an exhibition of 'bushfire art' that opened less than seven weeks after 7 February, when the curator's own home had been lost. Many of the projects depicted the extent of the devastation but also the process of regeneration in the bush, while others incorporated fire-damaged materials in startling, confronting or beautiful ways.

Some of the projects reaffirmed people's presence in the landscape. In Strathewen, a major project was to create new mailboxes to replace those which had been destroyed. Each was handmade and decorated with mosaics to reflect the environment before the fire, or people's interests and personalities. The boxes were not only functional, providing a needed service in reconnecting the community with the outside world, but were also markers in the land that reasserted human presence despite the surrounding devastation.

Other projects focused on the environment. Residents took thousands – probably tens of thousands – of photos of the bush as it soon began to put out shoots of green in both the native landscape and the developed one. The museum received offers of hundreds of images of tree ferns (*Cyanthea australis*) unfurling new fronds in the ash, and of eucalypts like messmate (*Eucalyptus oblique*) sending out new growth from epicormic buds, growth buds deep in the tree's bark that are triggered by exposure to fire. Exhibitions and publications documenting and celebrating the rebirth of the environment were organised, implicitly linking the recovery of the bush with the recovery of its residents.

Most of these creative responses can be seen as declarations of survival and resilience, an insistence that people and the bush would recover together, although the fires had altered the relationship between them. They also provided an outlet for the urge felt by many to do something physical and tangible to challenge the extent of the destruction. Rebuilding was a long way off but projects like the mosaic letterboxes made a significant difference in the landscape.

This chapter did not start with a photo of the original chook cushion (using instead a drawing from one of the children at Strathewen Primary) because it is not in the museum's collection. Barbara was reluctant to donate an object that still carried such emotional resonance for her, so we did what many institutions do in such a case and collected around it, catching its reflection in other objects and in stories. The Victorian Bushfires Collection contains the original instructions for the cushion, some of the drawings from Strathewen Primary, a sample of fibre from Cocoa left over from the original spinning, oral history interviews with Barbara and with Jane Hayward, principal of Strathewen Primary, and a cushion from St Andrews – what I think of as a 'third-generation' chook – donated by Stella Reid.

The story of Barbara's chook can be seen as a study of a changing society. The fibre from which it was made demonstrates both changes in livestock farming – it is made from alpaca rather than wool – and the evolution of land use from subsistence farming to hobby farms, inspired by dreams of living in the country but made possible by access to city jobs. Giving a name to an animal implies a very different relationship with one's livestock, based on a personal rather than agricultural aesthetic. Barbara's experience in spinning the fibre to produce the yarn not only evokes the alternative lifestyle in Strathewen that focuses on the handmade and natural materials (reflected in the many mudbrick houses, including Barbara's own, that dotted the landscape in Strathewen) but also the re-emergence of traditional work as an artistic endeavour. But most importantly,

THE CHOOK: BUSHFIRE AND GENDER

I think, is the way that Barbara's chook and all its offspring are connected to a long tradition of knitting in the face of conflict and disaster. From stockings and balaclavas for soldiers to blankets and toys for orphaned children, even mittens for injured koalas, women have knitted items of necessity and comfort for those in need.

In the weeks and months following Black Saturday many organisations, from official relief agencies to hospital departments to church and community groups, were flooded with donations of material aid. Much of this aid was made up of badly needed items like clothing, tools, furniture and electrical appliances, but there was also an extraordinary number of handmade gifts. Many of them were textiles: quilts, baby supplies, toys for children, household linens and – especially – knitted items. Socks, blankets, jumpers, baby wear and slippers were just a few of the knitted pieces that arrived, often accompanied by a note from the maker expressing sympathy for and solidarity with the unknown recipients.

In the museum's collection is a pair of socks donated by Ruby Tyler from Logan, Queensland. Like Barbara's chook, the original socks are still in use rather than in the museum; Ruby supplied us with replicas of the socks that she sent to the burns unit at The Alfred, Melbourne's major trauma hospital. In return for her gift she received a letter from one of the recipients. The letter read:

> Dear Ruby,
> My name is Peter Anderson. I am writing to thank you for your generous donation of bed socks. I am now a proud owner of a red pair. I have recently been discharged from the Alfred Hospital after I was airlifted from my brother's property after the fires. I stepped into an ember pit and required skin grafts

to my legs and hands. I am now recovering at home. Your work and thoughts help with the recovery.
Thank you again,
Kind regards, Peter.³

For Peter, and for all of the people who received a chook cushion, it was the process of creation – the thought and effort and emotion – rather than the finished product that was the real gift. And most significantly, it was the work of women.

Women and bushfire

Women in general have not been part of the grand narrative of bushfire. In the 32 days of testimony before Judge Stretton in 1939, only one woman was examined. Mrs Elizabeth Ashmore was asked to confirm that, during a period of her husband's absence from home, a fire had started burning nearby. It was her husband (even though he wasn't there at the time) who was asked to testify about the source, cause and progress of the fire, and who was asked for his opinions about fire prevention and control.

Most of the time women have appeared in bushfire stories as victims, grieving mothers, or widows, but there have been exceptions. Florrie Hodges was fifteen in 1926 and lived in Powelltown, a timber settlement in Victoria's northeast. On Black Sunday, 14 February, a major bushfire swept through the area and destroyed her home. Florrie saved the lives of her two younger sisters by covering their bodies with her own, suffering significant burns in the process, and spent months in hospital recovering from her injuries. Across

---

3   Peter Anderson to Ruby Tyler, n.d. Victorian Bushfires Collection, Museum Victoria, HT 25904.

THE CHOOK: BUSHFIRE AND GENDER

Australia, Florrie was hailed as a hero. She received commendations, speeches were made in her honour, and 50,000 schoolchildren in Victoria and Western Australia took up a collection to present her with a purse of £1000.

Until the 1980s CFA firefighting brigades were composed solely of men. Women's role, in the event of bushfire, was to provide support, mostly in the form of flasks of tea and vast quantities of sandwiches. A female reporter covering the fires near Strathewen in 1962 was told, 'You'll be more useful pouring out drinks than asking questions.'[4] But they were also the ones left on the farms to manage homes, animals and children while the men were fighting fires on other properties.

Norma Nelson remembered the 1962 fires, when her husband Laurie was away with the CFA. *My mother-in-law and I walked up to where those trees are, just there, and sat up there and looked across over to those mountains. And they were all twinkling because the fire had burnt that side and it was like looking at a red-hot twinkling side of a volcano. And we sat up there for hours. [...] We had no idea where the menfolk were, we just sat up there watching until it got too dark.*[5] She didn't expect the fire to reach the lemon grove that surrounded the homestead but, if it did, the lemon trees were believed to be fire resistant and there was a dam in which she and the children could take refuge as a final measure.

Alan Horne was also in the CFA in 1962 and was gone for two days, leaving his wife Joyce with a baby and the farm. Joyce's response to the fire was to open the gates between the paddocks so that the cattle could run freely if threatened by flames or smoke. As for herself

---

4   *Diamond Valley Mirror*, 17 January 1962.
5   Norma Nelson, Interview 7 September 2012.

and her family: *Well, if the fire came a certain direction, I'd go the opposite. And I had the pram packed up and Raymond would have been, I think, nearly two. And I was going to put him in the pram and I loaded it up with a few of my treasures, like my wedding album, and Alan's suit was draped over the handle, his one and only suit, and my – oh, I suppose some of my clothes. I can't remember what other things that I must have thought was precious at the time.*[6] Like most of their contemporaries, Joyce and Norma were the last line of defence for their children. They had no equipment, no training and no experience.

The use of battlefield language seems almost inescapable; I have just referred to Joyce and Norma as 'the last line of defence'. The military analogy adds a moral element to fighting bushfire, as if it were truly an enemy that needs to be (and can be) vanquished, and it is also overwhelmingly male. The Chook Project and Ruby Tyler's socks call to mind images of women knitting by the fireside while their men were fighting in the trenches far away. War narratives cast women in the role of nurturers, as the builders of emotional bridges across disaster, or as victims. They reinforce the idea of women as passive onlookers while battles are fought, heroes are created and the bonds of comradeship are formed. The same is true of the story of bushfire.

Disaster and gender

Like many things which are so familiar that they become invisible, the significance of the differences between men and women in bushfire stories took some time to emerge. By 'gender' I mean a culturally transmitted understanding of differences between men and women:

---

6   Joyce Horne, Interview 27 November 2012.

perceptions, assumptions, actions and interpretations based on the belief that men and women experience the world in different ways. It is not directly linked to sex but to the different ways in which society expects males and females to think and behave, and how individuals respond to those expectations.

The field of disaster studies has been around since the 1920s but it was not until the 1990s that researchers in gender studies began to explore the differences between men and women in relation to disaster. The consequences of being female, observed across a range of societies and types of disasters, included increased fatalities during the event itself, restricted access to assistance, greater long-term responsibilities, lack of financial and social support and increased risk of physical harm such as domestic violence and rape.

To begin with most attention was focused on economically and socially vulnerable women, many of them in developing countries, for whom the consequences of natural disasters were magnified. The work published in the wake of Hurricane Katrina, however, highlighted the intersection of class and race with gender and demonstrated that, even in wealthy countries, natural disasters increase and exacerbate existing risks for disadvantaged and vulnerable women. The increased incidence of domestic violence, regardless of socio-economic status, after an earthquake in New Zealand suggests that not only marginalised women are vulnerable.

At the same time, researchers have challenged the long-held view of women primarily as victims. Women have been particularly responsible for rebuilding community and family networks and providing long-term emotional and physical support. In the words of Helen Cox, after Ash Wednesday in Victoria 'women rewove the fabric of their communities while men rebuilt the structure'.[7] Cox's words recall Barbara Joyce's interview and how she spoke of reweaving or reknitting the community. It is an overwhelmingly feminine metaphor.

Cox's work was part of Enarson and Morrow's pioneering collection of essays *The Gendered Terrain of Disaster*, as was Doone Robertson's report on the absence of women from policy, decision-making and leadership roles in emergency management in Australia, in which she observed that 'emergency management has been, by tradition if not by right, a male prerogative in Australia'.[8] Cox in particular was writing about the Ash Wednesday bushfires, but early work in disaster and gender also included Australian women's experiences through drought and flood. Common to all of the Australian works are the findings that women play essential but often unacknowledged roles in disaster relief and recovery and that they are rarely part of larger discussions about prevention, mitigation, response or rebuilding. Cox also observed that, as emotional and social rebuilding is women's work, men were often excluded and isolated and they carried a psychological and emotional burden that could have a devastating impact. It is a reminder that, although 'gender' in research frequently means 'women', the consequences of gender-based social attitudes and policies are felt by both men and women.

This chapter investigates just a few of the ways in which gender is reflected in bushfire stories from Strathewen. The research is, by virtue of its lack of anonymity, limited in its ability to address

---

7   Helen Cox, "Women in Bushfire Territory," in *The Gendered Terrain of Disaster*, ed. Elaine Enarson and Betty Hearn Morrow (Westport CT: Praeger Publishers, 1998), 142.

8   Doone Robertson, "Women in Emergency Management: An Australian Perspective," ibid., 201.

serious social issues such as domestic violence and suicide, although these were found to have increased in some communities after Black Saturday. In-depth interviews in a small settlement are almost inevitably known to the wider community, especially as every narrator agreed to using his or her own name and to having the interviews deposited with Museum Victoria's Victorian Bushfires Collection. Such publicly accessible research reinforces narrators' reluctance to discuss subjects, such as suicide or violence against family members, which are already taboo in wider society. What I found were the more subtle, even unconscious, ways in which gender influences the stories told in the bushfire zone and the decisions made there.

Bushfire and gender

The most obvious place to start is with the admission that this is a highly gendered study. Not only am I a woman but most of the oral history narrators were also women. The men who did participate did so in company with or at the behest of a woman they knew. Many of the stories about men were relayed through and interpreted by women.

Most of the men who declined to take part in an oral history interview declared they did not have the time or interest. Strathewen, like Kinglake, Marysville, Steels Creek and other communities hard-hit by the fires, has been exhaustively studied by researchers, journalists, psychologists, bushfire experts and the Royal Commission. Taking part in yet another study may not have been important enough to take time and energy away from the myriad jobs of rebuilding a life either in or out of the bushfire zone.

Maybe there was also some reluctance due to the nature of the questions I asking. I wanted to know not just what happened to them during the fires but also about impacts on personal relationships and community dynamics, about intangibles such as sense of place, visions of the future, memorials and creative responses, and (eventually) about the differences between men and women. These can be seen to be gendered interests, focused as they are on personal and social issues that are often considered to be the province of women. They are not inevitably the only interests of a female researcher – the Senior Curator of our collection, Liza Dale-Hallett, engages in spirited conversations about the size of hose couplings and location of ember traps – but they were my interests.

On the other hand, at least one male respondent agreed to talk to me *because* I was a woman, and others, both male and female, observed that it was easier to talk to a woman about difficult subjects. It was also the area in which my own biases came most clearly to the surface, starting with the selection of an object that spoke to my own background with textiles and women's work. So before I even began my oral history interviews, gender was helping to shape who would or would not speak, what stories they would or would not tell and what interpretation they – and I – would put on those stories.

The aftermath

Tools and sheds: that's where it started. Nearly everyone I spoke to, both informally and in recorded interviews, said that men's greatest losses were their sheds and the objects they contained, from old tins of nails to tractors and chainsaws. To Barbara Joyce *it was as if they had lost their hands*.[9] Without exception, women speaking of men and

---

9   Barbara Joyce, Interview 18 June 2013.

their sheds did so with affection and sometimes even with an indulgent tolerance, but they knew how important a shed and its contents were.

Both Vicki Mitchell and her mother Norma Nelson observed how helpless their men seemed without tools with which to start clearing and rebuilding their properties. In the weeks after the fires Norma and Vicki spent a good deal of their time visiting relief centres looking for replacement tools. It was a relief and a pleasure to bring home something as simple as a shovel, for it was a sign of emotional support as well as practicality. *The guys were really struggling. They had to keep busy and they had to keep working and if we came back with a shovel, if we found a shovel or something that used to be on the farm before, you could see their eyes light up and you could tell that by you doing that it was helping the guys get through it a little bit.*[10]

The stories about men and sheds led to more comments about the differences between men and women with regard to the fires. It was generally agreed that such differences existed and that for the most part they followed traditional gender roles. Men were perceived as responsible for physical property, both in planning its defence against bushfire and in carrying out the plans. Women were responsible for emotional and social wellbeing, especially that of children but also of their male partners and of other people in their community. Men were more likely to 'stay and defend' while women were more inclined to evacuate. Men had a greater tolerance for physical danger in defence of their home, while women placed more importance on physical safety. Men were practical and women were emotional. Women were more able than men to recover from disaster because of

---

10   Vicki Mitchell, Interview 8 August 2012.

stronger social and emotional bonds, but men were more inclined to rebuild in the same place.

Some of these general assumptions have been supported by research into other communities. A study of rural landowners in a bushfire-prone area of New South Wales found that women tended to leave bushfire planning and preparation to male members of the family, and were also more inclined to evacuate in the face of bushfire threat. Another Australian study has suggested that the preference to leave early may be connected to women's traditional responsibilities for children's safety and wellbeing.

The gender split is also obvious in the testimonies before the Royal Commission, particularly with regard to bushfire preparation. The testimonies describe almost exclusively male activity in planning for and carrying out bushfire defence. Even where a man and woman were both involved in defence of their home, the preparations were generally perceived as the responsibility and the accomplishment of the male, and descriptions of bushfire preparations are usually focused on the man's work. Testifying to the Royal Commission about the deaths in Strathewen of Bob O'Sullivan and his partner Sue Evans, Sue's son Jon and two of his friends, one witness said, 'Over the years Bob showed me how he had been prepared. It wasn't like something had been rigged up for the day. He was so capable and so well prepared; he was not a risk taker.'[11] From the rest of the testimony it can be seen that Sue had also been active in the preparation and defence of their home, but it is clear that this was considered to be Bob's responsibility.

---

11   Kyle Westall, testimony to Royal Commission. Teague et al, "2009 Victorian Bushfires Royal Commission Final Report," Vol 1, 16:9.

THE CHOOK: BUSHFIRE AND GENDER

Many other women participated in bushfire preparation and defence. Peter Wiltshire's witness statement to the Royal Commission describes an equal partnership between himself and his wife Felicity, both of them trained CFA volunteers, in order to save their house in nearby St Andrews. Paul Nowak's testimony describes the efforts he and his wife Cathy made to defend Carseburn, the old Mann property in Strathewen that they bought in 2009. These are striking examples that the ability to face bushfire is not restricted to men but the perception, overwhelmingly, remains of bushfire as men's business.

Gender roles helped to determine what people did before, during and after a bushfire, but they also were important in shaping narrators' understanding and interpretation of their experience. Because men's sheds and their contents were consistently mentioned in the interviews as significant objects, they give the best entry point into the relationship between gender and bushfire.

Shed stories

When a man said that his greatest loss was his shed, he didn't mean only the structure. Inside every shed was a unique collection of tools, materials and bits and pieces: tractors; motor bikes; farming equipment from the days when orchards covered the valley; hand tools, many of them inherited; power tools; bits of wood and scraps of iron; gardening equipment; tins of paint; innumerable screws, bolts, nails and rivets; things that were essential for daily chores and things that might come in handy someday. Some sheds were immaculate and highly organised, while others were cluttered and dusty. Each shed reflected not only the common jobs of looking after a property in the bush but also the heritage, interests and character of the individual owner. For many men, their shed was their personal private space in a way that their house was not.

Shed contents were largely practical items, and their presence in the interviews helps to reinforce the perception that men were more focused on the nuts and bolts (so to speak) of bushfire recovery, but this does not explain the near-universal grief over the loss of a shed. Although managing without all the tools and implements was difficult, and replacing them was expensive, neither monetary value nor inconvenience was mentioned as reasons for men's distress at the loss of their sheds. Male narrators like Fred Bateman described how the loss resounded for years after the fires. *Even now [five years later] it still goes on, bits you had in your shed, [you] think you've got that and then you realise you haven't got it. So in the shed we had, that was just full of tools and bits and pieces, so I could go there if I needed a nut and bolt or a screw, it was always there. So when you haven't got any of those sort of things you've got to start replacing them and even though it's simple and easy to replace, it still means something.*[12]

Sheds and tools and buckets of nails were not, of course, the only things that men mourned. Each man in this admittedly small sample also talked about other significant losses: the photos and medals that were reminders of a long-dead father; jewellery and photographs of a wife and two daughters, all of whom had died years before the fire; an extensive library; a collection of antique cameras; garage-sale treasures that carried memories of the past and dreams for the future; the heritage of a family reduced to rubble and carted away.

Women also felt this kind of loss. Many of them spoke movingly of possessions, especially pieces that had been passed through the

---

12   Fred Bateman, Interview 27 June 2013.

family. Joyce Horne recounted: *My mother lived to 101 and I had a drawer full of some of her special things. Like, she did beautiful crocheting and there was a big supper cloth or big afternoon tea cloth crocheted that she had in her glory box. That was a treasure.*[13] Men and women both viewed personal objects like these in the context of their emotional value. For Leslye Chappelle, it was *my mum's wedding ring. Mum never had anything much in her life and it was just a small simple wedding band that I can't pass down to my daughter. It's those things, my great-grandparents' crockery, all that type of thing that I would have passed down, so they're all gone.*[14]

The men and women in this study shared a common grief for objects of emotional value, especially heirlooms, which represented the bonds of family and friends and the passage of time. Photographs, particularly of relatives or family homes and events, were a keenly felt loss. For many people, male and female alike, they were the physical embodiment of memories and they feared losing those memories on top of everything else. But women didn't mourn the loss of practical objects – professional equipment, kitchen tools, art materials or farm implements – the way that men mourned their sheds.

The true significance of shed stories lies not in the loss of useful equipment but in the emotional impact of that loss. Sheds represented men's relationship with their properties and symbolised their ability to take care of both the land and the family home. Shane Pugh observed that the shed was a symbol of men's responsibility to provide shelter for their families and that *most of the houses were either built or renovated by the men, so it's all their blood, sweat and tears*

---

13 Joyce Horne, Interview 27 November 2012.
14 Leslye Chappelle, Interview 27 June 2013.

*that they've put into creating that space.*¹⁵ Tools were important symbols of competence and self-reliance that contributed to a feeling of self-worth and a connection to the ideal of the rural Australian male. The shed was a potent symbol of that idea of manhood.

For men whose family had occupied a property for generations, the loss of tools was also a loss of family tradition and identification with male ancestors. Ian McKimmie mourned the destruction of outdated and useless equipment that had lain in his sheds for decades, seeing it as part of the greater loss of cultural heritage. *One of us, somebody, said, 'I just can't stand to see the truckloads of history going out of Strathewen.' And I thought that explained everything: truck after truck after truck, all that history going out.*¹⁶

There were, however, some men who did not share this grief and for whom the loss of tools was a minor consideration. When Robert Crisfield evacuated before the fire reached Strathewen he took his old family photos with him. He considered himself lucky to have grabbed them rather the chainsaws with which he earned a living as an arbourist. The greatest impact was the loss of his books. *I had five to eight thousand books – no wonder the house burnt!- and I still haven't read a novel since and I can't explain why. It doesn't upset me but it was like those books were my intellect and they were taken away and I still have trouble with that. [...] I'd been collecting those books since I was eight.*¹⁷ Darren Thompson lost all his possessions, including the tools he needed for his work, but what hurt most was the destruction of treasures he and his late father had collected over the years and which he hoped someday to turn into cash to buy a house in which to raise

---

15   Shane Pugh, Interview 13 February 2013.
16   Ian McKimmie, Interview 6 October 2010.
17   Robert Crisfield, Interview 7 August 2013.

his son. Darren lost not only the material evidence of the past but also his connection with his father and his dreams for the future. It is worth noting that, of all the narrators, Robert and Darren were the only ones who did not own the properties on which they lived. For both Robert and Darren, tools were objects of employment that had a monetary and practical value but no emotional connection to a specific property. Their unsentimental view helps to reinforce the significance of other men's strong attachment to sheds and tools.

I wondered if the shed stories told by women were an attempt to reassure themselves that men, once they were re-equipped, would recover from the trauma. Tools, unlike old photographs, could be replaced, and women like Vicki and Norma helped to source their replacements. In doing so, they hoped to aid men's healing, a process for which many women perceived themselves to be responsible, and so reduce their own feelings of helplessness in the face of male suffering. Perhaps also it was the case that men, especially outside their own families, were more comfortable mourning their sheds than crying about baby pictures. Grief could be cloaked in an aura of acceptable practicality, of loss related to 'doing' rather than 'feeling', especially a loss with such strong cultural connections to being an Australian man.

So shed stories reaffirmed the myth of the Australian rural male as practical, capable, self-reliant and able to deal with any emergency. They also undermined that myth, because every shed story had at its heart an overwhelming emergency, a failure to defend the home against an implacable destructive force and the loss of an intimate, beloved space.

Conflicting narratives

When I examined interviews I had collected in more depth, contradictions and complications began to emerge, making it clear that gender relations were neither as clear-cut nor as rigid as the narrators portrayed. Men were believed to be more willing to stay and fight, yet some men evacuated before the fire while Irma Winton, a widow in her 70s, refused to leave and attempted to defend her home. In her testimony to the Royal Commission her daughter, Karen Gardam, said that 'Mum wouldn't have a bar of it. She refused to leave. Mum told me she had been pumping water out of the dam and wetting down the gardens and the surrounds of the house in preparation for the severe weather. There was no way Mum was leaving the house.' [18]

Women were believed to be stronger emotionally and to recover more quickly after disaster yet Jane Hayward, principal of Strathewen Primary, was providing lunches for children two years after the fires because some mothers were still unable to cope. The Strathewen Community Renewal Association was dominated by men, and its Rebuilding Committee was composed entirely of men, but men also led community meetings to discuss grief and bereavement, or the emotional aspects of designing a memorial to the victims. Women were knitters, but both men and women were poets.

Oversimplification of gender roles leaves the impression that women were not involved in the physical labour of cleaning up and rebuilding, a perception that Rosemary McKimmie Young was careful to refute. For five years after Black Saturday she was *fixing fencing, fixing dams, fixing erosion, fixing rooves, fixing sheds, fixing paddocks, fixing weeds, spraying blackberries that have grown out of*

---

18   Teague et al, "2009 Victorian Bushfires Royal Commission Final Report," Vol 1, 16:9.

control, it just goes on and on and on. I worked like a man.[19] Rosemary's words challenged the idea of gender-based actions but at the same time reinforced them – after all, she worked *like a man.*

In the face of these and other exceptions, it seems that the descriptions of strictly gendered roles did not necessarily document only what happened after Black Saturday but also what people thought should happen. Many people subscribed to the idea that men and women thought and felt and did things differently, and they found comfort in that idea. It seems to me that one reason that Strathewen women were so emphatic about the prime importance to men of tools and sheds is that it was the point of divergence between the sexes, where men's losses could be expressed differently from women's and therefore reflected differences in gender roles.

The evocation of traditional gender distinctions in Strathewen, as expressed through gender-based stories of loss, may have provided a feeling of stability in a time when nothing seemed fixed or predictable. Shane Pugh said, *When you get something that stresses society like a fire, then women tend to go in as the nurturers and rebuild the society, help people rebuild on a personal level, where the male approach is much more practical.*[20] In the midst of chaos, gendered roles gave people a place in the social structure and a job to do. They also linked Strathewen's experience to the highly gendered rural Australian story of resilience and self-sufficiency in the face of natural disaster, providing a template for recovery. By doing so it brought strength both to individuals and to their community, at least for a time, when they needed it most.

Conformity to the idea of what a man or a woman ought to do during a crisis made it difficult for people whose narratives did not

---

19   Rosemary McKimmie Young, Interview 18 June 2013.
20   Shane Pugh, Interview 13 February 2013.

follow accepted gender roles to accommodate their story within the wider society. Robert Crisfield evacuated from his home in Bowden Spur Road before the fire, convinced that Strathewen was in severe danger, and headed to a nearby settlement to check on the safety of two female friends. He stopped to talk to his neighbours in Strathewen but was unable to convince them to leave as well. *And I just left, but I got a mile down the road and thought I was abandoning Strathewen, but then had a second thought, thought, 'No, no, there are things I have to do: see these girls, get them to safety and get myself to safety.'*[21] Robert lost his home and his neighbours lost their lives. In the interview he returned repeatedly to a sense of guilt over leaving Strathewen and to his belief that evacuation – mandatory, if necessary – was the only solution to conditions like Black Saturday.

I saw in his constant return to this theme a struggle to reconcile his actions, sensible as they were, with the gendered expectations of men. His eventual solution was to distance himself from the accepted form of masculinity, which he described as *male ego. A lot of it was male pride [...] saying, 'Oh no, we can beat this.' It became a personal thing between them and the possibility of fire and it's not like that. It's too big to fight.*[22] Robert developed, instead, an alternative concept of masculinity that was based on leaving his own home in order to persuade two female friends to evacuate to safety. It was still concerned with the protection of women, but in his version men shepherded women from the danger area instead of staying to fight the fire.

Stories like Robert's, that touch on ego and male identity, lead to darker narratives than those of men and their sheds. There are deeper and more deadly consequences of gender-regulated behaviour.

---

21   Robert Crisfield, Interview 7 August 2013.
22   Ibid.

THE CHOOK: BUSHFIRE AND GENDER

The increased incidence of domestic violence and male suicide is the side that no one talked about except in the most guarded of terms. Increased drug and alcohol use after the fires, particularly by men, was also informally reported.

Some men felt compelled to indulge in risk-taking behaviour, and Helen Legg at the Hurstbridge Bushfire Relief Centre organised sky diving and war games to channel their frustrations into safer activities. It was Helen who first raised with me the issue of masculinity as more than just a difference in gender roles, and as something that affected men negatively. *One guy from the bushfire-affected areas, he felt that he hadn't done enough on the day and he was beating himself up thinking that he was a weak man. So he was choosing this [skydiving] experience to prove to himself that he wasn't weak and he wasn't scared. And I remember he went up in the plane, he was crying all the way up in the plane. He was crying because he was obviously very, very scared but he was trying to overcome his fears. And this is one way he thought he could overcome fear, by doing this thing that was so scary, to prove to himself finally that he's a man.*[23]

Angela McKenzie and Vicki Mitchell, during a conversation recorded for the museum, reflected on the effect of the fire not only on the men as individuals but on the relationships between men and women. *I think the fires have locked us into boxes a little bit. We're still locked into boxes in relationships and we're not getting across how we need to – how we were before the fires. We're still running separate paths.*[24] Along with many other people, they observed how women were offered more counselling and services for emotional recovery, and that men often struggled to admit they needed and then to find

---

23 Helen Legg, Interview 25 June 2013.
24 Vicki Mitchell, Interview 8 August 2012.

emotional and psychological support. This was despite the situation in which many men, through their identification as protectors of their family and their home, frequently faced debilitating guilt and disorientation in a way that their partners did not. But all of this took time to come out; first of all, most people talked about sheds.

Throughout this project I have been aware of the tension between narrative and reality – between the stories I was told and what was happening inside individuals, in relationships and in the community. Every bushfire town, and perhaps Strathewen to a greater degree than most, has endured an unprecedented level of public scrutiny in the months and years since the fires. Everyone was watching to see how and when and whether they 'recover' and judged or rewarded them according to how well they were perceived to do it. This placed unimaginable pressure on people who already had enough to deal with, and I count my own study as a contributor to the pressure. All of the narrators were aware of the public audience for their interviews; Bob Crisfield started his interview with *Hello, viewers*.[25]

Increasingly, the stories about tools and sheds seemed to me to be a comforting narrative device through which people could tell their story in a way that made it acceptable not only to themselves and their community but also to me, and through me to the wider public. Men certainly mourned the loss of their sheds but they also grieved over lost homes, lost animals, lost keepsakes and especially lost friends and family. Sometimes this grief was turned against their families and against themselves, but this is painful to address and most narrators wanted to spare their community and themselves the additional distress.

---

25 Robert Crisfield, Interview 7 August 2013.

Shed stories can be seen as giving everyone – the public, the narrators and the men themselves – stories of loss that are palatable proxies for darker narratives about loss and despair that cannot be aired publicly. They are concerned with masculinity but at a level that includes pathos, humour and resilience rather than violence, self-harm or death. At a time when everything seemed uncertain and under threat, it was safe for men to mourn their sheds without compromising – either to others or to themselves – their identity as men.

Tough stuff

Both men and women tried to save their homes from destruction on Black Saturday by actively defending them. Some were successful and not only saved their homes but also their own lives and often the lives of others. Others, despite having what was in many cases a well-prepared and well-defended home, were not.

Women and men often worked side by side, as the Nowaks did, or in a partnership based on traditional gender roles. Barrie Tully, for instance, along with three other male firefighters, fought the flames outside the house while his wife Rae provided support to the firefighters, patrolled the interior of the house and looked after the people who had collected there as a safe haven. But many men fought the fires on their own, assuming a physical and psychological burden that has yet to be fully measured or understood.

Many people judged the risk of staying to defend to be too great, or the effort to be beyond their capabilities, and decided to evacuate. Some left the moment of decision too late and evacuated either in great danger or not at all. Others were caught by surprise and were unable to carry out their bushfire plan; yet others had not made any plan and left their survival to luck, or to the efforts of others. In many cases, women left the planning, preparation and decision-making – and frequently the active work of defence – to the male members of their household.

From the Ash Wednesday fires of 1983 to Black Saturday in 2009, the heart of Victorian bushfire policy was to 'prepare, stay and defend your property or leave early'.[26] I think of this as 'his and hers' policy, in which the first option reflects the 'masculine' acceptance of greater risk in order to defend one's home and the second caters to the 'feminine' tendency to place safety above protection of assets. It is hardly surprising, given that the policy developers were men, that the literature encouraged property owners to choose the former – if not explicitly, at least in the way it outlined the advantages of staying to defend. The watchword became 'People save houses. Houses save people.'[27] The default response to bushfire was to behave like a man – or, rather, the way that we think that a man should behave. This meant, in effect, to place the emphasis on protecting individual physical assets, to accept a high degree of physical and psychological risk, often to face the fire alone and not to admit to needing help afterward. More than anything, it meant believing that to stay and defend is the correct response for a man, and that leaving early indicated a lack of courage, strength or ability.

The practice of staying and defending is imbued with engrained ideas of manhood. This may have encouraged a false sense of

---

26 "Evaluation of Stay or Go Policy," Bushfire Cooperative Research Centre, http://www.bushfirecrc.com/projects/c6/evaluation-stay-or-go-policy [Accessed 20 November 2014].

27 J. Handmer and A.Tibbits, 2005. 'Is staying at home the safest option during bushfires? Historical evidence for an Australian approach.' Cited in Christine Eriksen, Nicholas Gill, and Lesley Head, "The Gendered Dimensions of Bushfire in Changing Rural Landscapes in Australia," *Journal of Rural Studies* 26, no. 4 (2010): 337.

competence or made it more difficult for men to admit fear or doubt over their abilities to fight the fire, and encouraged them to stay when the wise course was to leave. The men who insisted on staying to defend because of a dangerously misplaced idea of masculinity are not to be blamed. Gender roles are deeply ingrained cultural behaviours that most of us follow to a greater or lesser degree. But they lead to a question that I cannot avoid: did traditional gender roles contribute to avoidable deaths on Black Saturday?

I think they did. In a preliminary meeting one of the narrators told me of concerns about inadequate preparations by two Strathewen residents and of attempting to convince them to evacuate early on Black Saturday. The wife was afraid and wanted to evacuate but felt obliged to stay because her husband was determined to stay and defend. The couple were later found dead in the ashes of their home. By the time I recorded the interview, however, the narrator had smoothed out the gender difference into a description of a united decision to face the fire. Out of concern for the surviving family the narrator had altered the story so that the public record would portray a husband and wife fighting – and dying – together. In doing so, however, the story failed to acknowledge the difference between men's and women's reactions to threats. The woman's voice was silenced.

This deferral to the masculine point of view was not an isolated case. One of the most disturbing statistics about Black Saturday is that nearly 50 per cent of the fatalities were 'vulnerable' people: children, the elderly, the disabled or chronically ill. Many people mentioned off the record that they knew of women who stayed in the bushfire zone against their own wishes in order to support their husbands, because to leave would show a lack of confidence. Some people survived, some didn't; some had their children with them. No one would talk openly about it. Trying to catch these stories was like trying to catch smoke.

A report on Black Saturday from the Bushfire Cooperative Research Centre made reference to similar situations:

> There is evidence of disagreements as the fire approached. In virtually all cases this was between women who wanted to leave and take the men with them and men who either wanted to stay and defend or who felt they had to support others in that role. In some cases it appears that the difference in opinion was long standing, in other cases it was only acknowledged at the last minute. This led to some people changing their plans at the last minute. This appears particularly the case for couples. There are several instances where women who fled under these circumstances survived. Conversely, there is also evidence of such disagreements where males refused to leave, but relatives decided to stay, leading to additional fatalities – assuming that they would have survived leaving.[28]

I know that there are people in Strathewen who are still alive today because of men's courage and determination in defending a home against the fire, but there is also little doubt in my mind that some people who died in Strathewen would be alive today if the woman's desire to evacuate had not been overruled by the man's desire to stay and defend. This observation is not intended to inflict pain nor is it a futile exercise in 'if only'. We cannot do anything about deaths in

---

28 John Handmer, Saffron O'Neil, and Damien Killalea, "Review of Fatalities in the February 7 2009 Bushfires," (East Melbourne: Bushfire Cooperative Research Centre, 2010), Prepared for Bushfires Royal Commission, EXP.029.03.0022, 22.

the past, but we can use the experience to consider how we approach the future.

Thinking about bushfire

So deeply embedded is a gendered approach to how we think of, plan for, respond to, recover from – even speak or write of – bushfire that it is difficult to discern. A masculine approach permeates our assumptions to the extent that it appears to be not only the right way but the only way to relate to bushfire.

An example of the dominance of our gendered public discourse can be found in testimony by John Handmer to the Bushfires Royal Commission. Handmer is a leading researcher in natural disasters, especially bushfire, who was an expert witness to the Commission on a number of topics and received a Special Recognition Award from the Bushfire Cooperative Research Centre. He has written on the differences between men and women in perceiving and acting on bushfire risk and the consequences of those differences.[29] Handmer made an extensive presentation to the Commissioners on the language used in bushfire warnings and community education, with recommendations for changes to wording. He expressed the need for warnings to become more 'listener-friendly' and to shift from language that reflected an emphasis on physical assets to words that encompassed emotions and relationships. 'Properties' should become 'homes'; 'residents' should be become 'families'.[30] He also recommended that warnings should be varied in order to reach a number of audiences,

---

29 Ibid.
30 Prof. John Handmer, Testimony. Teague et al, "2009 Victorian Bushfires Royal Commission Final Report," transcript 16 June 2009. http://www.royalcommission.vic.gov.au/getdoc/32d93df1-8563-4f9e-b984-34a1fad25667/Transcript-VBRC_Day-024_16-Jun-2009.PDF [Accessed 14 November 2014].

among them teenagers, the elderly and people with chronic health issues. Yet at no point in his presentation did he suggest women as a specific audience for warnings, nor acknowledge that the shifts in language he recommended were essentially moving from the perceived masculine zone of interest to the feminine. The fact that an eminent researcher who was attuned to gender differences did not offer gender as a consideration – and none of the Commissioners picked him up on it – demonstrates the degree to which masculine thinking with regard to bushfire is both pervasive and invisible.

Since the formation of the CFA in 1944, bushfire policy has been conceived, developed and carried out by men. With the admission of women to operational duties in the CFA and the promotion of women in many emergency organisations (Christine Nixon was the Chief Commissioner of Police in Victoria at the time of Black Saturday), it might be anticipated that the gender-based culture of disaster management would change but, fifteen years after Doone Robertson criticised the absence of women from decision-making positions, Naomi Brown was still dismayed by the lack of women in positions of influence in Australia's emergency management. In a special 'gender edition' of the *Australian Journal of Emergency Management* Brown, the retired CEO of the Australasian Fire and Emergency Service Authorities Council, wrote that 'for too long we have been 'gender-blind' when developing policy, responding to and recovering from disasters'.[31]

A gender-conditioned response to disaster has affected what we think and do about bushfire. It is present in decisions about evacuation, in the way the 'stay or go' policy was carried out, in the relief

---

31 Naomi Brown, "Foreword," *Australian Journal of Emergency Management* 28, no. 2 (2013): 2.

and recovery efforts, in the language of warnings and in the whole way we, as a culture, engage with bushfire. It '[shapes] the environmental decisions we make and the contingencies we fail to plan for, the dynamics of our disaster-management organisations and relief operations, the disaster-responding household and emergent response groups, the decision-makers we choose and the heroes we create'.[32]

We need an approach to bushfire planning that incorporates the concerns and strengths of women as well as men. We need women to take part in bushfire education and to gain confidence in their own ability – and responsibility – to make informed decisions regarding their own safety and that of their families. We need a new definition of masculinity that recognises that sometimes, like on Black Saturday, the manliest thing may be to put life ahead of property and leave, and that getting psychological help is not weakness but a sign of responsibility to oneself and one's family. Changes like these can only come about through a shift not only in the number of women in positions of authority but also in the culture surrounding the decision-makers.

The question is whether we can change. There has been a surge of new research since Black Saturday, some of which focuses on the interaction of gender. Some of these papers report on the effects of bushfire on women while others examine the possibilities of new programs and initiatives to reduce gender differences in planning for bushfire. Yet there is in many of these papers the melancholy reflection that researchers have, since Helen Cox's essay of 1998, been arguing for gender to be acknowledged and accommodated in

---

32   Elaine Enarson and Betty Hearn Morrow, "Why Gender? Why Women? An Introducton to Women and Disaster," in *The Gendered Terrain of Disaster*, ed. Elaine Enarson and Betty Hearn Morrow (Westport CT: Praeger Publishers, 1998), 4.

bushfire policy, but even as late as 2013 there was 'little recognition in Australia, in either research or policy, that there are important gendered issues surrounding bushfire'.[33]

Yet I think there is hope. In public awareness programs from the CFA, there is now more emphasis on the dangers of staying and defending. 'Leave early' is now presented as a legitimate option – and on 'Code Red' days as the only safe option. The assertion made with heartbreaking confidence that 'People save houses. Houses save people' has been quietly retired in favour of 'Leave and Live'. The 2015 CFA survival guide follows John Handmer's advice about language: 'families' and 'homes' figure prominently in the guide, reinforced by a child's stick-figure illustration of a family.[34] These are not presented as gender-influenced choices, but they are a shift away from the 'masculine' preoccupations with protecting property and defeating a fire. The avoidance of gendered language may well be deliberate, as its use could further polarise an already sensitive topic.

Anecdotal stories also suggest that some women are starting to take more responsibility for their safety, whether it is refusing to rebuild in a region where they do not feel safe, or insisting on particular materials, designs and procedures to enhance safety during a bushfire. More women now intend to make the call of whether or not to stay on high-fire-danger days based on their own assessment of the danger rather than leaving it to someone else's judgement. Perhaps there is the same generational shift taking place in the bushfire zone that the historian Deb Anderson identified in the drought-affected

---

33 Meagan Tyler, "Gender, Masculinity and Bushfire: Australia in an International Context," *Australian Journal of Emergency Management* 28, no. 2 (2013): 20.
34 "Your Guide to Survival," ed. Country Fire Authority (Melbourne2015).

THE CHOOK: BUSHFIRE AND GENDER

Mallee, of younger women being less willing to defer to their husband's decisions and priorities.[35]

In the outer Melbourne suburb of Bayswater, Diana Ferguson was first female to lead an urban CFA unit. She said, 'We all know men and women think differently. At Bayswater this has given us the ability to see issues through many different lenses. It has also shifted our focus from fire trucks and equipment to our team and our fellow volunteers.'[36] I said earlier in this chapter that this was the issue in which my biases came most clearly to the fore. These changes suggest that it is becoming acceptable for a man to think more 'like a woman', and for a woman to think more 'like a man' – and I cannot help thinking that that is a good thing.

---

35 Deb Anderson, *Endurance: Australian Stories of Drought* (Collingwood: CSIRO Publishing, 2014), 94.
36 Diana Ferguson, *My C.F.A. Story, Digital story-telling: Women in leadership roles* (Victoria: Country Fire Authority, 2015).

Figure 9. Hard hat, Strathewen Primary School. Victorian Bushfires Collection, Museum Victoria, HT 27573.

Image: Marita Dyson. Source: Museum Victoria.

Chapter 7

THE HARD HAT: PLACE, HOME AND REBUILDING

'Jane' is Jane Hayward, principal of Strathewen Primary School. The personalised hard hat was a gift from one of her students and she wore it during her site visits supervising the rebuilding of the school after Black Saturday. On the back, in hand-lettered texta, it says 'Super teacher'.

In a tiny place like Strathewen, local social institutions like the primary school take on great importance. People described the school, the hall and, to a lesser degree, the sports pavilion as the centres of social connection and community activity for many decades. In many families, three generations of children had attended the school – some, like Bronwyn Apted South, sitting in not only the same room but at the same desk that older members of her family had occupied – but even for those who were relative newcomers the school represented social continuity.

Strathewen State School opened in March of 1917. Before this time the children of Strathewen walked through the bush up the mountain to Kinglake three times a week for instruction. In what was surely a school exercise May Giddons wrote to the *Weekly Times* describing the new institution:

> It was opened in March of this year, and there are 17 children attending it. It is situated on a small hill, and we can get a very nice view of Mount Sugarloaf from here. The creek is not very far away. A great deal of wattle is growing alongside it, and we can see it all from the school ground. [...] We have just started a flower garden.[1]

Most of the teachers assigned to Strathewen were fresh out of teacher training in Melbourne. They often found the isolation and lack of resources difficult: May's teacher, Miss Mary Golding, was 'so overcome by inadequacies and loneliness that, as she confessed to the District Inspector later, "I was tempted to take the first coach home."'[2]

Like many small settlements, Strathewen struggled to keep attendance levels high enough to justify the expense of its own school. One correspondent to the local paper (clearly not from Strathewen) described the school's opening as 'educational waste' in a time of war, and questioned the area's ability to meet the minimum enrolment requirements.[3] This was perceived not as criticism about the priorities of the Department of Education but as a lack of confidence in Strathewen's future prospects. Local sensibilities were offended:

> The Strathewen State School picnic was held on Thursday, 5th [April, 1917]. [...] Tables had been erected in the schoolroom and the display of silver and glassware filled to overflowing with good things, combined with the numerous decorations, would have done credit to the most up to date city banquet.

---

1 *Weekly Times*, 8 September 1917.
2 JW Payne, *The Plenty: A Centennial History of the Whittlesea Shire* (Kilmore: Lowden Publishing, 1975), 186.
3 *Evelyn Observer*, 28 September 1916.

Considerably over fifty parents and children took part in the feast. This speaks volumes for the success of the school for many years to come. One must pause to wonder where the Education or Public waste comes in.[4]

In 1941 Lyn Lewis arrived in Strathewen for her first rural teaching position. *There'd only be about 15, 16 kids there at the time and it was mainly bush. I boarded next door in a little two-bedroomed wooden cottage which was also the post office. [...] [The school] was just one big room of a wooden building, with a blackboard right along one wall and the alphabet was written on the top of the blackboard and you had to divide your blackboard up into eight classes and put the work in each group.*[5]

Little changed for decades after Lyn's brief stint in Strathewen. In the 1950s and '60s children like Ian and Rosemary McKimmie or their cousin Sylvia experienced the same style of education that their parents or even grandparents had: *one teacher with four classes, responsible for all levels and you're all in the same room. It was only a one-roomed school in those days when we went through.*[6]

Better roads, city jobs and a greater choice of schools might have meant the end of Strathewen Primary. Instead it experienced a reverse migration at the end of the 20th century as middle-class parents from nearby communities drove into Strathewen so that their children could attend a little bush school complete with gardens and chickens. The school's facilities expanded beyond the one-roomed building and the teaching staff developed a reputation for child-centred education with strong community participation.

---

4   *Evelyn Observer*, 13 April 1917.
5   Lynette Chambers, Interview 27 July 2012.
6   Sylvia Skinner, Interview 15 September 2010.

Black Saturday

On the afternoon of Saturday 7 February the school, like almost everything else in Strathewen, was consumed by fire. All that remained was a small outbuilding and the charred remains of some play equipment. What might have happened if the fire had come through on a school day is difficult to contemplate. *We thought we were very well prepared, with a sprinkler system on the roof tops and steel shutters on windows and all the fire-fighting gear we needed. But I don't think much would have protected us at all on that day.*[7]

On Monday the school community gathered in nearby Arthurs Creek. *That look that people have, just that shocked, dazed, broken look. That was us. [...] There were children arriving whose horses had died, there were children arriving who didn't have parents, or a parent. [...] So many families who'd left with nothing, and who had nothing, not a thing, left.*[8] A former student who had graduated from the school a few months previously was the only survivor of her family and had been hospitalised with severe burns. Her younger sister had been a student there.

What happened next has become the stuff of Strathewen legend. At that meeting the Department of Education announced that Strathewen Primary would re-open in two days' time, on Wednesday, 11 February. Complete with textbooks, teaching supplies, meals and parent support, the school reopened four days after Black Saturday in temporary quarters at Wattle Glen Primary School. *That first day everyone went home with a reading folder, and a reader. Locker tubs were all labelled, books were all given out. And we started again.*[9]

---

[7] Jane Hayward, Interview 3 November 2010.
[8] Ibid.
[9] Ibid.

THE HARD HAT: PLACE, HOME AND REBUILDING

For the next 18 months the school staff looked after the educational, social and emotional needs of the students and their parents, often at the expense of their own wellbeing. At the same time they were planning a new school. On 18 October 2010 Strathewen Primary reopened in a modern building on its original site above the Arthurs Creek. In the next few years the grounds were developed and play areas, gardens and chook runs re-established. The emotional and psychological consequences will take longer to overcome. *We're going to have children needing support for a long time to come. [...] These kids have seen things they shouldn't have. They know that the world isn't the safest place. They know that their parents can't always keep them safe, and that's a huge loss for children.*[10] The children have been involved in planning a contemplative garden and other reminders of the events of February 2009.

Jane Hayward's hard hat represents not only the loss and re-establishment of the primary school but also the relationship between the school and many of the residents of Strathewen. I had been alerted to the hat's existence by a number of people ('Get the hard hat,' they said) for whom it was recognition of the central role Jane and her staff played in helping the children and the community recover. The school's rebuilding was also more than simply replacing a lost piece of infrastructure. Just as the establishment of the school in 1917 had been viewed as an investment in the area's future, its rebirth was for many people a symbol of survival, a guarantee that Strathewen would continue to exist.

---

10   Ibid.

Other rebuilding

When the school reopened in late 2010, it was one of the few completed buildings in the Strathewen landscape. For the most part, the area was still dominated by empty sites or houses in various stages of repair or reconstruction. At the time of the fourth anniversary in 2013 more houses had appeared but there were still many empty spaces along the roads.

In the days immediately after the fires, political and community leaders spoke of the importance of rebuilding the homes and infrastructure that had been destroyed on Black Saturday. Governor-General Quentin Bryce told the national memorial service in Melbourne that bushfire communities would rebuild: "In time, what was will be restored – no matter how colossal the effort."[11] Prime Minister Kevin Rudd promised 'a solemn contract with each of these communities to rebuild: brick by brick, home by home, school by school, church by church, community by community'.[12]

The refrain was picked up by singer-songwriter Cam Tapp: 'We will rebuild, stone by stone, hand in hand, you and I.'[13] He and a chorus of Strathewen schoolchildren performed the song at the first commemoration of Black Saturday in Strathewen in 2010. On the eve of that first anniversary the head of the Victorian recovery effort, Christine Nixon, was quoted as saying that 'with a lot of resolve and the backing of communities, we will continue to rebuild homes, streets, businesses, townships and livelihoods'.[14]

---

11   *Sydney Morning Herald*, 22 February 2009.
12   Hon. Kevin Rudd, National Day of Mourning, 22 February 2009.
13   Cam Tapp, 'Lest We Forget.' Copyright 2009 Cam Tapp.
14   *The Age*, 6 February 2010.

THE HARD HAT: PLACE, HOME AND REBUILDING

Rebuilding was for most people a slow and intensely stressful and frustrating process. Home owners had to face innumerable challenges: clearing the site; new building codes rushed into legislation soon after the fires; the lack of materials that conformed to the new codes; finding acceptable house designs; a shortage of builders or the reluctance by some builders to work in the bushfire zone; navigating insurance claims; the inventory and replacement of lost goods. Even people like Rae and Barrie Tully whose houses had survived were faced with the loss of outbuildings, equipment and – throughout all of Strathewen – endless kilometres of fencing. All of this had to be managed at a time when most people were living in temporary quarters, visiting relief centres for essential goods, worrying about children and partners, maintaining jobs and trying to come to terms with the loss of friends, neighbours, pets, livestock and everything that had meant home.

For some people, rebuilding was not a possibility. Robert Crisfield and Darren Thompson were both renting properties in Strathewen partly because they loved the bush but also because, like many people in and near the Kinglake Ranges, they needed somewhere affordable. Cheap rents in old buildings attracted tenants who could not afford Melbourne's high prices. Many of them, like Bob and Darren, were not insured; even with financial assistance from the Bushfire Relief Fund they have not begun to recover their losses. People who were getting by before the fires have lost ground; those who were struggling to begin with have been pushed even further to the margins: *I walked out with five cents and a torch.*[15]

---

15 Darren Thompson, Interview 20 August 2013.

Other people could have rebuilt but chose to go elsewhere. Fred Bateman and Leslye Chapelle originally planned to build a modern house on the site of their former mudbrick home in Gregorys Lane. *But the whole lot, everything, needed doing and I just didn't think I was going to be capable of doing it all.*[16] They eventually decided to build in Yarrambat, where the land is more open, although it is still a high-risk bushfire area. They sold their block to a young couple who have since built a new home.

To an outsider, it is remarkable that so many people have been so determined to return to an area that was the scene not only of physical devastation but also of horror and death, yet for some Strathewen residents it was inconceivable not to do so. Vicki Mitchell told of her family's decision to rebuild even before the fire had passed: *From the time we stood up in the swimming pool and we all looked at each other and couldn't believe that we were all alive, there was no thought about going anywhere else.*[17]

Joyce and Alan Horne's sons tried to convince them to relocate from the family property to somewhere more suburban but they refused to consider it, because Strathewen was where they felt they belonged. *Every time we came back after the fires, […] even though everything looked ghastly and black, there wasn't a bird or an animal, I always felt right. 'We've come back, I'm right.'*[18]

Alan Horne's reasons for returning to the farm where he has lived for all of his 80-plus years are echoed in the sentiments of other residents: *Strathewen has always been home to me and I think that if I*

---

16   Fred Bateman, Interview 27 June 2013.
17   Vicki Mitchell, Interview 8 August 2012.
18   Joyce Horne, Interview 27 November 2012.

went somewhere else this place would still be home.[19] They show that the decision to rebuild – or not – is inextricably entwined with ideas of home and the place that is Strathewen.

Place and meaning

The close connection between physical environment and people is reflected in people's stories of Strathewen. Many of the narrators were at pains to make sure that I understood exactly where an old farm lay, where the path to school followed the creek or how a steep garden was terraced with redgum sleepers. I am therefore using the word 'place' to encompass both the physical location of Strathewen and the complex network of memories, experiences, stories, relationships and aspirations that overlays its geography.

Although the oral histories conveyed a strong sense of Strathewen, everybody meant something different in their use of the word. For Fred and Leslye, who were relative newcomers to the area and were not involved in the school or other community activities, Strathewen meant their own property, the mudbrick house and the garden in which they had invested so much time and effort. For people like the McKimmies, the Hornes or the Apteds, whose families have been in the area for over a hundred years, their understanding of the place was interwoven with memories transmitted through generations, and their sense of ownership – in the emotional rather than financial sense – extended beyond their own properties to include farms owned by relatives past and present. *You see, the Horne family – my grandfather, he bought all this land here and then he gave each of his sons*

---

19 Alan Horne, Interview 27 November 2012.

a block. There's 60 acres in this one and then my uncle had the next one, another uncle had the next one and they all were growing apples.[20]

Those who had grown up in the area and had experienced it as free-ranging children added little spaces in the bush to the definition of Strathewen, spots where they built cubbies and lit fires, and the quiet pools where they watched platypuses at play, far removed from the grown-up formality of roads, fences and farmyards. Memories of walking from the school to the hall for Christmas concerts embedded both the buildings and the path between them firmly into their definition of the place. *When I was little it was just a magical dream with Santa. You lived way out Woop Woop here and Santa comes flying in through the door with all these presents. And especially back when I was little – because it was pretty tough up here, no one had a lot of money – those were magic, magic moments. […] Apart from the school, the hall* was Strathewen.[21]

For Barrie and Rae Tully, who had moved their cattle and orcharding operation to Strathewen to escape the urban sprawl that swallowed their original farm, their property was part of an agricultural region and economy that extended beyond the idea of Strathewen as a residential settlement. For Bronwyn Apted South who is the business manager for Apteds, the last of the commercial apple growers, Strathewen was the centre of a network of orchards that stretched from Arthurs Creek up to Kinglake. For both of these families, and the Nelson and Mitchell families, Strathewen was not only home but also a workplace that was dependent on the land on which they were situated.

---

20   Ibid.
21   Vicki Mitchell, Interview 8 August 2012.

Bob Crisfield also regarded the settlement as part of a larger whole. Raised in the forests of Gippsland, he saw Strathewen as one point in a continuous Victorian bush that stretched all through the ranges and valleys east of Melbourne and brought him solitude and consolation through a connection he described as genetic. *So that's what I love about the country, is that peace and there's a real bond that I've got with the bush. [...] There are those parts where you can go and feel that sense of, I don't know, a bit of a sense of completion for me. I can sit in the bush and go, 'Oh, this is nice,' and I won't get that anywhere else.*[22]

These descriptions of Strathewen describe expanding circles of engagement, from an individual property to a network of former family farms to an extended agricultural region to the entire Victorian bush. Despite its seeming isolation, the idea of Strathewen as a place was in part defined by social, economic and environmental connections to the wider world.

Strathewen is based not only in the physical geography but also in time. Before Black Saturday, the evidence of Strathewen's past was apparent in many ways. Buildings like the school, the hall and many old homesteads, the vestiges of old orchards, the roads named after many of the original settlers and the legacy of both early families and later arrivals are evident in all the stories.

Visions of Strathewen carried traces of the past but they also reached into the future. People regarded Strathewen as a place to live out dreams. They envisioned a country upbringing for children, a peaceful retirement far from noise and congestion, a close relationship with nature, or continuity with family heritage. Many of the descriptions of Strathewen as a place emphasise what Strathewen is not.

---

22   Robert Crisfield, Interview 8 July 2013.

Strathewen is not 'the city', meaning not only that it is not Melbourne but it is also not afflicted with the evils that many people associated with urban living, including social dislocation, an unhealthy environment for children, stress, and a breakdown of community ties. Angela McKenzie said *the city isn't a good place to bring up kids;* Bob Crisfield believed *the bush can't hurt me, people can.*[23]

This negative view of the city calls on an Australian tradition of anti-urban (particularly anti-suburban) philosophy, from Henry Lawson and Oswald Barnett to Robin Boyd and Barry Humphries, but it also glosses over the fact that many people would not live in Strathewen without the benefits that 'the city' has provided, including electricity, the internet, made roads and good jobs within commuting distance. Despite the powerful emotional associations, Strathewen is not the bush, but a semi-urban enclave in the bush.

Given that the building blocks of 'place' include social relationships and personal experience in the past, it is hardly surprising to find conflicting ideas of the nature of a place. The importance of personal interpretations in constructing the idea of Strathewen is most vividly played out in histories that contradict an established story of a close-knit community. Although everyone in the oral history interviews shared Bob's love of their physical surroundings, social understandings of Strathewen also entailed grief, pain and anger. Vicki Mitchell, Karen Gardam and Angela McKenzie were outspoken in describing the difficulties they had fitting in to a community where, in their perception, behaviour was controlled and deviations from acceptable opinions were punished. Some of these incidents happened many decades ago, or involved people no longer connected to

---

23 Angela McKenzie, Interview 20 August 2012; Robert Crisfield, Interview 7 August 2013.

Strathewen, but their traces in the women's memories continue to influence their relationships with both the people and the place of Strathewen. They are hard to reconcile with the idyllic portrayal that many people project, and demonstrate the degree to which memories and emotions infuse the landscape and people's relationship to it.

Into this complicated and many-faceted sense of place came the disruption of Black Saturday. It affected everything: the physical nature of the surroundings; the memory of the past embedded in buildings, trees and waterways; the visions of the future.

'Lost' places

There is an extensive literature on place attachment and identity, but perhaps the most influential in terms of Australian history has been Peter Read's 1996 book, *Returning to Nothing*.[24] Read explored the deep sense of attachment people felt to their surroundings and used the terms 'lost places' and 'dead places' to describe landscapes that had been changed irreparably or made inaccessible through a range of causes, from change of ownership to major development projects to natural causes, including bushfires. In their study of Australian memorials, Paul Ashton, Paula Hamilton and Rose Searby picked up on the link between bushfire and lost places, noting that at Mount Macedon, the town that Read examined in his book, the memorial to the 1983 Ash Wednesday bushfires failed to acknowledge the 'landscapes lost to fire'.[25]

In both of these works, bushfire is linked to the irretrievable loss of place. I find this problematic. While the fires destroyed structures,

---

24 Peter Read, *Returning to Nothing: The Meaning of Lost Places* (Cambridge; Melbourne: Cambridge University Press, 1996).
25 Ashton, Hamilton, and Searby, *Places of the Heart: Memorials in Australia*.

fencing and roads, erased the history embedded in the built environment and radically transformed the landscape, Strathewen was not a lost place. As a matter of fact, many of the people who spoke to me would probably react angrily to the suggestion that it was. It was undeniably changed but not lost – and certainly not dead.

I think there is a fundamental difference between bushfire sites like Strathewen and Mount Macedon and other places, like Old Adaminaby or Yallourn, that Read described as lost. Those are irretrievable, the former having been flooded by a new dam and the latter being replaced by an open-cut coal mine. But bushfire is a part of the life cycle here; without the great fires to regenerate the mountain forest, the bush would be truly lost. After a major bushfire a community's continued existence as a place, with all the connotations of memory, relationships and stories that the word carries, is not inevitably doomed, but neither is it guaranteed.

May Proudley, one of the group of researchers who worked with the Bushfire Co-operative Research Centre, has examined the role of place attachment in resilience and decisions to rebuild after the bushfires of 2009. Her early findings suggested that a strong identification with a bushfire-affected place can make people more resilient and yet more vulnerable, as it intensifies both the joy of survival and the pain of loss.[26] Other researchers have found that a strong connection to place can positively influence people's commitment to bushfire preparations.

In many of the oral histories of people who continued to live in Strathewen, there is a clear connection between the regeneration of the environment and the sense of belonging. Helen Cox found the

---

26 Mae Proudley, "Place Matters," *Australian Journal of Emergency Management* 28, no. 2 (2013).

THE HARD HAT: PLACE, HOME AND REBUILDING

same synergy when interviewing people after Ash Wednesday.[27] Joyce Horne, who with her husband came out to their property regularly until the house was rebuilt, identified with the surviving wildlife. *I used to take bags of food – crusts of bread and lettuce leaves and apple peels – and put them out in the paddock. And if we happened to come back next day for some reason, everything would be gone, so there was something alive eating, and I was so happy that there must have been a kangaroo or a bird or a rabbit or something.*[28] Many of the poems on the Poetry Tree expressed the same identification with their surroundings, the belief that the place and the people would heal together. The permanent memorial that opened in 2012 also linked the recovery of the bush to the recovery of the residents.

Many of the people who recorded oral histories with me expressed a commitment to Strathewen that was, if anything, strengthened by the fires. One of the reasons Vicki Mitchell was determined to stay in Strathewen was personal loyalty that was deeply entwined with an historic sense of place: *I wanted to [rebuild] for my parents as well. They spent their whole lives here, they put everything [into it], they built the place from nothing to just a fantastic business that ran so well. [...] They deserve to be helped to rebuild and to have whatever happiness they can have in their later lives.*[29]

There were, however, many for whom the events of Black Saturday severed the connection with place. Fred and Leslye, whose attachment had been largely built on their irreplaceable mudbrick house, found that the difficulties and stress of the proposed rebuilding outweighed their commitment to the property, and they sold it. Bob

---

27   Cox, "Women in Bushfire Territory."
28   Joyce Horne, Interview 27 November 2012.
29   Vicki Mitchell, Interview 8 August 2012.

Crisfield never considered returning to Strathewen, as his commitment is to the larger idea of the Victorian bush rather than to a specific locality. Both Darren Thompson's and Angela McKenzie's relationships to Strathewen were, for different reasons, so relentlessly negative that to return was unthinkable.

There was inevitably some friction between policies that favoured rebuilding and some people's decision not to rebuild, even if that decision were the sensible course. Fred Bateman struggled for more than two years to get the financial assistance to which he was entitled. *The state government were going to reimburse all the local councils and they had to waive all the planning fees and building fees. We applied and they said 'No, because you're not living on the land. We're giving it to the people who bought your block of land.'*[30] The local authorities associated the financial support with the land, not with the people who had lost their home, and it was only with the change of state government that he and Leslye received their rebates. Implicit in the council's words was the assumption that those choosing to live in the bushfire-affected zone were more worthy of assistance, even if – like the new owners of the property – they had not experienced the loss.

There was, in time, a recognition that not everyone could – or should – rebuild. This was reflected in the changing language used to describe the recovery effort. By 2014 and the final report of the fire recovery effort, the term 'rehousing' was used to describe both the reconstruction of former homes and the transition of people to other areas. Crucially, 'rebuilding' was extended to include support for the environment, local economies and such intangibles as social

---

30   Fred Bateman, Interview 27 June 2013.

relations, arts programmes and psychological wellbeing, none of which are necessarily linked to a specific location.[31]

The question of rebuilding is not just about replacing houses but rebuilding homes, and a home encompasses much more than a house. It includes physical environments like gardens, neighbourhoods, roads, the bush and the wildlife who inhabit it, but also intangible qualities such as feelings of safety and familiarity, relationships with neighbours, memories of working hard to build something or enjoying rest and quiet. It also means that even when a house is saved or rebuilt, the feeling of home may still be fractured.

For some people, like Joyce, what remained became more precious: *I was so glad if a crow came flying. You know, nobody likes crows that much but I was happy to feed a crow.* For others, it may not have been so straightforward. Even when a home had been rebuilt and, in the eyes of the outside world, one's life was well on the way to recovery, there were unexpected emotional and psychological hurdles. *We were in the shed and we were ready to move into the house and in some ways you were really excited about wanting to move, but then when you moved in it was horrible. It was like you were in somebody else's house. I think the whole time you were waiting to move back into your old home. That's what it was, the whole time you were waiting to move back into your old home, and then when you moved in it wasn't your house.*[32]

I suspect that there are families who have rebuilt their houses only to realise that they could not rebuild their attachment to Strathewen. That they are not represented in this study is possibly a failure of the

---

31 Fire Recovery Unit, "Victorian Bushfire Recovery Five Year Report," (Melbourne: Department of State Development, Business and Innovation, Government of Victoria, 2014).
32 Vicki Mitchell, Interview 8 August 2012.

methodology, which necessarily relied on willing and public participation. It would be difficult to speak up about such a disappointment, especially in the teeth of public expectations about rebuilding. Zelma Gartner was able to do so, but from a distance of 28 years. She and her husband lost their house in Mount Macedon in 1983 and rebuilt the identical house, and its gardens, almost immediately. Only a few years later, they sold it and moved away; Zelma said in 2011 that *it just wasn't the same place*.[33] It wasn't home.

The places of oral history

There is another way in which place has helped to shape the oral histories upon which this book is based. The presence of Strathewen as a dominant element in the interviews, and the subsequent 'displacement' of many people after Black Saturday, also gives importance to the place in which the interviews occurred.

Each of the interviews was recorded at a location of the narrator's choosing. Bob Crisfield suggested an outdoor location near, but not in, Strathewen. His voice was accompanied by the continuous calling of lorikeets and parrots in the nearby gum trees, the presence of which sparked discussions of the bush and the changes that he had seen in it in the last few decades. Barbara Joyce offered to walk me through the memorial, talking as we went not only of the memorial itself but also its location by the Chadds Creek Road and the significance of its placing in the Strathewen landscape. It was, she said, close and yet removed: *the sound of people will be in the background but you'll have that sense of separate space.*[34]

---

33   Zelma Gartner, Interview 16 March 2011.
34   Barbara Joyce, Interview 13 February 2103.

THE HARD HAT: PLACE, HOME AND REBUILDING

Ian McKimmie and his sister Rosemary agreed to interviews at a number of locations: Ian's burned-out property, Rosemary's house which had survived the fires and at the Poetry Tree. In each of these the surroundings asserted themselves. Ian's property, on the lower reaches of Mount Sugarloaf, had always been a windy spot but after the loss of trees from the mountain's ridges the wind frequently blew in wild gusts, including during the recording. There were moments when we could barely be heard over the roar, and it sometimes seemed as if the wind itself were taking part in the conversation. At the Poetry Tree, the recording was frequently drowned out by the rumble of trucks crossing the bridge over Arthurs Creek. Eighteen months after the fires, they were still clearing properties of debris. And in the middle of the interview in Rosemary McKimmie Young's home, just as she and Ian were describing the effects on the bush of a ten-year drought and record-breaking heat before Black Saturday, the heavens opened and heavy rain on the tin roof added a fierce counterpoint.

The intrusion of noise seemed appropriate. In most of the oral history interviews, the bushfire was described more often in terms of what it sounded like rather than what it looked like. Narrators struggled to find the words, but most often turned to a comparison with enormous engines: *the noise was shocking, like a very large jumbo jet descending on you. A roar, just a complete roar, as if a jumbo jet was landing right on top of us.*[35] Ian McKimmie found *the roar from the flames was just horrific. You just couldn't hear. There was no conversation, the roar was just deafening. The roar, before the actual flames came, was probably more frightening than the flames.*[36] For Rae Tully, the memory

---

35   Norma Nelson, Interview 7 September 2012.
36   Ian McKimmie, Interview 6 October 2010.

of the noise during the fire was enhanced by the later knowledge of how close they came to losing the house: *the roof was making an awful noise when the roof was pulling off the beams, the screeching of the nails along with the wind and the noise of the fire, the roof was making an awful din, the nails screeching and then it started flapping so it was adding to the din.*[37]

In the context of recording quality, these sound-inflected interviews could be regarded as failures. Yet they document and help to describe through sound the nature of the place where the interviews happened, its changes and its effects on the narrators nearly two years after the fires. To be heard above the wind, the rain and the passing truckloads of rubble, the survivors had to assert their own place in the landscape.

Most narrators, however, chose to be interviewed in their own homes. Sitting in Fred and Leslye's new home, a soaring construction of glass and concrete, I was struck by how everything – absolutely everything, from kitchen implements to sofa cushions to art on the walls – matched. There was no trace of their previous life because none had survived. Everything in their new home had been purchased at the same time and conveyed, as perhaps words could not, both the extent of their physical losses and the work involved in recreating every element of a new home.

Where Fred and Leslye's surroundings seemed to emphasise the distance and disconnection between their former home in Strathewen and their new house, the Hornes found continuity and comfort in their new house on the site of the old one. This was derived not from the physical surroundings but from the social relations that

---

37   Rae Tully, Interview 16 October 2013.

were re-affirmed in a new setting. Seated at the new kitchen table, Joyce said: *The kids still love coming home to be with us and we make this table an extension and they sit around here on a Sunday for lunch and everybody talks together and it's nice and that's what I wanted to get back to.*[38] This could not be accomplished in the setting of their rented house in a nearby township. For Joyce, being together meant being in Strathewen.

The importance of 'place' as both a word and an idea surfaced time and again in bushfire stories, but nowhere more consistently or powerfully than in the story of Barrie and Rae Tully. In the hours immediately after the fire, rumours circulated that more than a dozen people had taken shelter at their property, although no one knew who, how many or even if they were still alive. It was not until CFA captain David McGahy and CFA volunteers Peter Jenkinson and Wes Stecher cut their way on foot through the still-burning bush at 3:00am on Sunday that they discovered 19 people alive and safe. The story of their survival resonated through many accounts as a symbol of hope and reassurance that not all had been lost. Although I was told the story many times, both in the interviews and outside them, by narrators and by others, not once did anybody call it 'Tullys' farm' or 'Tullys' property' or another term. It was always 'Tullys' place', as if the word itself were a talisman against loss and an affirmation of survival.

Other oral historians have discovered that the site of an interview affects not only the narrator but also the interviewer. I felt this in Fred Bateman and Leslye Chappelle's home: although they were welcoming and the house itself was beautifully furnished, I was

---

38   Joyce Horne, Interview 27 November 2012.

uncomfortable in the surroundings and the interview started awkwardly. It was not until later that I realised that my attachment to my own home – a place where things don't match, have accumulated over time and tell stories of people present and past – had been challenged and had interfered with my ability to listen to their story.

The most telling example of my own response to the siting of an interview occurred with Darren Thompson. Still living in temporary accommodation four and a half years after the fires in a house he did not consider fit for visitors, having no friends in whose house he felt safe or comfortable and repelled by the idea of returning to Strathewen, he asked me to find somewhere close to his workplace to record his story. In a rented-by-the-hour office in a nearby town, he spoke bitterly of his ongoing difficulties. After losing his home and subsequently his relationship with his partner and son, he felt that he had been used by former friends, failed by the relief organisations and abandoned by society generally. The cold and impersonal setting reinforced his story of displacement and loss and I felt that I had made a mistake in choosing it. It was all that was available in the small town but it seemed to put me on the same side as all the people who had already failed him.

Buyback

When 80 per cent of the buildings have been destroyed and over 10 per cent of the population killed, the continued life of a place is a fragile thing. That is why the rebuilding of the school was so important, and why so many people wanted Jane Hayward's hard hat to enter the museum's collection. It is also why discussions around the issue of rebuilding are so complex and so sensitive. Nowhere is the

THE HARD HAT: PLACE, HOME AND REBUILDING

importance of place more evident than in the question of the buyback scheme.

The final report of the 2009 Victorian Bushfires Royal Commission presented 67 recommendations to the Victorian Government. These covered a wide range of measures, including policy and planning, emergency management, warning systems, bushfire education, building codes and land management. It also included a recommendation that questioned the wisdom of continuing to live in certain areas of the bush.

In explaining what they undoubtedly understood would be one of the most controversial recommendations, the Commission acknowledged the emotions and issues around rebuilding.

> The Commission understands the imperative to rebuild, but to rebuild without any real thought being given to the future management of bushfire risk is to fail to learn from experience. The Commission notes the State's efforts to quickly rebuild homes and communities in order to help people heal and to deal with practical problems such as homelessness. It considers, however, that this has put short-term social welfare considerations above the longer term safety of the community.[39]

After outlining the measures that could be taken to reduce bushfire risk, the report considered that some areas, regardless of mitigation efforts, were simply too dangerous to be rebuilt. Properties that bordered national parks were deemed particularly at risk, and this included areas of Strathewen. The recommendation itself read:

---

39 Teague et al, "2009 Victorian Bushfires Royal Commission Final Report," Section 6.8.

> The State develop and implement a retreat and resettlement strategy for existing developments in areas of unacceptably high bushfire risk, including a scheme for non-compulsory acquisition by the State of land in these areas.[40]

The government of the day, led by Labor premier John Brumby, accepted 66 of the Commission's recommendations in full, in principle or with the promise of action. The 'retreat and resettlement' recommendation, which quickly became known as the 'buyback scheme', was the only one upon which they chose not to act. In August 2010, Premier Brumby was reported as being 'concerned that a government buyout scheme could undermine rebuilding efforts in regional towns like Marysville'.[41]

In the state election of 2011, Labor was defeated and the Liberals, under Ted Baillieu, took power. The new government endorsed the final recommendation of the Royal Commission and instituted the buyback scheme. Landowners in areas of 'unacceptably high bushfire risk' were able to sell their properties to the state. The properties were reabsorbed into Crown land or made available for purchase to neighbouring landowners for use as buffer zones between the remaining properties and heavily forested areas such as national parks. They could not be built on again. By the time the program closed in June 2014, eight properties in Nillumbik shire had been acquired, three of them in Strathewen.[42] Their locations, from the outer reaches of Strathewen to the centre of the valley, implied that all of Strathewen was considered an area of unacceptable risk.

---

40 Ibid., Recommendation 46.
41 *Sydney Morning Herald*, 2 August 2010.
42 Greg Christopher, Senior Officer, Risk and Resilience, Emergency Management Victoria, email to author, 10 September 2014.

THE HARD HAT: PLACE, HOME AND REBUILDING

The issue of the buyback scheme is less straightforward than it may initially appear. The intrinsic quality of being 'too dangerous to live' is restricted to very few locations on the planet. From the high Arctic to the desert, people have managed to make their homes in more inhospitable places than the Victorian bush. In writing their recommendations the Commissioners made assessments and judgements not just about environmental conditions but also about people's willingness and ability to manage risk. Their identification of properties bordering national parks as being especially dangerous also brought into consideration the management policies of public land, and these were further complicated by climate change. All of these factors – environmental, political and especially human – led the Royal Commission to make a recommendation that reflected what they understood to be the most reasonable compromise for 'longer term safety'.

Among the people I spoke with, reaction to the buyback scheme was mixed. Some saw it as a sympathetic solution for individuals who could not face the difficulties of rebuilding or the dangers of living in the bushfire zone, but many others were opposed to it on either environmental or economic grounds. They worried that buffer zones would not be maintained and the regrowth would increase the risk of bushfire for the remaining properties. They were concerned that the message the buyout program conveyed – that Strathewen was not a safe place to live – would discourage both current and prospective residents, damaging Strathewen's future viability as a community. The recommendation regarding 'retreat and resettlement', expressed in the language of defeat and displacement, counteracted the fierce attachment that many Strathewen residents felt and continue to feel to their homes. It threatened not only the continued occupation of the properties in question but also all the history, social relationships and dreams of the future that were inextricably caught up with living in the bush. But the strongest push to rebuild came from outside the bushfire zone, from the governments of the day.

In looking back at the immediate response by government to the fires, I wondered why the emphasis on rebuilding was so strong. The commitment to rebuild was intended to bring comfort and support to survivors, but I think it was also a political statement intended for the broader Australian community, for the power of the bush as a 'place' extends far beyond the bushfire zone.

Many urban Victorians feel a strong attachment to the bush, fostered through visits but also through cultural representations of the landscape as integral to Australian character. Victorians visit the bush, walk in it, take holidays in it, photograph it, paint pictures of it and perhaps dream of living in it someday, but it is more than simply a landscape or a destination. 'The Bush' is intricately woven into many people's understanding of what it means to be Australian. It is not, of course, the only way in which Australians associate their identity with place. The beach, the northern rainforests and the Red Centre are also important constructs in many Australians' identification as Australians. It is, however, one with which perceived national characteristics – egalitarianism, mateship, self-reliance and anti-authoritarianism, among others – are strongly associated. In a society that is increasingly global, the *idea* of the bush is unequivocally local, an antidote to cultural homogenisation.

This is the case even – or, perhaps, especially – for urban Australians. Graeme Davison has argued that the 'Bush' myth was a creation of an urban intelligentsia and had its origins in the city rather than in 'rural folk culture'.⁴³ This was reflected in the oral history interviews, where the people who used 'the bush' as a descriptor of their home tended to be those who did not make their living from the land. In contrast Rae Tully, one of the last farmers in Strathewen, insisted that she and her husband lived in *the country. We don't live in the bush. We have bush on our property but we don't live in it.*⁴⁴ Rae regarded the bush as a physical environment, where others regarded it as both a physical and an emotional, social or philosophical environment.

Davison has more recently written that the legend of The Bush 'no longer offers a sustaining myth for an urbanised, multicultural, post-colonial Australia'.⁴⁵ Catastrophic bushfire, however, is an event far beyond the imaginings of our cosmopolitan world. It just doesn't fit into the conceptual framework of an urbanised postmodern society in which nature is firmly under control. So when the environment no longer plays within the rules we are used to, perhaps we turn to older ways of seeing the world. Just as the bushfires led to identification with traditional gender roles, I think Black Saturday – perhaps paradoxically – reinvigorated an Australian identity based on our relationship with a uniquely Australian environment, complete with all the dangers it brings with it.

Motivated by Black Saturday, Grace Moore has recently begun to explore the literary role of Australian bushfire. Her preliminary results encompass a diverse range of sources such as English novels, Australian poetry, H.G. Wells' observations of the Canberra fires in 1939 and John Howard's remarks after the Canberra fires of 2003.

---

43 Graeme Davison, "Sydney and the Bush: An Urban Context for the Australian Legend," *Historical Studies* 18, no. 71 (1978): 192.
44 Rae Tully, Interview 16 October 2013.
45 Graeme Davison, "Rethinking the Australian Legend," *Australian Historical Studies* 43, no. 3 (2012): 451.

Tellingly, they point to 'a sense of collective identity that encompasses tragedy, loss, heroism, mutual support, neighbourliness and rebuilding'.[46] All of these themes were expressed in media stories, politicians' speeches, books and oral histories about Black Saturday. In an echo of the original proponents of The Bush, they make explicit links between the Australian bush and the best qualities of the Australian people.

These works connect our identity with a sense of place, but the buyback scheme is the ultimate negation of 'place'. It says, in effect, that people should not have been living there and they should not go back. I think the Government's commitment to rebuild was a statement of reassurance to all of us that our relationship with the bush could be restored, and along with it the founding myths of Australian identity. The message behind 'We will rebuild' is that we *can* rebuild, and we have the right to be here. It is not surprising that the Brumby government, after the heart-stirring rhetoric of 'brick by brick', was unable to endorse the recommendation and that it took a new government with more distance from the emotional turmoil of the aftermath to adopt the measure.

The buyback scheme attempted to define the limits of the relationship between people and the environment, acknowledging that, in some places on some days, nature cannot be controlled. The emphasis on rebuilding short-circuited a reappraisal of our relationship with the bush both in terms of safety, which was the Royal Commission's primary concern, and in terms of our national character. I think the commitment to rebuild was an attempt to answer, in the affirmative, the question that Manning Clark originally posed and Graeme

---

46 Grace Moore, "Fires, Literature, Politics and Mateship in the Bush," *Agora* 48, no. 4 (2013): 58.

THE HARD HAT: PLACE, HOME AND REBUILDING

Davison has suggested still needs to be answered. It is often expressed as an existential question of settler Australia and its relationship with Indigenous peoples and their land, but it might just as well apply to the specific houses, farms and acreages surrounded by bush that make up urban enclaves in the bush like Strathewen. 'Do we belong here?'[47]

I confess that originally this chapter ended with the previous sentence. It's a nice little trick, to finish with an unanswerable question, but the issue of place and belonging deserves more than a cute literary flourish. I have been thinking about the Royal Commission's 'retreat and resettlement' recommendation and how it is based on assumptions about the ways that people choose to live. In Australia, the choice that many of us make is to invest a lot of our time, effort, money and emotion in a permanent home and its contents, even when it is situated in a danger zone. The natural tendency of people everywhere to believe – to want to believe – that catastrophes will not happen, or will not happen again, adds an extra dimension of risk. The result is fundamentally at odds with the extreme and cyclical nature of the bushfire environment.

One option is to decide, as the Royal Commision did, that homes should not be built in certain places, but there are other choices. Many people have rebuilt with designs, materials and survival plans better suited to life in a high-risk area. Others have kept their homes and their fire plans as they were before but added last-refuge fire bunkers, acknowledging the possibility of losing a house but determined not to lose a life. But I keep returning to the idea of the 'ephemeral house' in Christine Hansen and Tom Griffiths' book *Living with Fire*.[48] In

---

47 Davison, "Rethinking the Australian Legend," 450.
48 Christine Hansen and Tom Griffiths, *Living with Fire* (Melbourne: CSIRO Publishing, 2012), 142.

Steels Creek, a small community on the opposite side of the Kinglake Ranges that was devastated to the same degree as Strathewen, Dave Gormly and Sally Ferres replaced their conventional home with a light wooden house fashioned from portable schoolrooms. It is, essentially, undefendable – one could even say that, like the mountain ash forests that overlook it, it has evolved to burn.

Dave and Sally's house suggest a dramatically different approach to rebuilding in the bushfire zone, one that not only challenges the established practices of building a defensible home but also the whole idea of how to live in a high-risk area. If there's a good chance that your house and its contents are likely to be destroyed, sooner or later, perhaps you are less likely to cling to material possessions. Perhaps, as Tom Griffiths put it, you value 'a society that invests instead in social and intellectual capital, in the sinews and fabric of community'.[49] And perhaps that existential question can be rephrased into one that not only has an answer but many answers, each as unique as the specific environment it relates to: 'How do we live so that we *can* belong here?'

---

49 Tom Griffiths, "The Language of Catastrophe: Forgetting, Blaming and Bursting into Colour," *Griffith Review* 35(2012).

Chapter 8

THE CHIMNEY: CONCLUSIONS

The Black Saturday chimney stands in the Forest Gallery, Museum Victoria's living display of Victorian flora and fauna. The seven-metre-high brick chimney was once part of The Uplands, a homestead in Kinglake just up the mountain from Strathewen. Built in the 1890s by the Lawrey family, The Uplands had been unoccupied for a number of years but it had been known as a gathering place for social and sporting events. The homestead was destroyed by the East Kilmore bushfire after the wind change drove the fire back through Strathewen and up into Kinglake and the neighbouring communities of Kinglake West, Pheasant Creek and Flowerdale. Thirty-eight people died in Kinglake.

The chimney was identified as a possible museum acquisition in March of 2009, soon after the fires and in the early days of the Victorian Bushfires Collection. Grocon, a major construction firm, had been contracted by the state Government to clear the sites of destroyed homes. Starting in early March, over the following four months they levelled nearly 3000 properties and cleared almost 400,000 tons of material. In June 2009 the owner of The Uplands, Mr Major Gill, Grocon and Museum Victoria formed a partnership to preserve the chimney. In only two days, working in a site contaminated with ash,

Figure 10. Chimney (bushfire-affected). Victorian Bushfires Collection, Museum Victoria HT 23963.

Image: Jon Augier. Source: Museum Victoria.

THE CHIMNEY: CONCLUSIONS

soot and asbestos, staff from the museum and Grocon numbered, dismantled, cleaned and packed each of the 1500 bricks. Within a week of being identified, the chimney was ready to be transported to Museum Victoria to be reassembled as a permanent exhibit.

The chimney now stands at the top of the path that winds up through the Forest Gallery. Its slender height echoes the vertical trunks of the eucalypts that surround and dwarf it. When there are not classes of schoolchildren clustered around, listening to the story of how bushfire is an integral part of Victoria's environmental and social history, it is a quiet spot dominated by birdsong. On the anniversary of Black Saturday, it is often a focus for survivors and the families and friends of victims to reflect on the events of that day. For many visitors it provides a place of quiet contemplation, a memorial as well as an artefact.

A chimney is a powerful symbol of the relationship between fire and the European presence in Australia. Part of its power comes from the recognition of a paradox: the hearth that contains and controls fire, making it serve the needs of people, is often the last remaining evidence of a building destroyed by uncontrolled fire. But I think that mostly it is because the hearth is the heart of the house and represents the lives, the relationships and the stories that are lived out around it. For many people, it is the symbol of home. In 1983 Zelma and John Gartner lived on their property in Mount Macedon while the ruins of their house were cleared after Ash Wednesday. Many years later Zelma said that the single worst day was when the workers demolished the chimney still standing in the ashes of their home. *That was when I knew it was really gone.*[1]

---

1   Interview, Zelma Gartner, 24 March 2011.

The Black Saturday chimney moves the story beyond Strathewen to include other areas affected in February of 2009. The Kilmore East fire that swept through Strathewen killed 119 people in total and devastated many other settlements, but it was not the only fire. In the fire season of 2008–2009, the Country Fire Authority (CFA) attended 16,103 fires; the firefighters at the Department of Sustainability and Environment (DSE), who are responsible for fires on public land including national parks, answered calls for 825 bushfires. By the time Black Saturday arrived, they had already been fighting fires for a fortnight, and would do so for another three weeks. On the day itself the CFA responded to 632 incidents; the DSE reported 117 active fires. Of these, the Royal Commission investigated 15 large fires that caused loss of life or major damage. In addition to the Kilmore East conflagration, 40 people died in the Murrindindi fire, eleven in the Churchill fire, two in Beechworth-Mudgegonga and one person in Bendigo.[2]

What happened in Strathewen during the fire and in the years after was the result of a unique combination of geography, history, social relations and individual personalities as well as environmental factors, weather conditions, the breakdown of emergency services and sheer bad luck on the day. There is nowhere quite like Strathewen, but there are still valuable lessons for all of us in what happened there.

From the people who told their stories, this is what I have learned.

The jack

The last 60 years have brought great changes to Strathewen. On Black Friday in 1939, almost all of the bushfire victims were sawmill

---

2   Ibid., 235.

workers and their families, who had few options about where to live. Now most people who live in the urban-bush interface do so by choice: hobby farmers rub shoulders with the descendants of the old settlers; retirees embracing a superannuation-funded tree-change are neighbours with people doing it tough. The physical stretching of the urban boundaries, the growing emphasis on the bush as a lifestyle choice and the greater reach of city amenities means that there is now a thick overlay of European structures, both physical and cultural, on a landscape that evolved without them. Strathewen is an example of what happens when those physical and cultural constructions collide with the extreme of environmental evolution, a force of almost unimaginable destructive power.

More people live in high-risk zones and fewer of them have experience, either their own or transmitted through generations, of bushfire. With expanding populations, the continuing appeal of living in the bush and the increased frequency of drought, extreme conditions and catastrophic bushfire due to climate change, this pattern will intensify.

The map

More people will be affected by bushfire, but there is no single experience that all will share. Even within the tiny geographic area covered by this book, there was great variation in what people saw, felt, decided, did, endured and survived. We rightly extend great sympathy to people who lost family, friends or homes, and to those who faced the terror of a catastrophic bushfire, but everyone was affected. Even those we count as 'lucky' – who lived below the fire line, or got out before the fire hit, or successfully defended their homes, or have rebuilt meaningful lives – will be dealing with the social, emotional and financial consequences of Black Saturday for many years to come. Everyone in the bushfire zone, to one degree or another, is burnt.

The Poetry Tree

How and what we choose to remember helps to determine how we shape the future. The Poetry Tree created a past vision of Strathewen as close-knit, supportive and at one with nature, thereby paving the way for a similar vision of Strathewen's future. It memorialised positive attributes and ignored unwise decisions, horrific deaths, suicide and community discord. It blurred our understanding of the event and removed any sense of personal responsibility from the victims.

But this is how we cope: the full tale of catastrophe, with all the mistakes, conflict, bad behaviour and failure that inevitably happen, is not what memorials tell. Instead, they tell the story that makes it possible for people to keep going. We just have to remember – especially when reminded by those whose experiences contradict the harmonising narrative – that it is not the whole story. Histories can and must offer a different account, one that is deeper, harder and more complicated.

The posters

Outsiders like us pass judgement on survivors of disaster in many ways: in the money we donate; the help we offer; the sympathy we extend; the stories we pay attention to. In the experience of many survivors, the generosity and kindness of strangers made it possible to face a difficult future. The reaction within the bushfire community to displays of generosity and kindness from outsiders was gratitude and the sense that they were connected to and supported by the rest of the world.

We also pass judgement when we donate useless junk, deny the impact of the fires on people, fail to listen to stories of conflict or failure, or treat struggling survivors as whingers and bludgers. As the posters from Helen's Place attest, this has also been the experience of some survivors. The reaction to words and actions that trivialised, dismissed or exploited their experience was anger, isolation and the erection of protective barriers between bushfire survivors and the rest of society. In the complex world of bushfire recovery, it is possible for people to feel both gratitude and anger, community and isolation, support and exploitation.

For those of us outside the bushfire zone, our reactions to survivors pass judgement on ourselves. We respond to stories of bushfire experiences in ways that serve our own needs and support our own narratives, whether through aligning ourselves with 'true Aussie courage' and resilience or through denial, cynicism and a sense of superiority.

The mobile phone

In the time after Black Saturday, many different narratives emerged about the fires and their aftermath. Story-telling and testimony helped survivors to make sense of what had happened and to regain a feeling of control over their lives. Their stories were concerned with the future as well as the past, and helped to frame and support decisions made during and after the fires.

Although narratives themselves have a beginning, a middle and an end, the story is never finished. It is a constantly evolving process in which attitudes change, perspectives are rearranged and decisions made or unmade. A narrative tells us only what is true for a person at one moment in time.

Story-telling by definition depends on a relationship between the narrator and the audience. Public testimony, whether it is through oral history, videos, digital story-telling or any number of other media, tells a personal history that is influenced by and influences public thinking. The testimony of bushfire survivors helps to create a public history that complicates and enriches our understanding of bushfire.

Story-telling overlaps history-making but it is not quite the same thing. When curators and other historians work with testimony, along with other sources, to make history, we must collect and interpret multiple accounts, explore their complex and contradictory meanings and create multivalent histories about the past, and its life in the present, of individuals and communities.

The chook

Bushfire planning and response is one of the most gendered areas of activity in Australia. Historically men have been responsible for the protection of property and, especially since 1983, for the active defence of individual homes. The act of 'staying and defending' has become inextricably mixed with ideas of masculinity, making it difficult either for women to have a voice in bushfire decisions, or for men to pursue alternative courses of action. On Black Saturday, some decisions to stay and defend (or to stay and be defended) were made not according to an assessment of risk and preparedness but according to gendered emotional concerns and relationship dynamics. This probably contributed to the high death toll, especially of women and children.

Policies and education programs have changed since 2009 and now emphasise the dangers of staying to defend, the need for more than one fit, capable and trained person to mount a successful defence, the wisdom of evacuating vulnerable people, and the conditions under which no defence should be attempted. Although the word 'gender' is unlikely ever to appear in public material, the changes indicate a shift from dominant masculine concerns to a more balanced, more gender-aware approach to bushfire planning.

The hard hat

Many people lived in Strathewen out of a strong affinity for it as a place, yet everyone defined this place differently. Sometimes it was described according to environmental or aesthetic values, sometimes according to historical associations, while other people defined it in the context of a working relationship with the land. The bushfires tested attachment to place, in some cases strengthening the emotional commitment to Strathewen and in other cases rupturing the relationship.

The debate about whether or not to rebuild after Black Saturday revealed the fragility of settlement in the bushfire zone but it was also a micro-version of a larger debate of where we, as a settler society, really belong. Support for rebuilding was strong outside the bushfire zone not just out of concern for survivors but also to reassure ourselves that we can make our own place in this country. In providing this support and reassurance, we managed to avoid uncomfortable questions of the conflict between the bush and an urban lifestyle, about the reasonable limits of settlement and about learning to adapt our desires and expectations to our environment.

The chimney

As a chimney from a single homestead reflects the larger experience, the stories told in and about Strathewen reflect Victoria's – and, by extension, Australia's – engagement with the bush and with bushfire. It has occurred to me that each statement about bushfire is like a brick from the chimney and, having dismantled the oral histories and examined them, my task now is to try to put them back together into something that, like the chimney, will help us to reflect on our relationship with bushfire.

The most significant discovery was the extent to which cultural attitudes inside and outside the bushfire zone interacted and helped to shape each other. This is a recurring theme in almost all of the interviews, whether we were talking of the fires, memorials, gender, hierarchies of suffering or decisions around rebuilding. What we say and do on one side has an impact on the other, regardless of whether we are the burnt or the unburnt. The debate about how to live with bushfire is not just the concern of people who live in the bushfire zone, or those whose job it is to defend them. Although there was in Strathewen a clear line where the fire stopped, with scorched earth on one side and untouched vegetation on the other, there is no such line in social relations.

The stories told about and by survivors elicit sorrow, horror and sympathy and influence our understanding of ourselves as a nation. They feed into a national mythology of endurance, resilience and generosity of spirit. This can be both a source of strength and a great burden for survivors who are expected to live up to these ideals, especially when doing so in the public gaze. The stereotype of the bushfire survivor may be one of stoic resilience and hardy self-sufficiency, but all of the people interviewed here were aware of and were affected both positively and negatively by the reactions of the public.

By choosing which stories we as outsiders value, which ones we pay attention to and reward (and those we ignore or dismiss), we reinforce certain ways of thinking and behaving in the bushfire zone. This is communicated through laws, policy and funding but is also apparent in what we value and how we define ourselves as both individuals and as a nation.

Tom Griffiths wrote, 'These bushfire towns – where the material legacy of the past can never survive for long – need to work harder than most to renew their historical consciousness. The greatest challenge of fire research is cultural.'[3] I was surprised to discover that the culture that needs the hard questions about bushfire is not the world of the survivors but our own world outside the bushfire zone. A lot of the time I think we choose to listen to bushfire stories that serve our own purposes, whether that is a national myth, a romantic vision of the bush, the desire to be associated with qualities like resilience and determination, or the dubious thrill of vicariously experiencing the adrenalin of the moment. We celebrate drama and heroics but not the quiet evacuations that also saved lives. We support decisions to stay and defend or to rebuild without asking if these are wise decisions. We praise those people who appear to recover quickly and criticise or question those who do not.

Bushfire stories that tell only of strength and resilience, of community building and of a renewed relationship with the bush are a source of pride, but I think they discourage us from asking difficult

---

3   Tom Griffiths, "'An Unnatural Disaster'? Remembering and Forgetting Bushfire," *History Australia* 6, no. 2 (2009): 35.5.

questions. As a final evocation of the military analogy, I think our attitude to bushfire before Black Saturday paralleled the mythologising of the Gallipoli campaign, a mythology in which there was no room for fear, doubt or criticism. Just over one hundred years after the landing at Anzac Cove, we are creating a more complicated and difficult – but richer and more human – history of war that incorporates not only fear, doubt and criticism, but love and sorrow. I hope that this book will help to change the conversation about bushfire and show that it too is far more complex than we have previously admitted. This new bushfire story is as concerned with ideas like home, masculinity and memory – not just the fact of remembering but how and what we choose to remember – as it is with fire danger ratings and education programs.

We need to listen to stories that reflect thoughtfully on the past and the future, not just the ones that quicken the pulse and give a shiver down the back, and describe many different ways of living in and with the bush. In that way we may be better prepared when the next catastrophic bushfire comes. If we do not do so, we risk repeating the events of Black Saturday – and that will be the greatest tragedy of all. As Rae Tully told me at the end of her interview, *you can't just live here and say, 'Isn't this nice?' That's not the end of the story.*[4]

---

[4] Rae Tully, Interview 16 October 2013.

Chapter 9

THE BACK STORY

Why am I doing this? I imagine it is a question that every historian asks herself at some point but the question has a particular resonance when the topic involves death, pain and other people's loss.

I spent 2010 working as a curator for Museum Victoria in an intensive collecting project to document the Black Saturday bushfires, the most fatal fires in Victoria's history. As most Victorians know, Black Saturday of 2009 was the latest in a long line of catastrophic bushfires documented since the early years of the colony of Victoria. Bushfire – a quintessentially Australian word for a phenomenon known elsewhere in the world as wildfire – is one of the defining features of life in southeastern Australia. Stephen Pyne, the leading international authority on wildfire, calls Australia 'the fire continent' and argues that it is one of three places on earth where fire has shaped and continues to dominate the relationship between people and the environment.[1]

Victoria is, in many ways, the epicentre of bushfire. Our state accounts for three quarters of the deaths and more than half of the economic losses due to bushfire. We give the big ones names – Black Thursday, Red Tuesday, Ash Wednesday – but nearly every summer has its share of bushfire events.

---

1   Pyne, *Burning Bush: A Fire History of Australia.*

BLACK SATURDAY

Within weeks of Black Saturday, Museum Victoria established the Victorian Bushfires Collection to preserve objects and oral histories connected to the state's history of bushfire. Although it was the first time the museum had specifically identified bushfire as a collecting theme, the collection fit in well with existing collecting areas of rural life and sustainable futures. In 2010, realising that a lot of the evidence of Black Saturday – both material and in people's memories – could change or be lost over time, the museum assigned two curators, Rebecca Carland and myself, to work with Liza Dale-Hallett, the Senior Curator of Sustainable Futures and founding curator of the Bushfires Collection. Our task was to bring into the collection as many objects and oral histories as possible that documented the many faces of this event: the fire itself, the emergency response, the aftermath, the recovery efforts and the ongoing challenges.

I was thrilled to get the job. I had spent several years working with groups of people, especially migrants, to develop museum exhibitions about their communities. Many of them had experienced trauma on their way to Australia, and emotional and cultural upheavals during their time here. I knew the power of objects to illuminate and communicate stories that are otherwise too painful to tell, and the validation that comes to people whose experience is for the first time acknowledged and included in the public record. Here was a chance to put my skills to work on a much larger scale. It was also, if truth be told, a chance to still the small voice inside me saying that I, an urban Melburnian, could have done more to help those people caught up in the inferno.

So with a mix of anticipation at the professional challenges and a hope that the work would be meaningful to both the survivors and the larger public, we embarked on a whirlwind year. The material we collected was both pitiful and profound: slumped glass; puddles of melted aluminium; the ruined remains of a home and its contents; defiant expressions of survival in the form of signs, poems, bumper stickers; oral histories that recounted hair-raising escapes or heartbreaking loss, determination and resilience or anger and bitterness. It was emotional stuff.

For a year, the three curators lived in a highly charged atmosphere; the air crackled around us. It was as if an invisible force-field separated us from the rest of the department, and the department's acquisition meetings fell silent when we presented our meagre objects: handknitted socks; burned farming tools; a melted plastic bucket. We were in the presence of death, and the pathetic had become sacred.

I was an experienced story-teller, so it was not difficult to shape such raw – in both senses of the word – material into descriptions and narratives that elicited sorrow, admiration and outrage. At public talks, I retold these stories and people invariably were moved, frequently to tears. But at the same time I was aware that the emotional response was the easy one. There are cheap laughs, but also cheap tears. (Amos Goldbloom put it more elegantly when writing of people's fascination with Holocaust testimony, calling it 'pleasurable identification with human suffering'.[2]) I had an uncomfortable suspicion that in some ways we were just a more highly educated version of rubber-neckers at the scene of a car crash. Perhaps we were both encouraging and then satisfying an appetite for the vicarious thrill of witnessing someone else's terror. Adrenalin, even at second or third hand, is a powerful drug.

---

2 Amos Goldbloom, "The Victim's Voice and Melodramatic Aesthetics in History," *History and Theory* 48(2009): 229.

The short time frame of the collecting project, our proximity to the event ('recovery' was, for many people, still a distant and fragile concept) and the space limitations of museum interpretation strategies did not allow a closer, more nuanced examination of the effects of the bushfires on people and communities. Six months after the completion of my contract, and nearly two and a half years after Black Saturday, I wanted to revisit the stories, examine the objects more closely, and follow the paths they suggested to some kind of better understanding of how the experience of bushfire has affected both the individuals and the society in which they live. This book is the result.

Methodology

There has been an enormous amount written about Black Saturday, from vivid accounts of what happened during the fire to detailed analysis of institutional responses to the massive Final Report of the Royal Commission into the 2009 Victorian Bushfires. I tried a different approach that is less focused on 'what really happened' and more on how survivors have told their stories and what this means both for those who tell the stories and those who listen to them. I used bushfire objects as literary devices to provide entry points into those stories, both in terms of organising the chapters in this book and also in the oral histories themselves, which frequently revolved around objects – lost, found and transformed – that conveyed bushfire experiences.

I am aware of the irony of examining an event noted for its destruction by starting with the objects it left behind. This is partly because my involvement with bushfire survivors started with collecting objects, although the oral histories soon became the main historical sources with which I worked. But I also chose this approach because survivors expressed complex, often contradictory attitudes to material culture, from regarding the shattered remnants of possessions as precious relics holding memories of great loss to embracing the chance to begin again without the burden of 'stuff'. It suggested to me that, for many bushfire survivors, objects – through their presence or absence, or their transformation through fire – are important symbols of their experiences. I thought I might be able to use similar objects on a larger scale, as starting points to explore ideas about Black Saturday, and to see if the stories they inspire might show not only how people in the bushfire zone but also outsiders like me respond to bushfire.

The objects opened many perspectives into the life of Strathewen. Some of them stretch back to early years of European settlement; others are more focused on life after the fires. For all of them, Black Saturday is part of the story they tell but it is not the only or even at times the most important story. At the time that each of these objects was collected, I conducted oral histories with the donors and other interested parties. I revisited those interviews and added to them with follow-up interviews and interviews with new narrators, supplemented by primary and secondary research.

In the original collecting project as well as in the new research, I met the narrators through a variety of avenues, including communication with the Strathewen Community Renewal Association, the local organisation largely responsible for dealing with the aftermath of the bushfire. Most people, however, came to the project through word of mouth and personal recommendations from other Strathewen residents. I often heard the words, 'You really need to talk to -' and this was usually followed up by an offer to introduce me to that person. Some people immediately agreed to the interview, while others spent a long time deciding whether or not to be involved, especially debating whether it was the right time and I the right person to be trusted with their stories. There was also significant 'story fatigue' as Strathewen, along with so many bushfire-affected places, had had significant exposure through the media. Some people declined and others eventually agreed, some of them only after two or more years of conversation and getting to know me.

This means that the people whose stories are told here are not representative of all Strathewen. I was careful to speak to as wide a range of people as possible based on both background and fire experience. The interviews included newcomers and long-time residents, farmers and urban workers, the politicised and the unenfranchised, those who stayed and those who evacuated, those who have rebuilt and those who have not, those who have been deeply involved in community rebuilding and those who have focused on their personal concerns.

There are gaps. I am particularly aware of the absence of young adults and the parents of young children. Although several families were approached on my behalf, none wished to take part. I can only speculate why they did not do so but possible reasons include lack of time, the priorities of their children's wellbeing or simply lack of interest. I was reminded time and again that this study, while important to me and the museum, did not carry the same urgency for people who had a daunting list of difficult problems to resolve.

I was aware that by the double process of self-selection and personal reference I was in danger of talking only to people whose stories represented an interpretation of events that was acceptable to the wider group. There was, however, a small number of people who were outside the tight social structure of Strathewen and who agreed to be interviewed. These are the outliers, the ones whose stories disrupt and challenge. Some of them contacted me directly upon hearing of the museum's collecting project, while others were introduced through community workers. None was immediately willing to participate but most of them eventually agreed to take part.

Before each interview, the narrator and I talked about our own backgrounds, the purpose of the project, and the role of the museum. We agreed on rules of engagement: what was 'on the table', especially when it came to stories of death and horror, and what was out of bounds; strategies for dealing with difficult emotions, both during and after the interview; the implications of creating a public record, as these interviews have become, especially in regard to accusations of illegal activity, and the rights of the narrator.

The oral histories were semi-structured in nature, in that I started out with a list of topics that I thought would be valuable to discuss, but they were only starting points for the conversation. In reality the interviews took many different paths, determined not only by the particular experiences of the narrator but also by the limitations of what they were willing to talk about. In addition to grounding the interviews in the life histories of each person, we covered the early history of Strathewen as passed down through the settler families; changes in the settlement in the last few decades; individual stories of the fire on Black Saturday (although for some people this was out of bounds); the difficulties of 'recovery'; the lessons learned or not learned, and the future of Strathewen.

Stories ranged from uplifting visions of a more caring future to bitter recriminations and accusations of dishonesty. They revealed some of the everyday realities of life in Strathewen before Black Saturday – lifestyle choices, farming practices, bushfire planning, neighbourhood relations – as well as the drama and difficulties endured since that day. They captured resolve, faith, anger, despair, joy, regret, fear and hope, as well as how many people you need to defend a house from a major bushfire and why you should not rely on an electric pump for firefighting.

I started to look for explanations of such varied and at times opposing interpretations of the meaning of Black Saturday, and the significance of these interpretations to the narrators themselves, the community and the larger society. I began to identify certain themes: gender relations; a sense of place; the need to justify decisions made after the fire; the struggle for power; the influence of the public gaze. These are all concerned with the social and emotional consequences of bushfire rather than with issues of its prevention or mitigation.

It was only in the final stages of this project that I was made aware that these themes are as much a product of my own interests as they are of the oral histories. My first awareness, apart from media reports, of Strathewen's experience through Black Saturday had been through a reference to the Poetry Tree. The tree intrigued me because it was concerned with words and, like most historians, I love words and am comfortable with them. I was attracted to the resilience and – let's face it – the romance of writing poetry in the midst of devastation. My first interviews in Strathewen were with the people who started the Poetry Tree and in their stories I heard affirmation of my own ideas about the power and comfort of words. These were things that, in the words of Charles Hardy, I had brought with me into the interview; I was 'calling into existence those stories of mutual concern'.[3] It took the introduction of opposing views from other people in Strathewen to awaken me to the contested role of the Poetry Tree and not only to record dissenting voices but to revisit those original interviews looking for more complicated messages.

This is not a conventional history. It is highly subjective, although what history is not?[4] Some people will think there is way too much of myself here, and too much emphasis on the dynamics between survivors and the world outside the bushfire zone. Others will be disappointed with the stories I tell, or dismayed by what they see as a focus on the negative: on community conflict; on division both before and after the fire, and on stories that do not tell a comforting narrative of recovery. It is perhaps part of the subversive heritage of oral history that it often focuses on the margins, where the stories of those who do not conform to the dominant narratives of mainstream culture can be most clearly heard. But it may be that this marginal focus will also reveal ideas and experiences that add to our understanding of Black Saturday, and offer some people the chance to become part of the public record.

Language

There are a couple of important points about language. Throughout the bushfire zone there is an unspoken agreement to keep the word 'victim' for those who died as a result of the fires, and to refer to

---

3   Charles Hardy, "A People's History of Industrial Philadelphia: Reflections on Community Oral History Projects and Uses of the Past," *Oral History Review (USA)* 33, no. 1 (2006): 4.

4   Since at least 1970 it has been argued that 'there are as many historical philosophies as there are historians; in other words, all history is subjective'. (H. Steele Commager, "Is There a 'Philosophy of History'?" In *Mind, Science, and History*, ed. Howard Evans Kiefer and Milton Karl Munitz. (Albany: State University of New York Press 1970), 304.)

everyone else as 'survivors'. I have respected this convention. I have also tried to avoid using the word 'community' to describe contemporary Strathewen, unless it is qualified as the view of a particular narrator. This creates some challenges in writing, as Strathewen is too small to be described as a village or a town (and 'hamlet' sounds rather twee) but it is an important distinction. Fairbrother *et al* have written about the 'conceptual murkiness and political baggage' of the word 'community', especially in relation to bushfire, and said that 'simply inhabiting the same space does not necessarily or automatically foster a sense of community, and so locality and community should not be conflated'.[5] Some of the narrators in this book would object to the assumption, implicit in the idea of community, that they share the values and attitudes of some of the other Strathewen residents.

Although it has become common to use the term 'wildfire' in the Australian context, my narrators were unanimous and adamant that we talk about 'bushfire'.[6] They insisted that 'wildfire' was an Americanism, and that Australian language must be used to describe Australian phenomena. I have kept to this request but it does raise the additional issue of how to differentiate between what might be described as 'normal' bushfires and events like Black Saturday (which is itself, for some survivors, a problematic term). There is no Richter scale for bushfires, nor is there a category rating such as for cyclones or hurricanes. We have the Forest Fire Danger Index (FFDI) which,

---

5 Peter Fairbrother et al., "Creating "Community"? Preparing for Bushfire in Rural Victoria," *Rural Sociology* 78, no. 2 (2013): 188.

6 For definitions of 'wildfire' and 'bushfire', which are considered to be the same thing, see Rural and Land Management Group, "Bushfire Glossary," (Melbourne: Australian Fire and Emergency Services Authorities Council, 2012). The use of 'wildfire' is, I think, a move by fire researchers to establish common ground in international research.

THE BACK STORY

as its name indicates, rates the risk of a bushfire occurring, but there is no nomenclature to describe its destructive power once it commences.

The most common description used by survivors of Black Saturday in Strathewen was to compare it to a nuclear holocaust. The term is no exaggeration: Kevin Tolhurst, a fire behaviour expert for the Victorian Country Fire Authority, testified to the Royal Commission in 2009 that the Black Saturday fires, in the space of a single day, released an amount of energy 1500 times that of the nuclear bomb dropped on Hiroshima. Both Stephen Pyne and Tom Griffiths have used the term 'holocaust fire' to describe those once-in-a-generation fires that burn deep into the ground and are so intense that it may be decades before regeneration even begins.[7] It was commonly used in Australian newspaper accounts of major fires. Black Friday in 1939, Ash Wednesday in 1983, Black Saturday in 2009: these were all 'holocaust fires'.[8]

The term, however, raised concerns among some of my colleagues as an appropriation of a word that has become irrevocably attached to the Shoah of World War II. I read into this reaction a concern that perhaps those who use it to describe bushfire are de-valuing the significance of 'holocaust' by meaning any event with significant loss of life. It is, however, a reference to the original understanding of 'holocaust'. The oldest meaning of the word, according to the Oxford English Dictionary, is 'a sacrifice wholly consumed by fire' and one of

---

7   Tom Griffiths, "We Have Still Not Lived Long Enough," *Inside Story*, no. 16 February (2009). Pyne, *Burning Bush: A Fire History of Australia*.

8   The earliest newspaper use of 'holocaust' I have found comes from the bushfires of 1898 (*Alexandra and Yea Standard*, 25 January 1898) and it was commonly used for coverage of each of the major fires.

the established meanings is still 'complete consumption by fire'.[9] Yet the word has become identified with an event of such magnitude and impact that any other use of it – even without the capitalisation – can raise concerns and obscure the issues.

Tom Griffiths has suggested using the word 'firestorm' to distinguish between ordinary bushfires and those like Ash Wednesday or Black Saturday.[10] It is an effective description, and one that resonates in its conflation of Black Saturday with the bombing of Dresden in World War II. I am hesitant to use it, for personal and possibly unprofessional reasons.

One of my earliest bushfire interviews was with Zelma Gartner, who survived the 1983 Ash Wednesday bushfires in Mount Macedon. Zelma used the word 'firestorm' to describe a specific phenomenon that happens during a major bushfire: the moment when super-heated gases in the atmosphere ignite without the presence of solid fuel, making it appear as though the air itself is burning. Her description of that moment was, according to her account, disbelieved by the scientists and researchers who investigated the bushfires, and the experience left her feeling patronised and belittled – a feeling that persisted for nearly 30 years and permeated our interviews. The scientific disbelief was not limited to Zelma's account. Basing their conclusions on data gathered from smaller, cooler fires, researchers in the 1980s dismissed eyewitness accounts of firestorms, fireballs and exploding houses, all of which were witnessed in the Black Saturday fires. It will take a few more years before I can use the word 'firestorm' with an alternative meaning without conjuring up Zelma's indignation and disapproval. For that reason I have adopted

---

9   Oxford English Dictionary online edition June 2015 *s.v.* holocaust.
10   Hansen and Griffiths, *Living with Fire*, 72.

the word used by the New South Wales Fire Service for the highest degree of danger: catastrophic.

And if the descriptors for bushfire have proved problematic, there is the whole question of the expression 'the bush'. From the breast-beating nationalism of the Sydney school as described by Graeme Davison to Don Watson's piercing, unsentimental analysis of the term and all the baggage it carries, 'the bush' has been a powerful cultural construction in Australia.[11] I am using the expression in the same way as the majority (but not all) of the residents of Strathewen refer to their homes as being in 'the bush' – that is, to describe a forested area beyond the boundaries of an Australian town or city.

Bushfire is deeply embedded in Victorian consciousness and in our culture, which is both shaped by bushfire and shapes the way we think, feel, act and remember about bushfire. That consciousness was renewed on Black Saturday, 7 February 2009. Perhaps the material legacy of Strathewen, as preserved in the Victorian Bushfires Collection at Museum Victoria, will reveal something beyond the disaster itself, something of our cultural assumptions and our complicated relationships with our environment and with each other, and enable us all to make wiser decisions. It is, in the end, the only acceptable reason for why I am doing this.

---

11 Davison, "Sydney and the Bush: An Urban Context for the Australian Legend." Don Watson, *The Bush: Travels in the Heart of Australia* (Penguin Australia, 2014).

ACKNOWLEDGEMENTS

I had just finished a meeting with two women about whether we could do an interview together about the 2009 bushfires. As we were all about to leave, one of them leaned forward and asked, "How do you do it – this job? How do you cope?" I must have looked as astounded as I felt, because on Black Saturday the woman speaking had lost her mother, her brother, her livelihood and her peace of mind, and had struggled for more than a year to get recognition and assistance. And she was asking me how *I* coped?[1]

That was in 2010, at the very beginning of my oral history work with bushfire survivors from Strathewen. Here, nearly ten years later, is the answer to how I did 'this job'.

I was inspired by the survivors with whom I worked, and humbled by their generosity in being part of this project, especially at a time when they were dealing with problems of an immensity that most of us cannot comprehend. They are named individually elsewhere in this book, but I am profoundly grateful for their involvement and hope I have justified their trust.

I had great advisers. Professor Al Thomson, an eminent oral historian and a key supporter of partnerships between Museum Victoria and Monash University, provided essential guidance in both the processes and the analysis of oral histories. I knew I needed someone

---

1   Liza Dale-Hallett, Rebecca Carland and Peg Fraser, "Sites of Memory: The 2009 Victorian Bushfires." In *Museum Theory: An Expanded Field*, ed. Andrea Witcomb and Kylie Message (Oxford: Wiley-Blackwell, 2015).

of his expertise and experience for this project and if he had said no to my request I would not have attempted this project. Dr Richard Gillespie, former Head of Humanities at Museum Victoria, is my former boss. He provided a steady curatorial perspective but also, more crucially, the ability to cut through to the essential questions of contemporary history-making in the museum and out of it. Both of them were constant supporters of the value of this work. I have also benefited from the advice of Dr Bain Attwood and Dr Ruth Morgan at Monash.

I had wonderful colleagues. I particularly acknowledge the pioneering work of Liza Dale-Hallett, Senior Curator of Sustainable Futures and founding curator of the Victorian Bushfires Collection, and that of Rebecca Carland, now the Senior Curator of Collections. For a year the three of us shared adrenalin, exhilaration, grief and black humour. Our efforts put strain on all parts of our department, especially the collection managers and our fellow curators, and I thank them all for their patience and assistance. I am grateful to Museum Victoria for the ongoing support shown by our senior managers and for the receipt of the 1854 Scholarship in 2011. I also thank Nathan Hollier and Monash University Publishing, who took this manuscript and turned it into a real book.

But more than anything else, I could do this job because I knew that Black Saturday was not my story. Unlike the survivors with whom I worked, I did not lose family, friends, pets, house, community or livelihood. At the end of even the worst day, I returned to a beloved home with a large garden full of animals, two happy adult children and my husband, Jules, who would take one look at my face, pour me a glass of wine and say, 'So, tell me about it.' Thank you.

ORAL HISTORY INTERVIEWS

All interviews conducted with the author; those indicated with a registration number were completed when I was a curator for the Victorian Bushfires Collection, Museum Victoria, before commencing this research project.. They are part of Museum Victoria's permanent collection.

Mary Avola, Whittlesea, 29 October 2013.
Lyn (Lewis) Chambers, Wonthaggi, 27 August 2012.
Leslye Chappelle and Fred Bateman, Yan Yean, 27 June 2013.
Robert Crisfield, Hurstbridge., 7 August 2013.
Karen Gardam and Sylvia Shaw, Diamond Creek, 15 September 2010 (HT 27089), 14 March 2013, 27 March 2013.
Zelma Gartner, Balwyn, 16 March 2011 (HT30465), 24 March 2011 (HT30473).
Alison Griffin and Bill Chisholm, Healesville, August 2010 (MM111813).
Joyce and Alan Horne, Strathewen, 27 November 2012.
Jane Hayward, Strathewen, 3 November 2010.
Barbara Joyce, Strathewen, 31 August 2010 (HT26886), 13 February 2013.
Barbara Joyce and Shane Pugh, Strathewen, 13 February 2013.
Helen Legg, Hurstbridge, 25 June 2013.
Helen Legg, Fiona Truscott and June Warburton, Hurstbridge, 23 February 2011 (HT28109).

Angela McKenzie, Strathewen, 20 August 2012.

Ian McKimmie and Rosemary McKimmie Young, Strathewen, 6 October 2010 (HT27093), 18 June 2013.

Vicki Mitchell, Strathewen, 8 August 2012.

Norma and Laurie Nelson, Strathewen, 7 September 2012.

Bronwyn Apted South, Strathewen, 21 November 2012, 5 December 2012.

Darren Thompson, Hurstbridge, 20 August 2013.

Rae and Barrie Tully, Strathewen, 16 October 2013.

Jim Usher, St Andrews, 29 October 2013.

SELECTED READING LIST

A list like this is by definition less than comprehensive. In the interests of keeping it manageable, I have had to jettison many valuable publications, a process that was remarkably painful. As you might expect, in trying to make sense of such a complex and sensitive subject as a fatal bushfire I explored beyond the usual preoccupations of historians, sometimes in unexpected directions. So from a great cauldron of history, psychology, sociology, museum studies, environmental science, oral history, performance practices, community analysis and social work, these are the works that most influenced and challenged my understanding of Strathewen, Black Saturday and its aftermath.

Local history

As in almost any account of a small Australian settlement, the most valuable sources have been the local papers and the work (frequently unpublished or self-published) of family and local historians. I am indebted to Lindsay Mann for his research into early Strathewen and to members of the Horne, McKimmie and Apted families for their stories.

Edwards, D.H. *The Diamond Valley Story*. (Greensborough VIC: Shire of Diamond Valley, 1979).

Mann, Lindsay. *James and John Mann of Arthur's Creek: A Brief History*. (Melbourne: self-published, c2004).

Marshall, Marguerite. *Nillumbik Now and Then*. (Research VIC: All Print Publications, 2008).

Murphy, James. *Early Settlers of Arthurs Creek, Victoria*. (Melbourne: self-published, 1971).

Payne, J.W. *The Plenty: A Centennial History of the Whittlesea Shire*. (Kilmore: Lowden Publishing, 1975).

Bushfire in Australia

I read anything written by Tom Griffiths. I particularly recommend his series of essays which appeared after Black Saturday and were collected in the collaborative book with Christine Hansen, *Living with Fire*. Griffiths' work illuminates the experience of survivors and the effects of fire of Black Saturday on larger society, and his unfailing empathy for survivors gave me a strong (if occasionally discomforting) moral compass when writing about negative or divisive issues.

There are a number of excellent front-line accounts of experiencing Black Saturday, such as those by Peter Stanley and Adrian Hyland, and Karen Kissane's book is a ruthless dissection of what went wrong on Black Saturday. In the immediate aftermath there were collections of emotional stories from survivors and of victims, often published as fund-raising efforts, but the book that mostly closely reflects the social and emotional upheaval that many of the narrators described to me is Robert Kenny's *Gardens of Fire*.

Stephen Pyne's seminal works provide perspectives on the natural and social history of fire along with some pretty searing commentary on how we interact (or fail to) with the splendid but lethal environment of southeastern Australia. The Bushfire Cooperative Research Centre out of Latrobe University has produced important work in their published notes, particularly in the areas of bushfire preparation and societal attitudes. The final report of the Royal Commission into the 2009 Victorian Bushfires provides a valuable record of personal

SELECTED READING LIST

testimonies after Black Saturday but I cannot help feeling that, out of consideration for witnesses' emotional states and respect for the dead, they soft-pedalled some painful but important issues. And, as always, looming in the background is the magnificent work of Judge Leonard Stretton.

I have limited myself to written publications but there are also many other media creations that make significant contributions to our understanding of Australian bushfire and its impact. The films 'Then the Wind Changed' by Celeste Geer and Moira Fahy's painfully honest 'Afterburn' are most relevant to the experience of the Strathewen survivors. You will also find many of the objects mentioned in this book, along with hundreds more objects, photographs and stories of Black Saturday on Museum Victoria's Collections Online website: https://collections.museumvictoria.com.au/search?query=victorian+bushfires+collection.

Fahy, Moira. "Afterburn: In the Tiger's Jaws." Melbourne: One Thousand Productions, 2014.

Gammage, Bill. *The Biggest Estate on Earth : How Aborigines Made Australia*. Crows Nest NSW: Allen & Unwin, 2011.

Geer, Celeste. "Then the Wind Changed." Melbourne: Rebel Films, 2012.

Griffiths, Tom. *Forests of Ash: an Environmental History*. Melbourne: Cambridge University Press, 2001.

Hansen, Christine, and Tom Griffiths. *Living with Fire*. Melbourne: CSIRO Publishing, 2012.

Hyland, Adrian. *Kinglake-350*. Melbourne: Text Publishing, 2011.

Kenny, Robert. *Gardens of Fire: An Investigative Memoir*. Crawley, WA: UWA Publishing, 2013.

Kissane, Karen. *Worst of Days: Inside the Black Saturday Firestorm.* Sydney: Hachette, 2010.

McGourty, John, ed. *Black Saturday: Stories of Love, Loss and Courage from the Victorian Bushfires.* Sydney: Harper Collins, 2009.

Pyne, Stephen. *Burning Bush: A Fire History of Australia.* 2nd ed. Sydney: Allen & Unwin, 1992.

Pyne, Stephen. *Still-Burning Bush.* Carlton VIC: Scribe, 2006.

Stanley, Peter. *Black Saturday at Steels Creek.* Brunswick VIC: Scribe Publications, 2013.

Stretton, Judge Leonard. "Report of the Royal Commission to Inquire into the Causes of and Measures Taken to Prevent the Bush Fires of January 1939." Melbourne: Government Printer, 1939.

Teague, Bernard, *et al.* "2009 Victorian Bushfires Royal Commission Final Report." Melbourne: Parliament of Victoria, 2010.

Usher, Jim, and Mac Gudgeon. *Footsteps in the Ash: The Story of St Andrews and Strathewen in the 2009 Bushfires.* Melbourne: Usher and Gudgeon, 2010.

Wettenhall, R.L. *Bushfire Disaster: An Australian Community in Crisis.* Studies in Australian Society, edited by Grant Harman. Cremorne, NSW: Angus and Robertson, 1975.

Memorials

A number of Australian historians have written about memorials and the original focus on war memorials is now expanding to include other forms of commemoration like roadside memorials. However, I found the most interesting work on the multiple and often conflicting meanings of memorials was being done overseas.

SELECTED READING LIST

'Performativity' – the idea that expressions of loss do not just commemorate an event but play an active role in creating social change – was an important concept for me in trying to understand many aspects of the bushfire's aftermath, especially the Poetry Tree and the naming of the cricket pavilion. It is explored in many of the chapters in *Grassroots Memorials,* in the context of both natural disasters and man-made ones such as the Madrid train bombings.

It is of course impossible to consider memorials without delving into the literature examining commemoration of the Holocaust. This is an enormous field and one I could only sample, but James Young's observations on the role of Holocaust memorials were valuable. So too were Graham Dawson's comments on how memorials to the Irish troubles were more concerned with the future than with the past.

Ashton, Paul, Paula Hamilton, and Rose Searby. *Places of the Heart: Memorials in Australia.* North Melbourne: Australian Scholarly Publishing, 2012.

Dawson, Graham. *Making Peace with the Past? Memory, Trauma and the Irish Troubles.* Manchester: Manchester University Press, 2007.

Inglis, Kenneth Stanley, and Jan Brazier. *Sacred Places: War Memorials in the Australian Landscape.* Carlton: Melbourne University Press, 1998.

Margry, Peter Jan, and Christina Sànchez-Carretero, eds. *Grassroots Memorials: The Politics of Memorialising Traumatic Death.* New York: Berghahn Books, 2011.

Read, Peter. *Returning to Nothing: The Meaning of Lost Places.* Cambridge; Melbourne: Cambridge University Press, 2000.

Young, James. *The Texture of Memory: Holocaust Memorials and Meaning.* New Haven: Yale University Press, 1993.

Gender and disaster

Elaine Enarson and Betty Hearn Morrow founded the discipline of gender and disaster studies in 1998 and their original book still rewards reading – perhaps a comment on how little has changed in public perceptions of disaster. The list below includes work surrounding more recent disasters, from drought to earthquake and wildfire, and it is heartening to see the number of Australian researchers now working in this field. However they were all preceded by Gretchen Poiner's disturbing first-person account of the Australian rural ideology and its inherent – frequently dangerous – masculinity.

Anderson, Deb. *Endurance: Australian Stories of Drought*. Collingwood: CSIRO Publishing, 2014.

Ariyabandu, Madhavi Malalgoda. "Sex, Gender and Gender Relations in Disasters." In *Women, Gender and Disaster*, edited by Elaine Enarson and P.G. Dhar Chakrabarti. New Delhi: Sage Publications, 2009.

David, Emmanual, and Elaine Enarson. *The Women of Katrina: How Gender, Race, and Class Matter in an American Disaster*. Nashville: Vanderbilt University Press, 2012.

Enarson, Elaine, and Betty Hearn Morrow. *The Gendered Terrain of Disaster: Through Women's Eyes*. Westport CT: Praeger Press, 1998.

Eriksen, Christine *Gender and Wildfire : Landscapes of Uncertainty*. Online: Ebooks Corporation, 2013.

Owen, Christine. "Gendered Communication and Public Safety: Women, Men and Incident." *Australian Journal of Emergency Management* 28, no. 2 (2013).

Poiner, Gretchen. *The Good Old Rule: Gender and Other Power Relationships in a Rural Community*. Sydney: Sydney University Press, 1990.

Stehlik, Daniela, Geoffrey Lawrence, and Ian Gray. "Gender and Drought: Experiences of Australian Women in the Drought of the 1990s." *Disasters* 24, no. 1 (2000): 38-53.

True, Jacqui. "Gendered Violence in Natural Disasters: Learning from New Orleans, Haiti and Christchurch." *Aotearoa New Zealand Social Work* 25, no. 2 (2013): 78-89.

Tyler, Meagan, and Peter Fairbrother. "Bushfires Are "Men's Business": The Importance of Gender and Rural Hegemonic Masculinity." *Journal of Rural Studies* 30 (4 / 2013): 110-19.

Ideas of Place and Community

Perhaps because settler Australia is such a young country, the idea of 'place' (and, more explicitly, how to find our place in it) reflects both philosophical and emotional complexities. Many of the narrators in this book expressed historic cultural attitudes to the land such as Davison and White have explored, as well as the attachment to place that Peter Read expressed, but they were also very aware of the resonances such attitudes carry in contemporary Australia. Proudley's work shows the ways – some of them contradictory – in which attitudes to bushfire interact with place attachment. I was also intrigued by J.M. Arthur's concept of the 'default country' and how an imagined sense of place influences our relationship with the real thing.

The concept of community is a slippery one and is frequently conflated with place, a mistake I made at the start of this project. (I was quickly put straight by some of the narrators.) Other researchers, such as Fairbrother *et al*, have also found the relationship between place and community to be complicated, especially in the emotionally heightened context of bushfire.

Arthur, J.M. *The Default Country: A Lexical Cartography of 20th-Century Australia.* Sydney: UNSW Press, 2012.
Davison, Graeme. "Rethinking the Australian Legend." *Australian Historical Studies* 43, no. 3 (2012/09/01 2012): 429-51.
Davison, Graeme. "Sydney and the Bush: An Urban Context for the Australian Legend." *Historical Studies* 18, no. 71 (1978).
Fairbrother, Peter, Meagan Tyler, Alison Hart, Bernard Mees, Richard Phillips, Julie Stratford, and Keith Toh. "Creating "Community"? Preparing for Bushfire in Rural Victoria." *Rural Sociology* 78, no. 2 (2013): 186-209.
Gordon, Rob. "Community Impact of Disaster and Community Recovery." *InPsych* (2009). Published electronically 2011.
Proudley, Mae. "Place Matters." *Australian Journal of Emergency Management* 28, no. 2 (2013): 11-16.
Read, Peter. *Returning to Nothing: The Meaning of Lost Places.* Cambridge ; Melbourne: Cambridge University Press, 1996.
White, Richard. *Inventing Australia.* Sydney: Allen & Unwin, 1981.

Difficult History

Difficult history is a two-edged term: it can refer to a history of difficult events (such as bushfires or genocide or terrorist attacks), or history that is hard to do. In almost all cases, these go hand in hand. I found many links between Black Saturday and other disasters both in the responses of those involved and in the challenges faced by historians documenting and interpreting those events, including the vexing question of historians' role in 'healing'.

SELECTED READING LIST

Some of these challenges I anticipated, such as questions about when to begin documenting disaster and the ethical use of emotional material. Others - such as the erotics of suffering as explored by Salverson, Goldbloom and Recuber - came out of the blue. It was in the minefield of difficult history that I most appreciated the power of the academic literature to offer guidance and share lessons – even though, as in LaCapra's case, it sometimes took several readings to appreciate the lesson.

Bruner, Jerome. "The Narrative Construction of Reality." *Critical Inquiry* 18, no. 1 (Autumn 1991): 1-21.

Clark, Mary Marshall. "Herodotus Reconsidered: An Oral History of September 11, 2001, in New York City." *Radical History Review*, no. 111 (Fall 2011): 79-89.

Fassin, Didier and Rechtman, Richard. *The Empire of Trauma: An Inquiry into the Condition of Victimhood*. Translated by Rachel Gomme. Princeton: Princeton University Press, 2009.

Field, Sean. "Beyond 'Healing': Trauma, Oral History and Regeneration." *Oral History* 34, no. 1 (Spring 2006): 31-42.

Gardner, James. "September 11: Museums, Spontaneous Memorials, and History." In *Grassroots Memorials: The Politics of Memorializing Traumatic Death*, edited by Peter Jan Margry and Christina Sanchez-Carretero. New York: Berghahn Books, 2011.

Goldbloom, Amos. "The Victim's Voice and Melodramatic Aesthetics in History." *History and Theory* 48 (October 2009): 220-37.

Gordon, Rob. "Thirty Years of Trauma Work: Clarifying and Broadening the Consequences of Trauma." *Psychotherapy in Australia* 13, no. 3 (May 2007): 12-19.

LaCapra, Dominick. *Writing History, Writing Trauma*. Baltimore: Johns Hopkins University Press, 2001.

Recuber, Timothy. "Disaster Porn!" *Contexts* 12, no. 2 (May 1, 2013): 28-33.

Rickard, Wendy. "Oral History- 'More Dangerous Than Therapy'?: Interviewees' Reflections on Recording Traumatic or Taboo Issues." *Oral History* 26, no. 2 (Autumn 1998): 34-48.

Salverson, Julie. "Change on Whose Terms? Testimony and an Erotics of Injury." *Theater* 31, no. 3 (Fall 2001): 119-25.

Sheftel, Anna, and Stacey Zembrzycki. "Only Human: A Reflection on the Ethical and Methodological Challenges of Working with "Difficult" Stories." *The Oral History Review* 37, no. 2 (2010): 191-214.

Williams, Paul. *Memorial Museums: The Global Rush to Commemorate Atrocities*. Oxford and New York: Berg Publishers, 2007.

Oral History

There is a lot of exciting work being done in oral history practice, some of which I have included in the section above. Time and again, however, I returned to the classics. These were the works that set me thinking about oral histories as more than interviews to be mined for information, teaching me to look at 'mistakes' as potentially valuable insights and to understand that oral history is a truly a performance in which the audience also takes part. I did not follow Michael Frisch's model of shared authority, for which I have frequently felt guilty, but that would have resulted in a very different book.

Frisch, Michael. *A Shared Authority: Essays on the Craft and Meaning of Oral and Public History*. New York: SUNY Press, 1990.

SELECTED READING LIST

Little, Edward and Steven High, "Partners in Conversation: Ethics and the Emergent Practice of Oral History Performance," in David Dean, Yana Meerzon and Kathryn Prince, eds. *History, Memory, Performance*. New York: Palgrave Macmillan, 2014.

Passerini, Luisa, tr. Robert Lumley and Jude Bloomfield. *Fascism in Popular Memory: The Cultural Experience of the Turin Working Class*. Cambridge: Cambridge University Press, 1987.

Portelli, Alessandro. "What Makes Oral History Different." In *The Oral History Reader*, edited by Robert Perks and Alistair Thomson. Abingdon: Routledge, 2006.

Shopes, Linda. "Commentary: Sharing Authority." *Oral History Review (USA)* 30, no.1 (2003): 103-110.

Thomson, Alistair. "Anzac Memories: Putting Popular Memory Theory into Practice in Australia." *Oral History* 18, no. 1 (1990): 25-31.

Thomson, Alistair. "Four Paradigm Transformations in Oral History." *Oral History Review (USA)* 34, no. 1 (2007): 49-70.

Yow, Valerie. ""Do I Like Them Too Much?" Effects of the Oral History Interview on the Interviewer and Vice-Versa." *Oral History Review (USA)* 24, no. 1 (1997): 55-79.

INDEX

Aboriginal people 42–43
  use of fire 54
Anderson, Peter 161–162
Anniversary of Black Saturday
  2010 196
  2013 88, 158
Apple-growing 33–34, 46–48
Apted, Edith and Lindsay 63–64, 91
Apteds Orchards 3, 48, 52–53
Ash Wednesday (1983) 80, 143, 150–155, 165–166, 208, 223, 244
Ashmore, Elizabeth 162
Avola, Mary 112–113, 116, 139–140
Avola, Peter 24, 76, 109–110, 112–113, 139–140
Bailleu, Ted (Premier of Victoria, 2010–2013) 214
Barnett, Oswald 39
Bateman, Fred 102, 172, 211–212
  Black Saturday experience 7, 10, 11, 14, 16, 20, 23
  Rebuilding 101, 198, 205, 206, 210
Black Friday (1939) 30–31, 58–62, 142, 162
Black Saturday (2009) vii, 1–28, 225–226
Black Saturday in Strathewen
  anniversaries 88, 158, 196
  arrival 10–12
  creative responses 67–69, 75–85, 158–160
  immediate aftermath 19–27
  lead-up 4–5, 65
  peak 12–17
  preparation 6–8
  warning 8–10
  wind change 17–19

Black Sunday (1926) 162–163
Black Thursday (1851) 56–57, 70–71
Brumby, John (Premier of Victoria, 2007–2010) 65, 214
Bryce, Dame Quentin (Governor-General of Australia, 2008–2014) 196
Bushfire poetry 67–79, 82, 84–85
Bushfire videos 124–139
Bushfires, major 233
  Ash Wednesday (1983) 80, 143, 150–155, 165–166, 208, 223, 244
  Black Friday (1939) 30–31, 58–62, 142, 162
  Black Saturday (2009) vii, 1–28
  Black Sunday (1926) 162–163
  Black Thursday (1851) 32, 56, 57, 70–71
  Dandenong fires (1962) 62–64, 163–164
  Hobart fires (1967) 96
Buy-back scheme 31, 212–216, 218
Carland, Rebecca 234
Chambers, Lyn (Lewis) 193
Chappelle, Leslye 22, 25, 173, 205, 210, 211–212
Chisholm, Bill 123
Chook Project *156*, 157–158
Country Fire Authority (CFA) 2, 123, 224
Creative responses 67–69, 75–85, 158–160
Crisfield, Robert 97, 174, 180, 197
  Black Saturday experience 5, 9, 13, 26
  Masculinity 178
  Sense of place 201, 202, 206
Croll, Herbert 38–39

Dale-Hallett, Liza 168, 234
Denial 105–108
Department of Sustainability and Environment 224
Drugs 50
Evans, Sue 170
Farr, Mona 72–73
Ferguson, Diana 189
Gardam, Karen 84, 86–87, 176
  Black Saturday experience 4, 6, 9, 11, 13, 16, 19, 20, 23, 24, 26
  Growing up in Strathewen 45–46, 49
  Memorials 89–90, 92, 111
Gartner, John 143, 150–155
Gartner, Zelma 80, 143, 150–155, 208, 223, 244
Geer, Celeste 134, 158
Gender and bushfire 157–189, 228–229
Gordon, Dr Rob 83, 97–98, 129, 143
Griffin, Alison 79
Grocon 221–223
Handmer, Prof John 185–186
Hayward, Jane 176, 191, 194–195
  Black Saturday experience 23, 25, 26
Healesville 158–159
Helen's Place 94, 95–97, 99–101, 106, 105–109
Hewitt, Herbert 43–44
Hierarchies of loss 94, 95–105
Hobart fires (1967) 96
Hodges, Florrie 162–163
Horne, Alan 84, 163, 198–99, 199–200
  Black Saturday experience 8, 17
  Strathewen history 33, 36, 42, 44, 47–48, 50, 52, 53, 54, 59
Horne, Joyce 84, 117, 163–164, 173
  Black Saturday experience 7, 11, 12, 14, 15, 18, 19, 20, 22, 24

Sense of place 198, 205, 207, 210–211
  Strathewen history 32, 35–36, 37, 44, 53
Hurstbridge 40, 49, 95
Hurstbridge Bushfire Relief Centre 94, 95–97, 99–101, 106, 105–109
Jenkinson, Peter 21, 211
Joyce, Barbara 53, 79–80, 99, 116, 123, 168
  Black Saturday experience 5, 9, 22, 23
  Chook project 157–158, 160
  Poetry Tree 66, 69, 75, 77, 82, 83, 86, 91–92
Kinglake 121, 221–223
Kinglake National Park 29–30, 54
Kingston Voluntary Relief Organisation 96
Langmead, Marilyn 69
Legg, Helen 95–97, 99–101, 105–109, 179
Lewis, Lyn 193
Mann family 31–33, 35, 57–58
Masculinity 177–185
McGahy, David 2, 21, 24, 110, 211
McKenzie, Angela 51, 104, 117, 179–180, 202, 206
  Black Saturday experience 8, 10, 13, 22, 25
  Bushfire videos 119–125, 128, 131, 135, 137
McKenzie, Dale 127–129, 130–131, 135, 137
McKimmie, Ian 45–46, 101, 174
  Black Saturday experience 6, 11, 12, 15, 18, 20, 23, 209
  Poetry Tree 69, 77, 79, 82
McLelland, George, and family 32, 56–57, 70–71
Memorials 73–93, 226
Mitchell, David (Mitch) 133

INDEX

Mitchell, Philip 132–133, 135, 137–138
Mitchell, Vicki (Nelson) 96–97, 101, 117–118, 119–125, 132–133, 169
   Growing up in Strathewen 49, 200
   Poetry Tree 49, 84–87, 89
   Rebuilding 80, 198, 205, 207
Museum Victoria 85–86, 91, 119, 151, 160, 221–223, 234
Negative public reactions 105–109
Nelson, Laurie 44, 45, 63, 132–133, 145, 163
   Black Saturday experience 6, 11, 21
Nelson, Norma 44, 53, 63, 132–133, 136, 163, 169
   Black Saturday experience 12, 13, 17, 19, 21, 209
Nillumbik Council 54, 206
Nixon, Christine 186, 196
Novak, Cathy and Paul 171
Opportunity 115–118
Orchards 33–34, 46–48
O'Sullivan, Bob 170
Outsiders 76, 105–109, 112, 226–227
Paulka, Donna and Terry 24
Pentreath, Albert Dudley 61
Perry, Libby and Phil 50, 157
Peter Avola Memorial Cricket Pavilion 109–113
Place 199–208
Poetry 66, 67–73, 77–79, 82, 84–85
Poetry Tree 66, 68, 67–86, 226
Public response 105–109, 226–227
Pugh, Clifton 49, 50
Pugh, Shane 50, 173–174, 177
Putt, Bill 84–85, 129–132, 135
Raftery, Geoff 110, 125–127, 135
Rebuilding 101, 195–208, 229
Reid, Stella 160

Retreat and resettlement 31, 213–216
Royal Commissions
   Black Friday 1939 30–31, 54, 58–59, 64, 142, 162
   Black Saturday 2009 31, 142–143, 213–216, 243
Rudd, Kevin (Prime Minister of Australia, 2007–10, 2013) 196
Sam the Koala 65
Sawmills 29–32, 54, 61
Search for meaning 144–146
Sense of place 199–208
Shaw, Sylvia 45–46, 193
   Black Saturday experience 4, 5, 15, 24, 27
Sheds 168–169, 171–172, 173–175, 180–181
Shepherd, Joe and Danny 76
Singing Water 40–42, 64, 66
South, Bronwyn Apted 91, 102, 103, 114–115, 116, 191, 200
   Black Saturday experience 1, 2–3, 5, 8, 21
   Strathewen history 43–44, 52–53, 55, 63–64
Sparkes family 29, 40–42
St Andrews 126–127, 158, 160
'Stay or go' policy 182–183, 188
Stecher, Wes 20, 21, 211
Steels Creek 219–220
Strathewen Community Renewal Association (SCRA) 87–88, 111, 113–115, 176
Strathewen Hall 32, 35–36, 38
Strathewen history 1, 2–66, 224–225
   apple orchards 33–34, 46–48
   Black Saturday in Strathewen 1, 2–27
   bushfire history 55–65
   changing demographics 43, 50–52
   early history 31–33

Strathewen Memorial 87–90, 92
Strathewen Primary School 35, 158, 191–195
Stretton, Judge Leonard 30–31, 54, 58–59, 64, 142, 162
Tapp, Cam 196
Testimony 141–148, 228
Thompson, Darren 100, 102, 118, 174–75, 197, 212
    Black Saturday experience 4, 6, 9, 12, 14, 16, 19, 24, 26
Three Stories Gallery 158–159
Trewhella jack *29*, 30–31
Tully, Barrie 49, 50–51, 98–99, 181, 200, 211
    Black Saturday experience 7, 12
Tully, Rae 49, 50, 98–99, 116, 181, 200, 211, 217, 232
    Black Saturday experience 10, 16, 17, 19, 21, 25, 210

Tyler, Ruby 161–162
Usher, Jim 15, 149
Victorian Bushfires Collection 85–86, 91, 119, 151, 160, 222–223, 234
Victorian Bushfires Relief Fund 107
Videos, bushfire 124–139
Volunteers 76, 107
Vreulink, Henk 69, 78
Wiltshire, Felicity and Peter 171
Wind change 17–19
Winton, Irma 24, 111, 176
Yarra Glen 123
Young, Rosemary McKimmie 109, 136, 146, 176–177
    Black Saturday experience 5, 8, 10, 15, 17, 21, 25
    Poetry Tree 69, 76, 81–82
    Strathewen history 41, 42, 45–46, 54, 64

Milton Keynes UK
Ingram Content Group UK Ltd.
UKHW021824100424
440890UK00007B/87